# A NEW REPUBLIC OF LETTERS

# A NEW REPUBLIC OF LETTERS

## Memory and Scholarship in the Age of Digital Reproduction

*Jerome McGann*

 Harvard University Press

Cambridge, Massachusetts
London, England
2014

*Library of Congress Cataloging-in-Publication Data*

McGann, Jerome J.
   A new republic of letters : memory and scholarship in the age of digital
reproduction / Jerome McGann.
      pages   cm
   Includes bibliographical references and index.
   ISBN 978-0-674-72869-1 (alkaline paper)
   1. Humanities—Research.   2. Humanities—Study and teaching.
3. Memory—Social aspects.   4. Learning and scholarship—Social
aspects.   5. Communication in learning and scholarship—Technological
innovations.   6. Digital media—Social aspects.   7. Internet—Social
aspects.   8. Globalization—Social aspects.   9. Social change.   I. Title.
AZ186.M35   2014
001.3—dc23        2013036538

For those future philologists, my instructors:
Alex Gil, Matt Kirschenbaum, Beth Nowviskie,
Steve Ramsay, and Andy Stauffer

*Dove sta memoria*

# Contents

# Preface

What we call literature is an institutional system of cultural memory—a republic of letters. The general science of its study is philology and its Turing Machine is what scholars call the Critical Edition. Driven by the historical emergence of online communication, this book investigates their character and relation.

Although it is cumulatively organized, each chapter has an integrity of its own, so a seriatim reading might not be best for every reader. As the titles of the three parts indicate, the book weaves a set of discussions around the relation of theory and method within the general horizon of an historical critique.

Part I engages the issues through the long-standing tension between the claims of philosophy and philology. It begins to investigate a key theme of the book: that a functional reflection on literature and culture should begin as a question of method rather than theory, and hence with a study of the critical scholarly edition and its historical and institutional character. Pivoting on the controversy between Wilamowitz and Nietzsche, the discussions in Chapters 1–3 accept the discourse of Continental Philosophy as their conceptual framework. This is done in order to give the relevant historical shape to the book's philosophical and theoretical issues.

Moving away from that discourse, Part II examines the relation of theory and method in the strongly procedural terms that have emerged under the horizon of digital technology. Chapters 4 and 5 are the most theoretical in the book since they sketch an interpretive method that maps digital to traditional philological functions. The centrality of the critical edition is reexamined in Chapter 6 in relation to its new digital problems and affordances.

Finally, the question "What is to be done?" frames the issues taken up in Part III, which reengages in more practical ways the historical and institutional issues raised in Part I. Chapter 7 argues the need to situate humanities research and pedagogy, including close interpretational practices, within our present (and changing) institutional horizon. Chapters 8 and 9 then lay out two exemplary case studies. Each suggests the interpretive expectations that have emerged for literary scholars because of the coming of digital technology.

The Introduction provides an overview of the book. The Conclusion is a set of cautionary reflections addressed most particularly to scholars of the West. Given the need for a new kind of philology, online and therefore global at an entirely new level, what ethos underpins that famous and still relevant question "What is to be done?"

# Abbreviations

ARP  Applied Research in 'Patacriticism. A Mellon-funded research lab to develop software for interpretive study of humanities materials: http://en.wikipedia.org/wiki/Applied_Research_in_Patacriticism.

ASCII  American Standard Code for Information Interchange. Code for representing text in computerized communication equipment.

DPLA  The Digital Public Library of America: http://www.dp.la.

ECCO  Eighteenth-Century Collections Online: http://gdc.gale.com/products /eighteenth-century-collections-online/.

Flickr  An image and video hosting website and an early model for social software: http://en.wikipedia.org/wiki/Flickr.

IATH  The Institute for Advanced Technology in the Humanities. University of Virginia's pioneering digital humanities research center: http://www .iath.virginia.edu/.

NCCO  Nineteenth-Century Collections Online: http://gdc.gale.com/nineteenth -century-collections-online/.

NINES  Networked Infrastructure for Nineteenth-Century Electronic Scholarship. A freely available online aggregator of long nineteenth-century scholarly research and publications: http://www.nines.org/.

PDF  Portable Document Format. ISO open standard document exchange format: http://www.nines.org/.

SCI  Scholarly Communications Institute. A Mellon-funded institute for promoting digital scholarship: http://uvasci.org/.

SGML  Standard Generalized Markup Language. ISO standard for e-text markup: http://en.wikipedia.org/wiki/Standard_Generalized_Markup_Language.

SSHRC  The Social Sciences and Humanities Research Council. Canadian national council for supporting scholarship in the social sciences and humanities: http://www.sshrc-crsh.gc.ca/home-accueil-eng.aspx.

TEI  The Text Encoding Initiative. A professional consortium for developing and maintaining standard models for digital texts: http://www.tei-c.org /index.xml.

XML  Extensible Markup Language. A standard encoding language for human and machine-readable documents: http://en.wikipedia.org/wiki/XML.

# A NEW REPUBLIC OF LETTERS

γραμμάτων τε συνθέσεις,
μνήμην ἀπάντων, μουσομήτορ᾽ ἐργάνην.

—Aeschylus, *Prometheus Bound* I. 460–461


And more than all, at last came memory,
Teacher of every art, mother of song.

—Translation by Thomas Medwin
and Percy Bysshe Shelley

# Introduction

I

Here is surely a truth now universally acknowledged: that the whole of our cultural inheritance has to be recurated and reedited in digital forms and institutional structures. But as the technology of cultural memory shifts from bibliographical to digital machines, a difficult question arises: what do we do with the books? This is a problem for society at large and many people are working at it, none more assiduously than certain expert persons, often technicians. Highly skilled and motivated as they are, book history and the complex machineries of books fall outside their professional expertise. Humanist scholars, the long-recognized monitors of cultural memory, register a problem in this situation. For humanist thinking has been shaped by the institutions and the technology of books.[1]

Prima facie, these problems must now be approached in digital terms and venues. Much of my work for the past twenty years has taken exactly that approach, through the founding of institutions like IATH and NINES, and in helping to build information machines like *The Rossetti Archive, IVANHOE,* and *Juxta.*[2] But I want to take up the question again in a more traditional form—this book and the older technology it represents. Now more than ever, I believe, we need to understand how bibliographical technology works. Designing optimal digital environments requires it. The notorious "Crisis in the Humanities," still with us, is by no means simply an intramural problem for an ivory tower and bookish academy.

Society at large is sorely mistaken when it views cultural studies as a surplus educational function—trivial, it is often thought, when set beside (for instance) those STEM fields of science, technology, engineering, and math. For all their importance, those disciplines are unequipped to investigate the relation of language and literature to society.

Why that understanding is a precious resource for our present presentist culture is one of the two primary concerns of this book. The other is practical: how to exploit that resource for societies now moving to organize their cultural memories in digital forms. The practical aim is primarily directed to the traditional custodians of cultural memory. It argues that textual and editorial scholarship, often marginalized in humane studies as a narrowly technical domain, should be shifted back to the center of humanist attention. Understanding the technologies of book culture is the beginning of wisdom for any practical approach to the so-called digital humanities. But you can't do *that* well unless you have an intimate acquaintance with the scholarship of textualities. That scholarship once had a name to conjure with: philology.

The interests of this book thus reach back to the nineteenth century, when philology gained an apex of achievement, and when advances in global communication began to pick up speed. Not without reason have the problems of cultural memory been the special interest of cultural critics and sociologists for the past 150 years, from Matthew Arnold, Friedrich Nietzsche, and Maurice Halbwachs to Raymond Williams, Paul Connerton, and Pierre Nora. Though studious of the work of those remarkable persons, my focus is different. I am interested in the materials, particularly the documentary materials that represent and misrepresent, that record and fracture, the cultures we inherit and transmit.[3]

Edward Said had something like that interest in mind when, in a late lecture, he called for a "Return to Philology":[4] "the least with-it, least sexy, and most unmodern of any of the branches of learning associated with humanism" (57). Said was not thinking about the so-called New Philology that emerged in medieval studies in the 1990s. A clear descendent of European genetic editing that we date from Friedrich Beissner and Adolf Beck's edition of *Hölderlin* begun during World War II, that work studies the complex production history of literature with a special focus on "the proliferation of [the] texts' intrinsic variants."[5] Such work is a version of what nineteenth-century German philologians called *Wortphilologie*—a philology of the word.

Said, typically, had something larger in mind—a reading practice he described as "a detailed patient scrutiny of, and lifelong attentiveness to the words and rhetorics by which language is used by human beings in history" (61). He called it "philological hermeneutics" (91)—a method for critically engaging "the constitution of tradition and the usable past" (75). It is a method "for making those connections that allow us to see part and whole . . . : what to connect with, how, and how not" (78).

I have great sympathy with Said's arrestingly unsexy word, which salutes the independent authority of the life—the lives—of the past in their most quotidian and minute particulars. Long contemned as greybeard monks, philologists are the custodians of that magical dryasdust repository Yeats called "the foul rag and boneshop of the heart." Not the least of philology's virtues is the relief it can throw upon—the relief it can bring to—the poverty of our fiercely just-in-time present. We can make no greater self-critical move today than to open ourselves to the judgment of the philological past, by which we might gain "some power"—thank you, Robbie Burns—"to see ourselves as others see us." For if we study the past with attention we discover how it can turn back our Faustian gaze and expose its secret follies.

I have less sympathy with the word "hermeneutics." For some time it has been used to shift our attention from the obstinate past and how it relates to the enterprising present. A "detailed patient scrutiny" of the language of our cultural record is indeed essential to *Humanism and Democratic Criticism*. That was what the old German philologists called *Wortphilologie*. But a purely linguistic scrutiny needs exposure to the social network, in all its particulars, that communicates with us from the past.

We need to reorient our study of the documentary archive. To do that well, we also need to recover certain neglected philological procedures for investigating the "implicate order" of human memory and its material representations.[6] The order was first engaged in this way by the great historicist philologians of the nineteenth century, most elaborately in what they called *Sachphilologie*—a philology of material culture.[7] The word signals an object-oriented and media approach to the study of history and culture. It solicits a larger perspective on the documentary record—in our context, the bibliographical as well as the digital record—and thus sets the agenda for what I am calling, after Susanne Langer, "philology in a new key."

The work asks to be recomposed in a new key because information technology is exerting significant practical and institutional pressure for change in humanities education and scholarship. Once lamentably glacial, the changes keep gaining momentum, fueled by various enthusiasms and interests both within and outside the academy. The drive that began in 2010 to establish the DPLA—the Digital Public Library of America—is symptomatic. The library, research as well as local-public, is the storm center of these changes because the library is the home base of general education for the citizen as well as the research and teaching humanist, as the laboratory is the home base of the physical scientist.

Nearly everyone now sees that scholarly communication will soon be largely organized in digital venues. The digital migration of our museum and library archives is well underway and will continue. So is the development of an integrated digital network for connecting those resources. All that is both good and inevitable—indeed, thrilling. But then—forgive me Wordsworth—a timely utterance brought my thrills to grief: "After we digitize all the books, the books themselves will still be there," as indispensable as they ever were.[8] No digital technology can replace them (with digital surrogates), no digital technology can embrace them (in an online network).

What kind of research and educational program can integrate the preservation and study of these two radically different media? Here I take book technology simply as a paradigm of the problem that digitization has brought to many traditional humanities disciplines and materials, not least of all audio, visual, and haptic materials. The problem is especially difficult because it requires a practical solution and nobody yet has found one. We've been experimenting with jerry-rigged approaches for over twenty years. But as the digitization of the traditional archive has gained inertia—a very good thing, let me reiterate—the problem for humanists has not diminished—if anything, it has grown more urgent. We see this in and as the emergence of the digital humanities, which both its promoters and its critics regard as a set of replacement protocols for traditional humanities scholarship. But the work of the humanist scholar has not changed with the advent of digital devices. It is still to preserve, to monitor, to investigate, and to augment our cultural life and inheritance. That simple truth is why, as we seek to exploit electronic environments, we want to think about them in traditional philological terms.

What is philology? Literally, it means the love of the word (or articulated thought). The term (and the discipline) grew to eminence in the nineteenth century and defined what we now call literary and cultural studies. The great German philologist August Boeckh famously defined philology as "Die Erkenntnis des Erkannten"—The Knowledge of What is and has been Known.[9] It is a brilliant formulation. Distinguishing two critical procedures—the Higher and the Lower criticism—philology studies the documentary record on the assumption—in the words of the late D. F. McKenzie—that the documents carry the evidence of "the history of their own making."[10] We study and pass on the human record that others before us have studied and passed on to us. Essential to the study of that record are the sociohistorical conditions of its creation and emergence.

"The knowledge of what is and has been known": the strength of that formulation lies in the equation it draws between what we know now and what has been known in the past. For the truth is that all knowledge comes at an historical deficit. Boeckh's words are an injunction to intellectual modesty, a warning against the illusions of enlightenment. He is arguing that we take the broken historical record—what we know from the past—as the measure of what we are knowing in the present. All knowledge is fractured and limited because acts of knowing are executed in the slipping-down life of the present when "The Moving Finger writes; and, having writ, / Moves on."

That famous text from Fitzgerald's *Rubaiyat* figures its skepticism as a script that can never be cancelled.

> The Moving Finger writes; and, having writ,
> Moves on: nor all your Piety nor Wit
> Shall lure it back to cancel half a Line,
> Nor all your Tears wash out a Word of it.

The passage fairly defines the philological conscience, which subjects all interpretation to the judgment of documentary facticities, as unevadable as they are unmasterable. Scholars may grow sick with what Jacques Derrida has called "Archive Fever" when they forget that the history of original documents includes their subsequent transformations and even their disappearance.[11] Archive Fever "is to have a compulsive, repetitive, and nostalgic desire for the archive, an irrepressible desire to return to the origin, a homesickness, a nostalgia for return to the most archaic place of absolute commencement" (91). But to be absent from the documentary record is yet to participate in the record. Like the concept of origin itself, original documents are fictions we practice in order to manage their losses and our limits. To understand that is the vocation of the scholar, to mourn it is the individual's fate, not least of all the scholar's. As Fitzgerald's poem goes on to argue, the ruptures that characterize the documentary record are an ever-present function, when the history of the making of the documents is continually rewritten and thence further revealed/obscured. For Literature is always and equally Obliterature.[12] The documents we fashion in the present record the same burden of their own making as the documents we inherit from the past.

Those documents are the heroes of my work. I begin there because the primitive coding protocols of the entire archive, material as well as documentary, are textual protocols, as they have always been: i.e., natural language and all of the institutional mechanisms that enable its communication systems. I shall be paying special attention to the textual machine that most completely models the operational functions of natural language: the critical scholarly edition. This amazing technology is scarcely known outside that tightest of little islands, literary studies, and even there it remains a mystery to many. The idea of such an edition is the Turing Machine of traditional information systems. Every book is a coded set of instructions for repurposing its design-accessible information. Some books are programmed for relatively simple reading operations (if indeed any act of reading could be called simple). Others are far more complex, and scholarly editions like J. C. C. Mays's edition of Coleridge's *Poetical Works*—discussed in Chapters 1 and 6—are so advanced that they expose the astonishing functional capacities of bibliographical machineries.

Starting at the documentary level, then, I mean to follow long-traveled philological roads, moving to explore the mechanisms of both production history and transmission history and their complex, unfolding relations. In that analytic point of view, secondary documents—posthumous editions and transformations, for instance—are as important as the authorial manuscripts and early editions. So are all those attendant materials—reviews and commentaries—that expose and further define the character and meaning of the materials. (What memory would we have of the ancient world—of Sappho and Homer, for example—except for those secondary materials? None whatsoever.) From a yet more comprehensive sociohistorical point of view, a strictly literary focus brings a special understanding to the cultural internetwork. Historians and sociologists, philosophers and anthropologists, necessarily subordinate this primitive textual understanding of the archive to their specialized interests. And yet it is equally true that textual investigations of the kind I am proposing draw heavily upon the knowledge pursued in those related fields.[13] For the truth is that our disciplines operate as codependent functions of each other. They are part of the implicate order of humanities research.

Literature and language scholars like myself, for example, work best when we don't wander far from what William Blake called "minute particulars": this prosodic movement in "Crossing Brooklyn Ferry," that edition of *Ivanhoe,* or that translation of *The Origin of Species;* this network of historical and literary allusions in *Portrait of a Lady;* those early reviews of *Tender Buttons.* Such works and documents are difficult to engage if they get disengaged from the internetwork of related documents and works, all very particular as well. For that is where they "live and move and have their being."

Or perhaps we have to say, at least initially: where they once lived and moved and had their being. For these are all what another great poet called "The dead, but sceptred sovereigns, who still rule / Our spirits from their urns." (Byron, *Manfred* III. 4. 40–41) Had I called attention to Ovid, Petronius, or Dante the problem of a fragmented cultural memory would have been clear. While all three are foundational for the transmission of the cultural memory of the West, they are now a conscious resource only for a small class of persons, a kind of secular priesthood: humanities scholars from the West. Indeed, the move to specialization in humanities research and education has greatly increased the difficulty of accessing such resources. So too has the focus on the present and recent past in humanities education. What is most "relevant" to present needs and concerns may well be hidden from us by what Shelley called "veils of familiarity."

The problems I am addressing have grown increasingly acute during the past 200 years. Eliot published *The Waste Land* in major part to argue—to demonstrate through the recollection of ancient exempla like Ovid, Petronius, and Dante—that a cultural crisis was already well advanced. His poem merely replicates another famous poem published more than a hundred years earlier—Byron's *The Giaour*—which made the same argument using very different but quite equivalent stylistic means. Both Eliot's Modernist collage and Byron's Romantic fragment were written to expose the dissociation of Western cultural memory. Eliot's is perhaps the more extreme and alienated work because his focus is so literary and aesthetic. *The Waste Land* only gained its social authority through specialized academic mediation. Byron's poem, by contrast, was an immediate popular success because it represented the cultural crisis not in Eliot's narrowly aesthetic terms but in an immediate social and political relation: the contemporary history of Western imperialism observed at a revealing point of focus, modern Greece.

Byron published his lament in 1813, Eliot in 1922. Today the situation appears even more stressed. There are few ready-to-hand readers for Scott or James, least of all for Pushkin or Stendhal. Having now become either ruins or movies, their works have to be pedagogically—artfully, philologically—recreated. And so the questions we now ask of those self-conscious ruins, *The Giaour* or *The Waste Land,* will be: can readers see them as cliff notes—signs that we are brinked at a cultural emergency, as Byron and Eliot did; or through Cliff's Notes—the target objects for standardized school tests?

In the terms of an earlier lexicon, poetry is the art of memory, rhetoric a set of memory techniques, and philology the science of memory. Their contemporary names are art, media, and scholarship. I take those as generic terms since all three mark a broad set of related practices. The sciences of memory themselves—my chief concern here—constitute that broad range of cultural studies whose general fields—say, history, anthropology, literary criticism—ramify to a host of sub- and cross-disciplines.

These are the Human Sciences, and while they are always enlisted for various instrumental social purposes, they are fundamentally self-reflexive and, in social terms, conservative.

Given the often violent struggles of competing human interests, the term "conservative" might signify, particularly today, only some special set of ideals or interests: a *Book of Virtues,* for instance. In that respect the word will command forgetting, refusing, deleting: "I am the Lord thy God, thou shalt not have strange gods before me." But even that famous monotheist injunction lets us know that strange gods, like the poor whom Jesus loved, will always be with us, however we may neglect or try to expel them.

Here I take a more conservative view of the word "conservative." As to cultural heritage, though much is always forgotten, refused, and deleted, we should, I believe, disapprove and resist all such moves. Standing thus—it is a philological, not a moral stand—all words become like the word "Jesus," Living Words exactly because they can only save their lives by losing them, like the gods themselves. The poets are not the only ones who work to shore those fragments against those ruins, although they are more acute to remember than most.

> Our little systems have their day;
> They have their day and cease to be.

That's Tennyson, whose works register as well as any the paradoxical experience, and legacy, of globalization: that with knowledge accumulating in the imperial archives of Enlightenment comes "The crumbling memory of modern societies."[14] Nineteenth-century philology and German historicism in general made the initial secular engagement with the problem of understanding historical traditions and cultural memory in the accelerating conditions of Modernity. The famous dispute between Nietzsche and Wilamowitz at the end of the nineteenth century, which I take up in Chapter 3, created the conditions for new, sociological investigations into these matters. Here Maurice Halbwachs's work on the social structure of *Collective Memory* would prove pivotal exactly because its most important ideas were received so belatedly.

Reading Halbwachs against the catastrophic histories of the twentieth century, his postmodern inheritors would reshape his confident sociohistorical determinism. Halbwachs's studies of human memory argued that because "it is individuals as group members who remember,"[15] the memory of both the individual and the group is sustained through their localized constellation. The past is thus always received and reconstituted by these dynamic collectives, which preserve their character by various kinds of ceremonies and commemorative events. "In reality," Halbwachs observed—or we should say, *in this kind of an embracing reality*—"we are never alone" (23; emphasis added). "I turn to these people, I momentarily adopt their viewpoint, and I re-enter their group in order better to remember . . . and recognize in myself many ideas and ways of thinking that could not have originated with me" (24). In the context of the social and historical problems exposed by Marx and Nietzsche, by Bergson and Freud, Halbwachs introduced an attractive model of social and psychological stability. But pressed forty or fifty years forward, it becomes a model that helps to illuminate a global array—a network only in a cybernetic sense—of social groups that have become radically atomized. Transacted in a postmodern condition by "ideas and ways of thinking that could not have originated with me," I discover my splintered sodality.

In this respect Paul Connerton's work sharply focuses the problem of memory, and hence of culture, in a world caught in its cybernets. "We are living in a culture of hypermnesia," he remarks, only to add immediately that "we are living in a post-mnemonic, a forgetful, culture."[16] But the paradox is for him only apparent because he sees these conditions as codependent functions.

> By accelerating time computer usage immerses individuals in a hyper-present, an intensified immediacy which . . . makes it ever more difficult to envisage even the short-term past as "real." . . . The onset of forgetting and the longing for the moment proceed in tandem. . . . Exposed to what Debord has called "diffuse spectacle" . . . [people] find historical knowledge annihilated . . . as a perpetual present is installed in its place. . . . Present time is packed to bursting point; past time is evacuated. (87–88)

What Connerton worries about here is a person's fractured experience of the present, i.e., a present that seems "packed to bursting" with everything that has ever been known as well as everything that is even now being known; and worse still, the prospect of a future that will keep augmenting this disoriented condition. For the scholar—even for that creature of fable, the General Reader—we seem to have been pitched into Borges's Library of Babel.

> An insidious oppression invades the lives of people who, while they concentrate on one piece of information, are forever subliminally reminded that they are losing the possibility of concentrating fully, or even just attending peripherally, to another item of information. Sharp in the background is the

thought that they might be in other places, or with other men, or other
women, or at other meetings, or exhibitions, or reading other books, or
pursuing other goals [and] other ways in which they might be spending
their time. (87)

Connerton's dour representation of online multitasking gains its special
force by having marked itself as an imaginary move. Unlike Marx's account of the commodity fetish, distinctly recalled in this passage, Connerton does not set himself apart from "the lives of people" moving in
virtual and subjunctive conditions. His consciously sympathetic style—
his negative capability toward his subject—gives us fleeting access to the
actual experience of living in the drifts of a "present time" that is "packed"
and "evacuated" at once.

A central concern of Connerton's work, as of so many now, is the "information overload" in a digitally globalized world. Literature scholars
gain a special view of that large social problem by virtue of our narrow
vocational investment in book culture. As our libraries move toward
digital organization, their primary traditional commitment—to collect
and maintain the heritage of manuscripts and books—has raised acute
problems. These emerge through that event now to become an accepted
fact of social policy: the migration of our traditional cultural inheritance
to a system of digital storage, access, and reuse.

How then are we to save the traditional inheritance in its original material forms; and to integrate those objects—the *realia* of the depositories—
to our new born-digital cultural works? We are living in the Last Days of
book culture; that is clear. Of course this doesn't mean we are in the Last
Days of reading culture, least of all of our textual condition. But it is also
clear that as we proceed to digitize our print and manuscript objects, and
hence as our engagements with those objects become primarily digital
engagements, the living culture that created and sustained them becomes
itself an object—something, in Connerton's words, "that is *known about*"
rather than "something that is *known* . . . in one's continuing life" (32).
For the literary scholar, it is as if we had entered a bibliographical Day
of the Dead. (For the digeratus, however, engaging with book culture is
more like watching George Romero's famous zombie movies.)

Book culture is dying, and for millions of people it has already died.
Cultural forms, like the people who gave them life, die all the time: the
global economy of sailing ships, the civilization of the Etruscans, Cathar
culture. But religious authorities—priests, Brahmans, shamans—mediate
the rituals and ceremonies operating a global truth that permeates perpetual loss: things that die need not therefore be dead. As the poet observed,

Nature *is* a Heraclitean fire, and if there is not to be a precisely Christian comfort of resurrection, there may instead be, as Joyce later observed, a *commodius vicus* of recirculation.

In that perspective, this peculiar moment in the life and death of book culture is handing its belated secular custodians an unusual gift: alienation. This is the theme of Mandelstam's famous essay "The Word and Culture" (1921).[17] It comes through with great force when he quotes the opening of Ovid's *Tristia* I.3:

*Cum subit illius tristissima noctis imago,*
*qua mihi supremum tempus in urbe fuit,*
*cum repeto noctem, qua tot mihi cara reliqui,*
*labitur ex oculis nunc quoque gutta meis.*

When the ghost of that terrible night approaches,
Which was for me my last hour in the city,
That night when I was abandoned by everything dear to me,
Even now tears are dropping from my eyes.

Mandelstam knows that Ovid's *Tristia* is an alienated cultural resource—as alienated for him by the proletarian revolution as it is for us even now— "*nunc quoque*"—in our world of global finance capitalism.[18] He quotes the Latin text without a translation in order to reperform the loss that Ovid originally experienced. For he is convinced that a (Russian) translation of the passage is exactly what one mustn't give now (1921) if one wants to call attention to the presence of the living dead.[19]

I have supplied a (free) English translation now (2013) to emphasize the impertinence of any translation, which forces itself upon us in that final, untranslatable line. Ovid is punning on the word "*gutta*," which means both "drop"—as in a teardrop—and the never-to-be-translated "*gutta*," which references the small ornaments on the architraves of Doric columns. The function of these scarcely notable projections was to protect the columns from water damage. To register Ovid's wordplay is to realize that Ovid is reconstructing—a key idea for Mandelstam—an image of the moment of Ovid's exile from Rome. His sorrow and sense of loss is so extreme—he is clearly recalling Aeneas's departing view of ruined Ilium—that he sees it through his tears, as a city whose glories are fled. A mere poet, what need has Rome of Ovid? Yet the lines do supply an answer: it is the need of the great columns for those small *guttae*, a need known only to those who remember how civilizations, like people, come and go. A need for these tearful reversings. The requirement of *Collective Memory*.

Ovid wrote those lines when Rome was at the peak of its greatness. Some commentators—recent ones, born in the epoch of Modernity—read them and the whole story of Ovid's exile as a self-promoting fiction. However the verse is inflected, its significance as a commentary on the relation of culture to poetry remains. The Roman World is passed away but it lives on in Ovid, Lucretius, Virgil, even Petronius. Some would say, with justice, that it lives on as well in its legacy of law and public administration. But it is the writers, the poets perhaps especially, who show us their faces and the lives they led.

I recall Mandelstam here because he pledged his allegiance to philology. This is an explicit part of the Acmeist Movement as he represented it. Significantly, and as is clear in the famous Nietzsche-Wilamowitz controversy of the previous generation, his pledge is made to miscegenated Hellenistic culture rather than to the ideal Hellenism of Nietzsche or Wilamowitz. Mandelstam does not hanker for realms beyond good and evil—quite the contrary. This is why, as Renate Lachmann has noted, memory for him must be catholic and not selective.[20] Though we forget, de-accession, and digitize, all that is deficit spending. The losses involved will never be redeemed by the gains we try to secure.

That is one moral we realize from the digital transition we are moving through. When I've suggested this in the past, some took it as a depressing view. But why should it be? It seems a gift and an opportunity. A fate of our time calls us to engage this transition and, as scholars, to help oversee, monitor, and first of all—given our vocation—understand it. We will do all that poorly if we don't try to imagine what we don't know: what/how/why (I'm even unsure how to frame the issue) literature as we have known it will be known again. Whatever that event, this seems to me certain: we won't achieve such an imagining without a sympathetic engagement with the Way We Live Now. Like Mandelstam or that other legendary philologian *de nos jours,* Walter Benjamin, our humanist vocation gives us an important vantage our current historical emergency.

## II

Recent initiatives like Europeana and DPLA demonstrate how much has changed at the center of humanities research and education—in our museums and libraries—since the turn of the century.[21] *Radiant Textuality* paid little attention to those kinds of institutional changes because they were nowhere so far advanced as they are today.[22] Rather, taking the experimental focus of *The Rossetti Archive* as its point of reference, that book tried to give a report on the growing relevance of "theoretical models [of interpretation and study] that have been perceived until now as odd, idiosyncratic, nonnormal" (*Radiant Textuality* 1). And while those matters remain important ones, their limitations became clear even as we pressed at their investigation. Circumstances, including the advancement of our recent learning, have shown how works like *Radiant Textuality* scarcely addressed a pair of key subjects: the institutional and instrumental character of the problems involved; and the historical reference points—one in the late nineteenth-, the other in the late twentieth century—that textual studies, history of the book, and memory studies have been forcing to greater attention since the mid-1980s.

Here's a relevant personal story. The theoretical design of *The Rossetti Archive* in 1993 was grounded in this working hypothesis: that a fully integrated online network of depositories was already theoretically operational and prepared to integrate with projects like *The Rossetti Archive*.[23] Such an internetwork, particularly for humanistic materials, did not *in fact* exist in 1993, although the hope toward it was well advanced among those who took an interest in the matter. But the hypothesis was judged necessary if the logical design of *The Rossetti Archive* was to be, from the *Archive*'s point of view, implemented within an online environment. Needless to say, it had to be a black box hypothesis since the design structure of an encompassing digital network and its constituent parts could not be known in its particulars, even though its evolution could be predicted as a general condition.

The design hypothesis laid a functional demand on the process of building the *Archive*. Its internal structure had to match a globally internetworked organization that was technically and institutionally feasible. That conceptual horizon meant we had to execute every local action in conscious relation to the imagined internetwork. Practically, we had to monitor in a regular way the global state of an unfolding and highly volatile set of institutional networks. That internetwork was realizing itself during the years we were building *The Rossetti Archive*—that is to say, between 1992, when the internet began to project a global interface, and 2012, when entities like Europeana and the DPLA were in full development. In turn, the evolving internetwork kept exerting critical pressure on our understanding of what we were doing with the *Archive*.

And so *The Rossetti Archive* got built. But that event produced as well a set of surprising results. For in building the *Archive* we were imagining what we didn't know. For instance, our initial design harbored internal flaws that only became visible when we tried to implement the design under the horizon of the unfolding global internetwork. Initially these flaws appeared as technical limitations and contradictions. Dealing with them brought a second surprising realization. The de facto historical status of certain problems could only be managed but not removed from the design without tearing it all down and starting with a new design. The problems also exposed deeper design issues that we had no idea how to address, much less resolve: for instance, how to design automated analytic relations between traditional materials and their digital surrogates. They could be linked and, as on a lightboard, compared, but beyond that lay the mysterium.

All this amounted to learning by doing, which is to say as well, learning by failing. At first these failures seemed conceptual and technical, but with the rapid expansion of the technical capacities of the internetwork we could see that the most intractable problems were political and institutional. That realization forced a decisive change in direction signaled by the founding of NINES in 2002. Designing and implementing online environments for research-based education in the humanities required more than a technical laboratory like the *Archive* or a think-tank institutional location like IATH. Without firm connections to the regular programmatic work of university operations—intramural degree-granting mechanisms as well as the supporting extramural professional system—research education must be fundamentally constrained (see Chapter 7).[24] The sign of those constraints is the institutional divide separating traditional from digital humanities. But it is more than a sign. It is a divide built into a complex set of quotidian institutional operations.

No one can seriously doubt that the discourse of the humanities research community will be digitally organized—in our traditional lexicon, that we will give up books like this one for online publishing and will take up digital tools for studying our cultural inheritance. But even as that is granted and understood, the importance of our traditional resources—material, methodological, and theoretical—is much less well understood. This seems true on both sides of the humanities divide. Digital humanists tend to see their traditional colleagues and the inherited research system as needing to be brought up to date. And while that view has its truth, equally true is the digital community's increasingly attenuated historical sense. Nearly everyone misses the problem here because the Web has made available such vast amounts of historical data. We can now quickly annotate just about anything we've never heard of. But there lies the problem, as Connerton, among others, has made so painfully clear. Perhaps never before have we been able to "know about" so much and to "know" so little of what we know.

Connerton is drawing an important distinction between forms of memory—i.e., the stored data, "the knowledge of what is known" (Boeckh), "the inorganic organization of memory" (Bernard Stiegler—see Chapter 2)—and the human persons who access and use it. We speak of computerized "memory banks" and we've naturally tried to organize digital environments after our library and museum models (and now, vice versa). Then the scale of the data and information deposits explodes in online aggregated systems and cloud computing. So we talk of drinking information from a fire hose.

Though our language often misleads us to think otherwise, none of that data or information is "Memory," not even the software that facilitates its retrieval and use. No one drinks from a fire hose, and only living things—perhaps even only people—have memories. It's imaginable that machines might take a Lucretian swerve and develop what we call consciousness and therefore what we understand as human "Memory." It's being imagined all the time. But I suspect, with Olaf Stapledon, that such an event requires an unimaginable time scale. *Blade Runner* is a sweet and sentimental dream of escape from a society that has lost its mind and its memory.

So I want to say that human memory means pretty much exactly what it meant to Montaigne, to Tolstoy, to Proust, to Sebald. I don't say that is what it meant to Gibbon or to Churchill because the forms of their memories were imperially inflected—a condition that transforms human memory, that most personal experience, into . . . what shall we call it? A sense of History? Perhaps. And I don't say that is what it meant to Plato or Augustine, or even Aristotle, because their interest in memory is theoretical, either metaphysical or theological. My approach to memory is through philology, a science that grounds its knowledge in an assumption of its own limit-conditions.

In this perspective, memory is how we take care of what we love and lose. (Tormented memory is when we remember that we forgot to take care.) We create machineries to help us remember—the arts, or rather the artifactures, of memory. Libraries, museums, digital environments. Families. Nations. Ceremonies. No question but these machines are unreliable and often destructive. And they get out of hand, some dangerously out of hand. The story of the *Tower of Babel* and the myth of *Faust* are ways of reflecting on memory machines that have gone out of control. Both are philological reflections, the one from a theological view of the world, the other from a philosophical and scientific one. The one is an imperial tale, the other is personal. Personally I prefer the personal ones. Faust and Margaret, Manfred and Astarte.

The transition to digitally based research education is being imagined and driven as a global internetwork—diverse, transnational, and collaborative. Broad and embracing in its geophysical perspective, the effort is at the same time shaped in severely presentist terms: an all-encompassment of the just-in-time, a marketplace of users and providers. It is a place with a great need to remember that all of those agents bear along with them their ancient household gods.

So as we now try forging our passages to India, even two-way and radial routes, we might also remember what E. M. Forster imagined at the conclusion of his novel *A Passage to India*. Though the book is an imagination of failure, that imagination also held out a promise of possible success. The promise lay recorded in the details of the place of failure, whose memory Forster urges us to cherish.

> "Why can't we be friends now?" said [Cyril Fielding to Dr. Aziz], holding him affectionately. "It's what I want. It's what you want."
>
> But the horses didn't want it—they swerved apart; the earth didn't want it, sending up rocks through which riders must pass single file; the temples, the tank, the jail, the palace, the birds, the carrion, the Guest House, that came into view as they issued from the gap and saw Mau beneath: they didn't want it, they said in their hundred voices, "No, not yet," and the sky said, "No, not there." (Chapter 37)

Forgotten gods lurk in those small things of the world and they have long memories. Philology tells us we should listen to their hundreds of voices as we try making our ways to India. It also shows us how difficult that "Longest Journey," as Forster called it, will be.[25]

# I

# FROM HISTORY TO METHOD

# 1

## Why Textual Scholarship Matters

I

Why does textual scholarship matter? Most students of literature and culture who worked in the twentieth century would have thought that a highly specialized question, and many still do. But a hundred years ago the question would hardly have been posed at all. Until the early decades of the twentieth century what we now call literary and cultural studies was called philology, and all its interpretive procedures were clearly understood to be grounded in textual scholarship. But twentieth-century textual studies shifted their center from philology to hermeneutics, that subset of philological inquiry focused on the specifically literary interpretation of culture. From the vantage of the nineteenth-century philologist, this "turn to language" would have been seen as a highly specialized approach to the study of literature.

To the philologian, all possible meanings are a function of their historical emergence as material artifacts. The investigation of those artifacts is the foundation of literary and cultural studies. The Lower Criticism devotes itself to the analysis of the textual transcriptions; the Higher Criticism studies the sociohistory of the documents.

That comprehensive historical method was gradually displaced in the twentieth century, and the very term "philology" fell into disuse. In the horizon of Modernism, scholars turned to hermeneutics of many kinds and thence—after World War II—to the meta-interpretive interests that played themselves out, in equally diverse ways, under the general banner of Theory.

In that Modern and Post-modern historical perspective "Why does textual scholarship matter?" is perceived as a technical or subdisciplinary (or even predisciplinary) question, as René Wellek's influential mid-century handbook *Theory of Literature* (1949) makes very clear. Bibliographers and other dryasdust scholars investigate and edit the documents in their monkish cells so that serious students of literature and culture can read and interpret what the works mean for the world of living people.

But the emergence of digital media in the late twentieth century is forcing a shift back to the view of traditional philology, where textual scholarship was understood as the foundation of every aspect of literary and cultural studies. Here I shall give a brief explanation about why this shift in perspective is happening and how we should respond.

A simple observation throws the issue into sharp relief: "In the next fifty years the entirety of our inherited archive of cultural works will have to be reedited within a network of digital storage, access, and dissemination. This system, which is already under development, is transnational and transcultural."[1] Published in 2001, that comment underscores the massive changes that digital technology is bringing to our schools, libraries, and museums. Because all of our educational work, intra- as well as extramural, depends upon the clarity and comprehensiveness of the documentary record, these changes in the fundamental character of the record have a correspondingly significant effect on public education.

With relatively few exceptions, this editorial work—the migration of the paper-based archives to digital forms—is being undertaken either by librarians or by the agents of commercial entities like Google, Chadwyck-Healey, Gale, and Kluwer. The commercial examples are the most troubling from a scholar's and educator's point of view since these entities operate to maximize profit. The "public good" is a concern only insofar as the vocational agents for that good—educators and their institutions—can be induced to pay these entities for their products. Their work on our cultural inheritance, while often very useful, is always marked by cost-cutting procedures that damage or endanger the cultural record. For example, while The English Poetry Database (Chadwyck-Healey) provides a vast depository of books of verse, all the prose materials in those books were removed as an initial—a disastrous—editorial decision. For its part, Gale's Ecco database (Eighteenth-Century Collections Online) was generated by what is called "dirty OCR"—i.e., Optical Character Recognition software was run on a set of (old) microfilms of the original documents. Google Books is the same. The resulting digital transcriptions are often lamentable. And while Google Books has begun its work in a relatively benign way, it is a monopolistic enterprise. These cases, of special concern to scholars and educators, reflect but a small part of the ongoing "information revolution" that is bringing such promise and danger to the pubic good. They are important to society at large because they implicitly and practically argue that the Advancement of Profit rather than the Advancement of Learning should finally determine—"in the last instance," as Marxists used to say—our cultural heritage.

When materials are migrated through entities like university presses—here JSTOR is the outstanding example—the results are much more satisfying because the presses have always operated in close collaboration with educational institutions. Most impressive of all is the free culture approach that is the foundation of the Library of Congress.

Research libraries—the University of California, the University of Michigan, Stanford University, and the University of Virginia are notable examples—are also committing themselves to the migration of the paper archive to digital form. In these cases the transcription of the primary documents is generally executed with care. Accuracy is a great concern here because reliable preservation is the primary goal. But this laudable work by librarians throws into sharp relief a crucial point about textual studies. From a scholar's and educator's point of view, textual accuracy (along with basic documentary metadata about the process of transcription) is only a minimal sine qua non for textual materials. Librarians do not readily move beyond that specialized focus, nor should scholars or educators expect them to. Filling out and exposing the richness of our cultural inheritance is precisely the office of the scholar.

These examples remind us about two very broad obligations that scholars have by virtue of their vocation as educators. We are called to surveil and monitor this process of digitization. Much of it is now being carried out by agents who act, by will or by mistake, quite against the interests of scholars and educators—and in that respect, against the general good of society. So we must insist on participating. At the same time—as Umberto Eco, Robert Darnton, Nicholson Baker, and Roger Chartier, among others, keep reminding us—we have to protect our paper-based inheritance.

Implicit in these vocational obligations are a set of basic ideas about the meanings of our cultural records and about how to investigate them. The twentieth century's retreat from philology involved a specialized view of the interpretation of texts. Instead of taking a broadly based sociohistorical orientation, scholars and literary critics worked out various ways for treating social and historical factors as interpretive constants rather than complex variables. The model for the act of interpretation was an individual reader engaged with a particular "text," with the "text" being understood not as a document with complex histories, but as a linguistic construct per se. But our literary works—informational as well as imaginative—are not simply alphanumeric entities waiting to be engaged by a particular reader.

The need to migrate our cultural heritage to a digital condition has exposed the serious limitations in such an approach to the study of our cultural inheritance. The historical record is composed of a vast set of specific material objects that have been created and passed along through an even more vast network of agents and agencies. The meanings of the record—the interpretation of those meanings—are a function of the operations taking place in that dynamic network. Only a sociology of the textual condition can offer an interpretive method adequate to the study of this field and its materials. And this field is dynamic because agents in the present—Google and Kluwer, the Library of Congress and JSTOR—are all shaping and interpreting the record in particular and—from a humanist viewpoint—too often in very unfortunate ways.

Digitizing the archive is not about replacing it. It's about making it usable for the present and the future. To do that we have to understand, as best we can, how it functioned—how it made meanings—in the past. A major task lying before us—its technical difficulties are great—is to design a knowledge and information network that integrates, as seamlessly as possible, our paper-based inheritance with the emerging archive of born-digital materials.

## II

One doesn't have to be a textual scholar to register a certain alarm at the general situation I've just described. Nonetheless, it should be obvious that we won't bring reliable judgment to these complex problems without a good understanding of manuscript, book, and digital technologies—and traditional audio and visual technologies as well. Because here I want to focus on textual criticism specifically, I set aside the issues—significant though they are—that relate to audio and visual materials. My focus is, in any case, more fundamental since when cultural information is digitally transformed, it is still indexed through natural language.

So, let's begin by thinking again about these two technologies, bibliographical and digital. It is commonplace now, even among scholars, to distinguish between "static" paper-based documents and "dynamic" digital environments. If we negotiate these materials at the level of their immediate self-representations, the distinction is clear. If, on the other hand, we want a more critical understanding of these two modes of communication, we have to expose the social agencies that power and structure them. When we do that, we discover how the distinction is seriously misleading.

Today such an analysis is important for the reason already given: the entirety of our paper-based inheritance is being digitally remediated. A "Digital Condition" is overtaking and in certain respects replacing our "Textual Condition." How will this unfold? No one knows because no one yet understands the social and institutional implications of these technological changes. But while our Digital Condition is now only beginning to emerge, we have inhabited a Textual Condition for millennia, the Age of Print being the culminant phase of its astonishing emergence. That history has much to teach us now. Our Textual Condition has forged an extensive record of its own making—which is to say, a process of critical reflection in manuscript and print that is itself part of the character, shape, and meaning of the history.

Whether we work with bibliographical or with digital technology, scholars want an optimal access to and understanding of our documentary materials. In this respect we can see, at our historical moment, the relevance of philology and its textual critical foundation. We have to go back to the future. We need to recover what Trotsky called "the privilege of historical backwardness."[2]

In the 1980s editorial theory and method made a significant move into what became known as a "social theory of text." For Anglo-American scholarship, two books defined this turn: *A Critique of Modern Textual Criticism* (McGann, 1983) and *Bibliography and the Sociology of Texts* (McKenzie, 1986).[3] The move entailed rethinking a distinction we traditionally make between a text and its context. For the past twenty-five years many scholars have been exploring the fault lines of that distinction. Recent work in antebellum American studies has been especially interesting. At the outset of her inquiry into "the Poe Circle," for instance, Eliza Richards gives an admirable summary of a social text approach to literary study: "the poetics of creation are inseparable from the poetics of reception."[4]

The complete genetic information about any cultural work is coded in the double helix of its DNA, which defines the codependent relation of its production history and its reception history. While much more could and should be said about the structure of that codependent relation, the essential point to realize is that each strand of this double helix is produced by the collaboration of multiple agents. The terms "the poet" and "the reader" are high-level generalized descriptors of a dialectical process of a host of distributed persons and institutions.

In that frame of reference one can lay out a complete matrix for a sociohistorical interpretive method. The method is prescribed by six foundational protocols defining the mechanics of a social text. Briefly these are:

1. The social text is a Bakhtinian space (heteroglossia)
2. For a social text, *a* equals *a* if and only if *a* does not equal *a*
3. Textual fields arise codependently with interpretive action
4. Interpretive action is always performative/deformative
5. Interpretation of a social text proceeds at an inner standing point
6. Textual fields are *n*-dimensional

As I have explained these protocols elsewhere, I leave that aside in order to focus on a key practical question.[5] In different ways, all of the antebellum scholars who were my point of departure are either explicitly or implicitly calling for a "model of literary production that . . . is intersubjective and interactive" (Richards 5). What would such a model look like? The question can be sharply defined if we pose it with respect to the essential philological form that any "model of literary production" must be able to take. That basic form is the scholarly edition.

The quest for Richards's model has been pursued with greatest rigor in the tight little island of textual theory and editorial method. D. F. McKenzie became The Hero of Our Own Time not because he discovered the sociology of the text—we've known about that for a long time. He became The Hero because he knew that the idea of the social text had to be realized as a scholarly edition.

Such an edition would be addressing and answering some key—basically philological—questions. Could one develop a model for editing books and material objects rather than just the linguistic phenomena we call texts? To pose that question, as McKenzie did, was to lay open the true dimensions of what he was after: a model for editing texts in their contexts. So the initial question is a palimpsest concealing other salient questions. Could one develop a model for exposing and comparing relationships between phenomena that are radically discontinuous: different authors and their authorized texts, say, as well as the relations between various agents—individual as well as institutional—in an eventual field disposing more than just textual or bibliographical things? Could the model expose and examine relationships between phenomena—various works and their various agents—located in fields that are discontinuous in social time and space? Finally, could such machines be designed and actually built, the way the critical editions we inherit were designed and built?

The (alphanumeric) critical edition—developed and modified over many centuries, and well before the coming of print technology—is one of the most remarkable machines created by the ingenuity of Man. Its importance cannot be overstated, for it is a complete model of the enginery that has come to sustain nearly the whole of the cultural memory of the West. Its design flexibility is amazing both with respect to the numbers and kinds of materials it can represent, and to the network of social relations it both models and engages. But that is to put the matter too abstractly. We can see what these machines involve if we reflect briefly on a representative example—for instance, J. C. Mays's recent edition of Coleridge's poetical works.

This edition deserves the closest kind of study and I will return to it in Chapter 6. Let me here focus on certain key formal properties that it shares with scholarly editions in general.

The object of such works is to supply readers with a more or less comprehensive view of the current state of what we know about the works to be edited. Mays's critical and synoptic edition of Coleridge aspires to give a comprehensive view of the production and reception histories of all Coleridge's poetical works. This means that the edition is obligated to examine and represent every salient documentary witness of every poetical work and, in addition, to represent the social and historical relations in which these witnesses stand to each other. The key critical means for displaying that information is the text/apparatus device. Linked to that elementary machinery are various commentaries, annotations, indexes, bibliographies, maps, chronologies, and appendices that help to elucidate the materials in brief or extensive ways.

Most important—and rarely noticed as such—is the use of various symbols and abbreviations in these works. So in Mays's edition we have notes like the following (to the title of poem no. 156, "This Lime-Tree Bower My Prison": "C's predilection for TP's bower—or 'Jasmine Harbour'—is corroborated by other sources, e.g., Poole I 202, H Works XVII 119, Cottle Rem 150–151. TP's walnut-tree and elms (lines 52, 55) likewise had a real existence." A list of abbreviations in the edition fills out these truncated references, and the procedure allows the editor to save a good deal of paper-space.

But the references, abbreviated or not, are far more significant than as space-saving devices. They are, in fact, vehicles for traversing space and time—the edition's hyperlinks to the received sociohistorical network of materials with which the author's work is meshed and implicated. They are the elementary signs that Coleridge's works are social texts and do not make explicit all of their meanings or all of their conditions of meaning.

Joseph Cottle, Thomas Poole, and William Hazlitt—the lives of these men are closely bound up with the life and the works of Coleridge. More to the specifically textual point of the matter, we know about their relationships through specific manuscript or printed sources, some direct sources, most indirect. The abbreviations in the quoted passage reference those sources and, in so doing, expose yet another remarkable truth about scholarly editions: they assume the existence of reference depositories of a highly sophisticated kind. "Literature was never only words": although Kate Hayles's words draw attention to a book's typographical and design features, a work like Mays's edition plunges far more deeply into the precise significance of bibliographical materiality. The edition is a model, a theoretical instantiation, of the vast and distributed textual network in which we have come to embody our knowledge.

So The Critical Edition—the idea of it that Mays learned about through his scholarly studies—supplies him with a machinery for delivering a summary representation of the production and reception histories of Coleridge's poetical work. It then links that representation—along with all its imbedded parts and sub-links—to the social and institutional networks that made those histories possible. The edition thus involves a comprehensive meta-interpretation of Coleridge's poetical work—at once a reflection of what it has come to mean in its historical emergence, and a forecast of how it might be taken to mean in the future. In observing this of Mays's edition I am not saying that the work is (for example) empirically comprehensive in its summary of the poetical materials or the meanings that have been or could be built from those materials. It is not nor could it be. Mays scants some materials and overlooks others, and of course there are materials—production and reception materials both—that undoubtedly exist but have not yet come to light. Nonetheless, the edition is both theoretically and methodologically complete. What is not there could be there; nothing about Coleridge's poetry has been alienated as such.


### III


We are now called to design and build digital equivalents of such a machinery. These scholarly devices will have to comprehend works like *The Rossetti Archive* (1993–present), which is a born-digital representation of nondigital work, as well as works like *From Lexia to Perplexia* (2000),[6] which is without explicit connections to nondigital materials. Such machineries have at this point only the most primitive existence. A library that houses manuscripts, books, and digital works is precisely such a machine, storing these materials and providing access to them. But the machinery of our emerging digital environments is at this point primitive to a degree since we have yet to demonstrate how these different kinds of materials can be integrated for study. Nor does anyone yet have a good idea about how online scholarly works will be sustained beyond a twenty-year horizon. And while that may be an entrepreneur's horizon, it is not a scholar's. We don't have the necessary knowledge.

Philology and textual criticism can help us gain that knowledge. The first thing to realize is that the general conceptual character of the machinery we require can be theorized. We're looking to deploy the system of philology as a digital emergence. Second, because the history of the emergence of traditional scholarly editions represents the material history of pre-digital philology, we can be confident about realizing the theory of a new philology by building models of what we now think the theory must involve. *The Perseus Project* (1987–present), *The Rossetti Archive,* and *The Canterbury Tales* project (1989–present) are early attempts at building such models. In the case of *The Rossetti Archive*—about which I can speak from an inner standing-point—building the model exposed the theoretical limitations of the model. That exposure led next to the undertaking of NINES, which attempts a more comprehensive realization of the theory of the new philology.

As a philological endeavor, this machinery has to meet the following functions and requirements. The first two reflect what traditional philology calls the Lower Criticism, the second two, the Higher Criticism.

1. The depository of artifacts must be comprehensive.

D. G. Rossetti's original works, *The Rossetti Archive* and *From Lexia to Perplexia,* all share the common space of an emergent cultural history. Although I've set aside all discussion of audio and visual materials (including film and television), I mention them here in passing to underscore the requirement that the archive be comprehensive.

2. Its different parts must be organized in a network of internal links and external connections that can be represented as conventions.

Fundamentally, this is a process of identifying and classifying artifacts and their component parts. Any given artifact will have many identifiable parts and can be variously classified. Such and such an object is (for example) at once a poem, a printed page, a sonnet (of a certain kind), a proof sheet (corrected or uncorrected, authorial or nonauthorial), a section of a larger poetical object, a translation, and so on and so on. Its parts are similarly multiple. Daniel Pitti likes to begin his XML classes by handing out a recipe printed on a single page and asking each member of the class to take five minutes making a list of the object's formal features. The ensuing class discussion quickly reveals the range of possibilities.

For materially different types of artifacts—printed texts, maps, photographs—sorting and classifying become yet more complicated when the ultimate purpose is to arrange them in a system that permits coherent analysis and study. The problem is greatly amplified when the manipulable physical properties scale to radically different measures, as is the case with a depository that includes paper-based objects and born-digital objects.

> 3. The total system must rest in a single perspective that reflects the conception of the system generally agreed upon by its users.

In terms of traditional philology, this rule explains the codependent relation that holds between the Lower and the Higher Criticism. That relationship reflects the social character of the system generally considered. In a nonhistorical system—Aristotle's for example—the parts and classifications are conceived a priori. That is the theory of the system. In philology, however, Aristotle's categories and topoi are understood as socially inflected and historically emergent.

Designing a system in the horizon of philology, then, requires building critical devices that require the system to be modifiable through use. If the system is not "open" in that way it is not, in the philological perspective, theoretically complete.

> 4. From that general conceptual vantage, the system must have the flexibility to license, and ultimately store, an indefinite number of particular views of its artifacts and their relations, including different views of the system as a whole.

That set of functions reflects the fact that a philological system is fundamentally a system of social software. It may be modeled and then instantiated in the paper-based form that we have inherited and still use, or in the online network that continues to emerge today and acquire more precise definition. Realizing this important homology between bibliographical and digital networks is crucial as we try to design the latter to the needs of scholars and educators.

Thus, the initial design of the Collex software that powers the NINES initiative was conceived to allow users to

> search, browse, annotate, and tag electronic objects and to repurpose them in illustrated, interlinked essays or exhibits. By saving information about user activity (including the construction of annotated collections and exhibits) as 'remixable' metadata, the Collex system writes current practice into the scholarly record and permits knowledge discovery based not only on predefined characteristics or 'facets' of digital objects, but also on the contexts in which they are placed by a community of scholars.[7]

Developing a practical interface for realizing that general goal will only emerge from building, testing, and modifying design models. Collex was redesigned for NINES (December 2008) to simplify the access and usability of its key functions. Redesign will doubtless continue as new search and repurposing functions—some planned, some not yet conceived—are implemented.

The quality of online information and the knowledge we expect to gain from it thus remains crucial. Scrupulous minds regularly, and rightly, urge caution in using online materials. As we know, they can be quite unreliable or worse. Enthusiastic educators add that the problematic state of online information presents an opportunity to help train students in methods of critical assessment.

Scholars assume that if we make something available for study—online or in print makes no difference here—the material should be accurately disseminated. A stable URL for an online work ensures a certain level of authority for materials that are so easily copied and represented; but of course the data at that URL can also be easily modified without notice. It can also disappear.

A scholar necessarily sees that situation as a problem. So if they create a website, reliability and sustainability are (or should be) primary concerns. In fact, however, most scholars who create online materials—the "content" is often excellent—often give little serious thought to either issue. For instance, most—nearly all—websites created in HTML will not outlive their creators, and the duration of the materials may well be much shorter even than that. Furthermore, suppose the materials are corrected or modified. Has provision been made to preserve those changes or even to keep an accurate record of them?

Most scholars who use online resources don't think about these matters for a very good reason: they are accustomed to operating in a paper-based environment, which has worked out—built into its machinery—forms and procedures for dealing with such issues. These forms and procedures are not infallible but they are reliable. As McKenzie understood so well, our paper-based documentary record bears within itself the history of its own making. How will the digital record do that? We don't yet know. What we do know—listen to the philologists—is that most of the record will be lost. So the problem is not to save this record: the problem is what we will choose to save, and why, and how will we do it?

If you look at most online scholarly editions—I leave aside the question of their structural stability—you will access a certain text or set of texts the scholar has chosen. The edition will perhaps be meshed with commentaries and notes and linked to other materials remotely located. Assuming all this is done knowledgeably and with care, how useful—in a scholarly sense—is the result? The answer comes if we compare such a work with an edition one might publish in print. Not without reason does the profession sanction the latter and look skeptically on the former. The printed book is immediately gathered into a complex network of trusted information and institutional relations that prepare it for further critical and scholarly engagements. The online work is more widely accessible, it's true, but only in a relatively abstract sense. It threatens to become what digerati call a "siloed" object—linked everywhere . . . and nowhere. It lacks the professional infrastructure that the scholarly book possesses by virtue of the mature social network in which it is located.

And there are further problems with the way online editing is regularly imagined. With rare exceptions, when scholars create such works they transcribe a single text. Indeed, the common "digital view" of scholarly editing is that all one needs is a single, carefully produced digital transcription—complete with facsimiles of course—of a good copy of a particular work. Put that online, make it stable, and voilà, a scholarly edition.

But think again about the Mays edition of Coleridge, which is a critical interpretation of all the salient witnesses for each of Coleridge's poems. More than that, the edition assumes that every single copy of every published (and unpublished) Coleridge work is potentially relevant to the critical survey. That assumption is what makes scholars assemble libraries of early materials and pressure their institutional depositories to augment their collections.

One can certainly design and, to an extent, build an online version of a work like the Mays edition—*The Rossetti Archive* and the *Canterbury Tales* project are good examples. More, digital resources have brought exciting new critical opportunities to scholarly works of that kind. Replete or innovative as they may be, however, they lack the institutional infrastructure that would integrate them, equally and simultaneously, to their bibliographical inheritance and their emerging digital network. Consequently, necessarily, these projects starve as scholarship.

That situation is rapidly changing—for better *and* for worse, I'm quite sure. I sketch this history, and end with these problems, to help guide the needed changes along lines that will meet our educational demands—the traditional requirements of what was anciently called *philologia perennis*.

# 2

# "The Inorganic Organization of Memory"

I

Let's try to imagine philology as the ground of literary and cultural studies. Philology, not philosophy, because philology's horizon is not a history of ideas but an institutional and programmatic history. And not philology as Wilamowitz presented it to Nietzsche, or as post-Nietzscheans expelled it from humane studies, but Philology in a New Key—a new arrangement of that canonical discipline so neglected after the nineteenth century.[1] Those huddled, dryasdust positivists are yearning to be free.

An imaginative recovery of philological method means revisiting some salient moments in our recent institutional history. I begin by telling two stories. One is personal but is relevant because it connects to my second story. With the latter I'll be retelling a story we *have* all heard, many times, but perhaps not as I'll be telling it.

One other preliminary. It's important that these are stories, not "narratives," and least of all "metanarratives."

So then the stories.

1975 was an important year for me. It was the year I left the University of Chicago for a fifteen-month stint in England and Europe working on my edition of Byron, and after that, seven years working at Johns Hopkins, then a key center for the advancement of Theory Studies in the United States. It was the year I read the just-published English translation of Jürgen Habermas's *Legitimation Crisis*. And most important for present purposes, it was the year I had a conversation with Stanley Fish about our different views of humanities research and scholarship.

The conversation happened in the spring of 1975—I didn't actually take up my work in Baltimore until the fall of 1976, after I came back from Europe. Stanley was showing me around the Hopkins campus and we were talking about the work we were each doing. I asked him what he thought about the library. He gave it a perfunctory approval—I don't recall his exact words—but then he added a comment I *do* remember: "I don't need a library for what I do." And I remember as well my reply: "Stanley, I can't do what I do *without* a library."

In 1975 this question of the library seemed to me pretty important, and Habermas's book signaled why. The legitimation crisis that Habermas saw emerging in the general social and political sphere was emerging as well in the institutions of humanities research and scholarship. *My 1975 view of humanities legitimation was growing more and more inflected by philology and editorial method.* That way of thinking—once Germanically celebrated as *Altertumwissenschaft*—was decidedly *not* in the main francophone stream of things at the time. On the other hand, Stanley and his view were very much in that 1970s stream of consciousness. As evidence I cite three defining—in the lexicon of those days—three *hegemonic*—institutional events we can trace to those years: the installation of Theory—of *philosophy* rather than *philology*—at the center of academic discussion; the explosion of the system of professional conferencing; and the liftoff period of humanities think tanks, institutes, and centers, all extraprogrammatic. A lively set of conversations on every aspect of literature and culture began to dominate humanities education and research. Indeed, if you wanted to take part in those conversations, a key move would be to invent a new topic altogether and then try to get a conversation going around it. An Interpretive Community might be waiting for you.

An Interpretive Community and (or) a Legitimation Crisis, as we soon realized when *The Postmodern Condition* appeared in 1979. Like Habermas, Jean-François Lyotard saw the crisis as a problem bequeathed to philosophy by modern science and its techno-performative criteria of legitimate knowledge.[2] Where modern secular societies grounded their knowledge foundations on instrumental reason, Lyotard called for a "postmodern science," which would change "the meaning of the word knowledge, while expressing how such a change can take place. It is producing not the known, but the unknown. And it suggests a model of legitimation that has nothing to do with maximized performance, but has as its basis difference understood as paralogy." (PC 60). Not fully explained in *The Postmodern Condition,* paralogy is Lyotard's term for a philosophical method that exposes the limit conditions of any traditional form or state of knowledge. See Lyotard's *Le Différend* (1983), where the idea is more fully explored.

Those ideas quickly became a *point d'appui* for a broad-ranging discussion across the humanities. And of course Lyotard's institutional position helps to explain why. He was a member of the faculty of philosophy at the University of Paris VIII, Vincennes. Founded in 1969 as a direct result of the student upheavals in 1968, Paris VIII quickly became the center of a strongly politicized Theory Movement through the influence of its faculty of philosophy, whose members included Foucault (as chair), Lacan, Lyotard, Guattari, Deleuze, Badiou, and Negri, among others less celebrated. As the Theory Conversation metastasized in the academy, the significance of Lyotard's specific focus—to rethink programs of advanced academic research—slipped from attention.

A little historicizing here is definitely in order—this is my second story. For despite the book's famous attack on instrumental reason and "performativity" as measures of legitimation, Lyotard's philosophical reflections had very definite instrumental purposes. The *Conseil des universités du Québec* had asked him to write a "Report on Knowledge" that would help guide the Council in shaping policy initiatives for its university programs. The first state of Lyotard's book was a typescript submitted to the Council under the title *Les problèmes du savoir dans les sociétés industrielles les plus développées.*[3]

That explicit institutional context, neglected but not forgotten in the discussions that ensued, has obscured an even more interesting dimension of the book's pragmatic focus. Though prepared as a report for higher education authorities in French Canada, it was clearly written as a guide for a radical reorganization of higher education in France, and at Paris VIII in particular. The final sentence of the Introduction to *The Postmodern Condition*—it is no part of the original report—is revealing: "I dedicate this report to the Institut Polytechnique de Philosophie of the Université de Paris VIII (Vincennes)—at this very postmodern moment that finds the *University* nearing what may be its end, while the *Institute* may just be beginning" (my italics). The significance of this dedication is explained in footnote 133 of the original report. Having posed the question whether "philosophy as legitimation is condemned to disappear" in face of the power of positive science and technology, Lyotard gives this answer: "it is possible that [philosophy] will not be able to carry out [its] work, or at least advance it, without revising its ties to the university institution." See on this matter the preamble to the *Projet d'un institut polytechnique de philosophie* (typescript, Département de philosophie, Université de Paris VIII [Vincennes], 1979). Lyotard carried this note over to the published book.

The full significance of all that would not begin to come clear until later. The dedicatee of Lyotard's book, that *Institut Polytechnique de Philosophie* of the University of Paris VIII (Vincennes), was not in fact about to supplant what Lyotard regarded as the outmoded research programs of the traditional university. His *institut polytechnique* never achieved institutional realization beyond a typescript of its program, perhaps still lodged somewhere in the records of the philosophy department of Paris VIII. A proposal for reorganizing the university must have been a topic of discussion at Paris VIII throughout the 1970s. If Lyotard actually thought the plan might be realized in 1979, as his book's dedication suggests, the next year he would know otherwise. Paris VIII was moved from Vincennes to St. Denis in 1980 with its departments intact and without that postmodern *institut polytechnique* Lyotard hoped to see.

Why do I tell this story? Three reasons. First, it illustrates an interesting fault line in Lyotard's approach to the university's crisis of legitimacy. Though based in a critique of instrumentalism, Lyotard's report was itself instrumentalist. It projected an institutional reorganization as the means for promoting the practice of "postmodern science." After 1979 he turned from his intra- and extramural political work in order to pursue philosophy as such, and in particular aesthetics.

Second, and much more important, we can now also see how that turn would become widespread in the research academy, building into the much-publicized "Crisis in the Humanities." Stanley Fish's recent reflections in the *New York Times* on the 2012 Modern Language Association (MLA) Convention have a backlog of more than twenty years.[4]

Most important of all, however, Lyotard's failed project can help us toward a different point of view on that crisis, which is my object here. I begin by looking more closely at Lyotard's proposal. I will then consider Bernard Stiegler's interesting move to rethink the proposal within its own discursive terms (Continental Philosophy). Finally, Stiegler will help me shift the investigation from philosophy to philology, where the problems of humanities research and education, and especially our current problems— digitally enhanced, so to speak—would be better located and addressed.

For Lyotard, the central "function" of a research institution is "speculative legitimation" (PC 39). Pound's early slogan, "Make it new!" forms the background of *The Postmodern Condition*'s explicitly avant-garde "agonistics" (PC 16). Here are several of Lyotard's formulations. Postmodern knowledge is a research program:

"to make a new 'move' (an unexpected statement)" (16)

"[for] the promulgation of new norms for understanding . . . a new field of research for the language of science" (61)

"[to promote] new norms . . . new rules" (61)

"[to] model . . . an 'open system', in which a statement becomes relevant if it 'generates ideas', that is, if it generates other statements and other game rules." (64)

"[which] properly conceived is to "generate ideas, in other words, new statements" (65)

"[for pursuing] the invention of new rules of the game" (80)

Those passages recall nothing so much as Fish's recent remarks in the *Times* on the 2012 meetings of the MLA. Commenting ironically on "the topics that in previous years dominated the meeting and identified the avant-garde" of the profession, he scanned the program for what "those in the know" now see as the "cutting edge" of disciplinary work. Though focused on the 2012 MLA, his essay implicitly evoked some forty years of proliferant humanities conferencing.

Stanley didn't attend the sessions in Seattle but he didn't have to. The printed program told the tale. The latest "avant-garde" is "the digital humanities," which delivered, he observes, "upwards of 40 sessions" to the conference. Sketching a parodic kind of Long Revolution in the humanities, Stanley was pushing a skeptical pin point into the *idea* and *ideal* of a latest "rage" or "new insurgency" for the humanities. What Lyotard took up in 1979 as a looming institutional tragedy, appeared to Fish in 2012 as an amusing, long-playing farce.

Now I've been as involved as anyone with those "digital humanities," which locate, I think, something at least as important as the theoretical conversations of our once-upon-a-not-so-very-long-time ago. But I do not see digital technology as a "new dispensation" for the humanities. Fish's *New York Times* essay points toward our profession's fifty-year preoccupation with Making it New. He reminds us that we have grown a habit of locating humane studies in a presentist, just-in-time horizon. A philological conscience presses against such habits. The past and the future are not simply opportunities to be exploited, they are also—perhaps even more—obligations we keep forgetting and neglecting.

And it isn't true, as he averred in his essay, that "disciplines like physics or psychology or statistics discard projects and methodologies no longer regarded as cutting edge." I hesitate to say anything about psychology since—let me confess—I don't see that the psychology and dream studies in Aristotle, Herodotus, and Plutarch are any less useful and interesting than those of Freud, Klein, Erikson, or Rogers. And as for the eighteenth-century physics of Newton or the statistics of Bayes, both are alive and well, even indispensable. Surely we're all aware that "cutting edge" may be no more than academic rhetoric; *and,* something even more important, that scholarship thrives on the privilege of historical backwardness. Whatever the discipline, the "projects and methodologies" of *Wissenschaft* only get discarded when they can't contribute to disciplinary obligations.

Like, say, astrology? Well, it once had much to contribute to astronomy, cosmology, politics, psychology, and of course literature. But now astrology has attenuated disciplinary obligations. It is only, as we say, "historically important." But that it *is* "historically important" is itself important, certainly for the humanist, as our daily newspapers daily remind us. From the *Times* to the tabloids, the ancient wisdom of Terence is repeated: *Homo sum; humani nil a me alienum puto*—which I'll render freely as "I'm a human being so there's nothing about human beings that doesn't interest me." Even as dead a discipline as astrology will always be as vital and important *now* as the dead or extinct languages we humanists cherish and sometimes even pursue as research fields.

Right there, in those most ephemeral of documents, I see the essential disciplinary obligation of the humanist scholar. As already noted, my polestar, August Boeckh, called it "the knowledge of what is and has been known." When Lyotard argued that "postmodern science "is producing not the known, but the unknown," he was explicitly setting his face against Boeckh's famous definition of philology, which Lyotard, like Nietzsche, read in narrowly positivist terms, as I never have. But since Boeckh did cast his thought in those hard nominals, Lyotard may be excused on this matter. Myself, I would recover the infinitives that rest latent in Boeckh's nouns. For what we know and what we have known are ongoing. So Philology: *to* preserve, monitor, investigate, and augment our cultural inheritance, including all the material means by which it has been realized and transmitted. Infinitives are better because they signal the conscious obligation that a discipline undertakes. So we would rewrite Terence just a bit: *Homo sum; sit humani nil a me alienum puto*—or, "Nothing human *should ever* escape my interest." Terence in a new key.

## II

Research aiming to produce "not the known, but the unknown"; and a *program* of such research, institutionally located. That is what Lyotard wanted. He was thinking critically about minds like August Boeckh's, of course, but also of Marx and Feuerbach. That's why his book proposed not simply to understand the world of knowledge production, but to change it. His projected polytechnic institute would transform the works and days of the Paris VIII philosophy faculty into an exemplary, and most of all an institutional, *Novum Organum Scientiarum.*

Fifteen years later, Bernard Stiegler would begin his critical reflections on what was right and what was wrong with the philosophic orientation of Paris VIII. The key book in this regard is his first, *La Technique et le temps* (1994)—a seriously dense work whose central argument is yet simple and important.[5] (It was anticipated, let me add in passing, by Marshall McLuhan's studies of "the extensions of man," and has been a decades-long focus of the phenomenology of the Radical Constructivist movement.)

So, the critique. Lyotard proposes that an adequate science must seek "not what is known but what is unknown"—as it were, *Die Erkenntnis des Unerkannten.* What is not known lies open to the progress of Enlightenment, with its repeated critical reflections toward "new norms for understanding." Stiegler inverts that prospective by rethinking the status of established forms of knowledge—i.e., the technical and systematic facticities by which knowledge gets materially implemented. These are the regular concern of instrumental reason. Among those "technics" of knowledge, Stiegler focuses on written language, which has served as the paradigm of *techne* ever since Socrates got so worried about it. It has been the focus of philosophy for most of twentieth-century philosophy. And of course it is the focus of philology.

In a traditional critical perspective, these systems generate determinate forms ("facticities") of a knowledge that seeks (in the language of the technicians of science) continuous "self-correction" or (in the language of the philosophers of science) *aufhebung.* But when Stiegler names these systems—and the System of these systems—"the inorganic organization of memory" (TT 172), he radically shifts both of those interpretations of productive knowledge. Deploying the language of Continental Philosophy, Heidegger especially, he explains the significance of the inorganic condition of material things:

> A tool is, before anything else, memory: if this were not the case, it could never function as reference. . . . The tool refers in principle to an already-there, to a fore-having of something that the *who* has not itself necessarily lived, but which comes under it . . . in its concern. . . . A tool functions first as image-consciousness. (TT 154–155)

This way of thinking is close to Wittgenstein's reflections on learning a language in the *Philosophical Investigations.* A word or a wheel; an alphanumeric script or an electronic circuit: before anything else, each of these minute particulars is an established memory of the complex system in which it is a codependent function. When the great philologist *de nos jours* Don McKenzie remarked that every document carries the history of its own making, he was saying much the same thing. Or in a lexicon we may be familiar with from digital humanities: "all text is marked text."[6]

When Stiegler calls the systematic technicity of science "the inorganic organization of memory," the pivotal word is "inorganic." For Lyotard and the Hegelian tradition, "inorganic" signals a state of fixedness, a negation that must be negated. (Coleridge defined this negative condition, lucidly if also romantically, when he observed that "all objects (as objects) are essentially fixed and dead": *Biographia Literaria,* chapter 13). The fixed material conditions of any science—its established methods, tools, data, and institutions—are what a "postmodern science" must repeatedly correct and overcome. The history of those repetitions, the *temps* of Heidegger's famous book, becomes a figure of the spirit's redemption from inorganic facticity.

Stiegler's book *Technics and Time* recollects Heidegger's *Being and Time* in order to translate its terms: specifically, to redeem its argument from the idea of spiritual transcendence. For Stiegler, the inorganic character of any science is not a negation to be negated, but one to be embraced and explored. To imagine otherwise is to lose sight of the importance of the past in the present. Like our genetic code, the past is an inheritance pervading the present, but always as a history that can't be known because it can't be experienced, though it can be studied, translated, and—as we say these says—repurposed. But always as it is inorganic inheritance. The institutions of a science thus appear a kind of *felix culpa*, the gift they return, sometimes consciously, more often blindly, to the infatuated Faustian world they ordinarily serve.

Stiegler's science is positive, inorganic, objective. It is the "image of a consciousness" that keeps forgetting, that keeps trying to forget—as it were, *for good*—its primal human awareness, which Stiegler calls "destitution." He argues that if it is sometimes good to try to forget, it is always *better* to try to remember, even if (and as) we always keep failing. This failing to remember is what his book subtitles "The Fault of Epimetheus," a fault which Epimetheus's brother Prometheus will institute, positively and objectively, as "the Advancement of Learning." For Stiegler, Prometheus (Science) does not (and cannot) repair the fault—the memory lapse—of his brother Epimetheus. What he can (and does) do is repeatedly fix and reestablish that fault so that it can be unpacked for further exploration.

A note on Stiegler's procedure: Tying his discussion to a commentary on the ancient Greek myth of Prometheus and Epimetheus, he argues that technology and science are forms of cultural memory and should be pursued and investigated as such. That is for him their deepest instrumental function. But something else is important here. Stiegler fails to invoke two other cultural deposits even though each has been, historically considered, common points of reference for these topics. I mean the story of the Tower of Babel and the doctrine of Original Sin. Their absence from his book is unlikely to have been accidental, but even if it were, it remains important. Closely related, both are monotheist myths that warn against forbidden knowledge. They organize knowledge into the permitted and the unpermitted, and threaten death if the prohibition is breached.

Two comments are worth adding here. First, Stiegler argues against the view of a person as redeemable spirit imprisoned in corruptible flesh. Indeed, he regards the distinction as invidious. Rather, Death and mortality are presented as human life's primal limit conditions. Hence his approach to his subject through Hellenic rather than the available Judeo-Christian traditions. Second, Stiegler assents to the basic myth of all science: that knowledge, though fated to fail, is nonetheless an absolute human good. This is why, looking at science in a philosophical perspective, he calls "the history of philosophy . . . *a history of mistakes,* awkwardnesses, distortions, and sinister failings *that had to be*" (TT 210). No matter that knowledge is often, even most often, at fault, mistaken, in error. That fault line is essential to the dynamic of the pursuit of knowledge, giving a relational definition to its shifting phases.[7]

The practical work of science—the "inorganic organization of memory"—produces an open documentary archive of human self-study. This archive is to be consciously exposed as a condition of infinite limitation. Or as the poet shrewdly observed:

In play, there are two pleasures for your choosing,
The One is winning, and the other, losing. (Byron, *Don Juan,* Canto XIV)


## III


Replacing traditional science with a science of the unknown, Lyotard saw the need for disciplinary change at the institutional level. Reflecting on legitimation crisis, Lyotard, and the Theory Movement in general, Stiegler recovers the fixed forms of instrumental reason. Facts, data, ontologies, and the network of academic institutional structures comprise an archive of occluded human memory.

Stiegler's argument restores historicity as a requirement for the human sciences. But his pivotal category, "the inorganic," while philosophically appropriate, leaves the *science* of his concept wanting. We see this because the reference of Stiegler's "inorganic" is not Nature, whether classical or quantum. It is the human, the factive historical world. Stiegler's philosophical approach, like Lyotard's, inevitably abstracts our attention from the expanding universe of historiated particulars.

His philosophical argument does not make a practical engagement with the archive he is so concerned with. Indeed, the argument tends toward what a Marxist might call a *surplus* ignorance about the actual "inorganic organization of memory" now ready to hand for us: that is to say, our libraries and archives straining with the pressure of digital change. Yet there *is* a science of archival memory. It is philology, an organized method for giving practical access to our inorganic organizations of memory. It is the science whose ground is the long tail of our awkward, fractured, and sinister history.

The method of philosophy, like science, seeks to generalize its detailed investigations, whether conceptual or empirical. The method of philology, like history, is different. Its orders of procedure are philology's various subdisciplines: paleography, bibliography, stemmatics, textual criticism, hermeneutics, and so forth—the entire array of what was organized in the nineteenth century as "the lower and the higher criticism." The primary operations of philosophy are to test, reconstruct, or falsify its subjects of attention: think of Plato, Kant, Heisenberg, or Popper. But these are the subroutines of philology. Its chief operation is to thicken what it knows and fill out its field of attention: think of Herodotus, Wolf, Grimm, or Boeckh. Or Milman Parry when he observes of philology's "historical method": "I make for myself a picture of great detail."[8] Truth in the ordinary philosophical or scientific senses of the term is a heuristic concern of philological method. *Nil alienum.* For the philologist, astrology is as true and as rich in consequence as the Pythagorean theorem, dialectics, or Planck's constant. And philology has a science, an order of method, for accessing its kind of truth.

The particular need we now have for philology is thrown into focus by a recent book by David Weinberger, *Too Big to Know* (2010).[9] It is a book for the scholar and the interested citizen alike—not the least of its virtues. Another is its critical understanding that "the Internet"—the hero of the book—"by its nature contains much diversity and many, many disagreements" (46). Here I want to pursue one line of disagreement, and

I'll begin with a key sentence that invites me to do so. Weinberger is addressing the difference between the traditional library and the internet. "We need to understand what of the old is worth holding on to, and what limitations of the new technology are going to trap and tempt us (46)." When I imagine a philologist parsing that sentence, this is what I think:

—as to "understand[ing] what of the old is worth holding on to," the sobering truth is that we cannot understand, and further, that we will always be too late recognizing our failure to understand. On this matter many examples could be cited, though one may suffice, being so notorious: the burning of Byron's *Memoirs*. A group of men, most of them friends of the recently deceased poet, several among his oldest and most devoted friends, assembled in the late spring of 1824 to decide what to do with the *Memoirs* Byron left in trust with his close friend Thomas Moore. They decided that the memory of the great poet would be best served if the document was burned. And it was.

In truth, everything of the old is worth holding on to. Still, most of it will be lost in one of two ways. It will either disappear through what we might call, adapting Robert Frost, "the slow smokeless burning of decay" and neglect; or it will get—wonderful word—*deaccessioned*. Alas, the latter process regularly happens "behind the backs," as Marx was wont to say, of seriously interested parties. Of this we were recently reminded by the Google Settlement discussions, which took place behind the backs of the educational community.

—and then as to "the limitations of the new technology [that will] trap and tempt us" into error, the volatile state of our new technology has multiplied those dangers. But one particularly serious danger is very old: the temptation to think we can "understand what of the old is worth holding on to."

With that past as prologue, let's look more closely at Weinberger's useful take on the character of the Internet. "We are in a crisis of knowledge," he remarks, "at the same time that we are in an epochal exaltation of knowledge." The crisis comes from "our fear for the institutions on which we have relied for trustworthy knowledge," the traditional archival systems; our exaltation "comes from *the networking of knowledge*" being driven by information technologies (xiii).

As knowledge becomes networked, the smartest person in the room isn't the person standing at the front lecturing us, and isn't the collective wisdom of those in the room. The smartest person in the room is the room itself: the network that joins the people and ideas in the room, and connects to those

outside of it. . . . [K]nowledge is becoming inextricable from—literally un-
thinkable without—the network that enables it. (xiii)

Weinberger's book will unpack the implications of this provocative and
useful passage. I mean the practical implications, for *Too Big to Know* is
a very good example of what Continental Philosophy calls instrumental
reason. The book knows how to think about building and using "the inorganic organization of knowledge."

But more needs to be thought and said on that matter so let me begin
with Weinberger's representation of "the network." If I agree that "knowledge is . . . inextricable . . . from the network that enables it," as I do, I
also think that this is not "becoming" the case because of the digital information network. It was the very thought that led Ptolemy Soter to
found the Library of Alexandria, which was conceived as a network for
organizing the study of the documents of the known world. Every library, archive, and museum only functions if it has some kind of standardized procedure for networking its materials. The encoding system
for the library of Alexandria was the Greek alphabet.

Of course the digital character of the internet and the scale of its interests present special organizational problems. Not the least of these is the
one I began with: the skew between our traditional cultural inheritance
and the emerging digital corpus. But the fundamental symmetry between
any library on one hand, and the internet on the other, is important to
understand, especially now. For a traditional library is always also, like
the internet, a library of libraries. Besides, when we think about the problems of scale that come with digital information systems—knowledge
that is too big to know—our digital focus often obscures the true dimensions of the problem of scale. But more on that point in a moment.

Nor is it true that "the smartest person in the room is the room itself."
The smartest person in the room is always some person in the room. This
is the case because someone in the room must *think* and use the room,
even if the room appears—what it can never be—a full automaton. The
complex functions of a room like the internet or a library system determine that it could be any person and always is someone. When Socrates
said that he was wiser than other men because he had a keen sense of his
own ignorance, he made a representation—a second order image—of the
wisest person in the room. But he also made a third order representation
of the idea of a complex network. Socrates was using the functions of the
Platonic academy, which was another network of information. It evolved
into the aggregated educational network we might well call, with Lyotard,
a polytechnic institute.

But if it isn't the case that the room is the smartest person in the room, to think and say so is both important and smart. The thought is a heuristic move directing our attention to the problems of organizing inorganic materials for human use. The digital network is, crucially and like every library, an *inter*network. A traditional library is always more or less extensively internetworked, as Union Catalogues suggest and as a project like Georgia's GALILEO shows.[10] But the digital internet's global condition exposes the instrumental scale of the problems, and opportunities, it presents.

That instrumental scale is by no means narrowly digital. The internet is being built by and for various parties who regularly work independently of each other (but often not), or at cross purposes (or not) and with very different agendas (or not). Invincible ignorance is as pervasive as the spirit of cooperation, and as disparate as the languages and cultures involved—national, ethnic, professional, technical. And so, miraculously (and ominously) the construction proceeds.

Philology long ago worked out methods for negotiating these kinds of amazing environments. Consider for a moment two of philology's elementary rules: first, in researching a problem, always examine the original materials *in situ*; second, consult the primary materials at least twice, once at the beginning and again at the end of your work. Surrogates, digital or otherwise, may serve the work at some point, but they cannot substitute for those first hand visits.

The full significance of those rules, particularly the second, is less apparent than it should be. As to the first, any person can appreciate that a xerox or photo or other relatively primitive copy is not a reed on which you want to lean. But a reasonable person today might demur and suggest that, say, if you had your documentary evidence in 1200 dpi color-corrected digital facsimiles to scale, that would be fine. It would indeed be fine. Nonetheless, to imagine it could substitute for on-site work is both a practical mistake and, worse, a misunderstanding of philological method.

I give two examples from my own pedantic history, one with Byron, the other with Rossetti. Both involved the great Houghton Library. The examples are nothing unusual since scholars have similar experiences all the time.

In 1973 I went to the Houghton armed with a list of manuscripts made from records I had available to me in Chicago. Working from the main Houghton catalogue on the first day, I discovered to my horror (and surprise—I was very young!) that three manuscripts on my list weren't catalogued. It was then I learned that libraries have multiple catalogues and organizational protocols, and that the older the library the more complex their order will be. Searching different catalogues for several days, and with the help of some learned librarians, the manuscripts were located. We also turned up a Byron manuscript that wasn't on my list.

The experience taught me a great deal about the history of those manuscripts, both before and after they entered the Houghton, as well as a great deal about how complex archives work. I learned that archives like people have memory lapses that they've forgotten. You can never be sure what's there, or if it's there, where it is. Most important, I began to see that the documents are far from self-transparent. They are riven with the multiple histories of their own making.

Rule two was brought home to me more recently. Working on *The Rossetti Archive,* I again visited the Houghton—it was 1994 I think—to check out their Rossetti materials. I did my work and left. Then in 2007, as we were in the *Archive*'s final year, two project colleagues returned to the Houghton. Noticing an unusual catalogue reference to Rossetti in the Edmund Gosse papers, they discovered a folder of Rossetti manuscripts and corrected proofs that I had not seen in 1994. It had been miscatalogued in 1941, it was recatalogued in 2003.

Let me add that this research exposed far more than a cache of primary materials. Studying those documents thickened our understanding of two significant histories: Rossetti's early reception history, when he was widely considered the most important cultural figure in England; and the revision history of "Hand and Soul" between 1850, when it was first published, and 1870 when Rossetti reprinted it privately, after deciding not to publish it with his famous 1870 volume of *Poems.* "Hand and Soul" is one of the Victorian period's half-dozen most important aesthetic manifestos.

So we draw a practical moral: you go in the first place because the archive can't be trusted to know itself; and you go in the second place because it still can't be trusted, since it will have changed its view of itself over time.

But these pedantic experiences conceal a more general and deeper significance. They are a veritable emblem of the field work of human imagination and human memory. "The smartest person in the room is the room itself"? Not in the rooms of imagination and memory. Indeed, the more enormous the room—think of Borges's tale "The Library of Babel"— the more certain that it will lose track of itself. In that sense, perhaps, we might agree that the room *is* the smartest person in the room. But then we might well be sobered, even frightened, at the thought. If that happens we again become, if not the smartest person in the room, a sadder and a wiser man.

These Legends of the Philological Fall, trivial as they are, can help us navigate through our emerging internetwork. We gain a better perspective on the limits and capacities of our digital rooms because others have worked in the same rooms in different times and circumstances and with different interests and purposes. Consider once again the Library of Alexandria. We rightly remember and celebrate certain of its purely technical breakthroughs—for instance, its coding mechanisms: alphabetization in Greek characters operating codependently with Aristotelian ontologies. But its acquisition and study policies were equally impressive because so demandingly catholic. It assembled manuscripts from various lands and in diverse languages and otherwise incommensurable scripts—Greek, of course, but also Egyptian, Persian, Hindu, Ethiopian, Hebrew. Internetworking such heterodox materials in a coherent system was the whole point. To that end, Ptolemy and his successors set about building an organization that was much more than a library narrowly conceived, even more than a library of libraries. It was also a study center for scholars from every corner of the Alexandrian world. The *museion* for the scholars was integral to the mission of the library, and the scholars came, like the library's deposits, from everywhere.

An internetwork of knowledge always functions as an institutional and social mechanism. And it functions over time, in history. Because our Enlightenment ethos shapes that history after Bacon's *Advancement of Learning,* we incline to imagine that if "we are not passive in [the] arrival" of the emerging internet, we will be able *to make the network a better infrastructure of knowledge* (Weinberger 46) than we have ever had. Absolutely we must be eager and engaged in that effort. But building a better mousetrap, or even a better automobile or computer, is not the same kind of problem as building a better library or internetwork of knowledge. The scale is radically different. While automated information systems are complex—card catalogues, MARC records, computer clouds—social networks, even pre-electronic ones, are vastly more complex and volatile.

The room of philology is more extensive than the internet room because it is a fully historiated enterprise—because it is, so to say, conscious that its current use depends upon the strength and depth of the belatedness it can never escape. Shaped to a vast presentness—blogging, texting, tweeting; LinkedIn and Facebook—the internet makes it difficult for us to see—to remember—two things about itself: that as a knowledge tool it is "before anything else, memory"; and that as a memory system, it will keep on forgetting. So current commonplace regards books and other physical things—"objects as objects"—as "fixed and dead," whereas the internet appears dynamic, even in a way *alive:* the smartest person in the room! But in fact it is an "inorganic organization" like any other artificial information system. Imagined otherwise, the internet—like Prometheus, like Faust, like science—forgets that it forgets. The special virtue of the knowledge internetwork shaped as philology is this: it is a research method, a science, for preserving a practical memory of the importance of memory.

The problem of integrating paper and digital materials is indeed a problem of scale. But large scale social and institutional problems like the ones we now face are much more difficult and complex *as such* than large scale engineering problems. Designing hardware and software is demanding work, but designing and putting into operation the knowledge industry that will use them is far more demanding. At the moment we think our PhD programs in humanities do not adequately prepare students for the knowledge and information internetwork that continues to develop around us. Because that is true, we also think about programs in Digital Humanities. But thinking that way, humanists help themselves forget what our resources and skills are *for:* to work with the entire archive of human memory. Python, XSLT, and GIS are important, but one might better think that descriptive bibliography, scholarly editing, theory of texts, and book history are now even more pressing programmatic needs.

I make a hero of the philologian, rather than the critic or even the scholar, because the figure is so resolutely alienated. Critics like Lyotard call to task the work of instrumental reason, forgetting how that work put in place methods and machines for studying and preserving the precious remains of our own alienated lives. Philology is the fundamental science of human memory (ethnography, archaeology, and anthropology are among its great derivatives). It is itself a derivative of history, but it is quite different—as different as "the canon" is from "the archive," or as Burckhardt's "texts" are from what he called "traces." What we think is important now, even if we pluck it from that archive, even if our thought is validated by a rapid response in a twitter network, one thing is certain: we will have forgotten much, perhaps much more, of great or perhaps greater importance. Social software and forward filtering carry both great promise and great danger. They have short memories.

Aleida Assmann's work has drawn a useful distinction between canon and archive, the former being the focus of criticism, the latter of philology (what she calls "cultural history"). The archive's materials are important because they "have lost their immediate addresses; they are decontextualized and disconnected from their former frames which had authorized them or determined their meaning. As part of the archive,

they are open to new contexts and lend themselves to new interpretations."
So she observes how the archive may bring us to "counter-memories" and
to "history against the grain."[11] And those are indeed well and good. But
for those moves to be possible, the lost material souls of the archive must
be held at a level of primal attention, where we will mark the significance
of their apparent insignificance.

From a philological vantage, the elementary act of preservation marks
the value of these materials when their normal values, whether for use or
exchange, have been lost. More crucially, philological attention continues
to be paid even as we recognize that the value of what we preserve may
*never again* be realized. "Never again" is crucial. For the philologian, materials are preserved because their simple existence testifies that they once
had value, though what that was we can never know completely or even,
perhaps, at all. If our current interests supply them with certain kinds of
value, these are but Derridean supplements added for ourselves. For the
philologian, the dead and their trace memories are precious and honor-
able as such. And besides, they may even return to consciousness.

That is the knowledge to which the science of philology is devoted. It
is, I believe, the ground on which all humane studies must finally take
their stand. Our great and neglected American poet Charles Reznikoff
celebrated that ground in a poem which bears its more common name:
*Testimony*. Alas, a work of little note nor long remembered in a Modern
Memory increasingly shaped to the machineries of the just-in-time.

# 3

## Memory
### History, Philosophy, Philology

I

Just about a hundred years before Lyotard and the Paris VIII philosophy department tried to reform both the theory and practice of humanities education and knowledge research, a famous controversy broke out in Germany around the same issues. The publication of Nietzsche's *The Birth of Tragedy* (1872) provoked Ulrich von Wilamowitz-Moellendorff to a sharp attack—at once witty, trenchant, and ad hominem. Nearly everyone agrees that Wilamowitz largely swept the field. In a confident if nasty peroration, he called for Nietzsche's resignation as professor of philology at the University of Basel. Six years later Nietzsche did just that, shaking dryasdust philology from his feet, as he made clear in the *Untimely Meditations* (1873–1876) and especially in the posthumously published aphoristic notes he called *We Philologists* (1874).

Wilamowitz went on to become one of the most celebrated and influential scholars in the world. He won the war with Nietzsche and he won the peace that followed. But the peace did not last, or perhaps we might say, after Tacitus, that for philology the peace became a solitude. Whereas philology and historical method were the source and end and test of humane knowledge for Wilamowitz and the *philologia perennis* he epitomized, a powerful anti-historicism began to dominate higher education by the mid-twentieth century. When *The Postmodern Condition* was published, Nietzsche had long supplanted Wilamowitz as the presiding presence in humanities research education, and history as "genealogy" replaced the historical methods developed by the various strands of philology, from *Wort-philologie* to the more capacious *Sach-philologie*.[1]

But this Nietzsche Redivivus was not the Nietzsche attacked by Wilamowitz. It was a Nietzsche *des nos jours,* brought back as an ally in the humanities' continuing struggle with instrumental reason and uncritical authority in the social sciences and humanities. And if this Nietzsche has been a powerful ally in certain respects, he has also become a stumbling block and a snare. Our volatile world of global intercourse and promiscuous information has exposed the fissures and contradictions in some of Nietzsche's cardinal points of reference: education "for life" of the "sovereign individual," the ideal of "aristocratic radicalism," and even the critical method of "genealogy." In considering the mission, the limitations, and the promise of philology now, we can profit by revisiting our Nietzschean legacy, which has so deeply affected our conversations about history, globalized culture, and human memory since Foucault.

Nietzsche's quarrel with the philologists is an insider's, an educator's, quarrel ("I know them—I myself am one of them": WP 70).[2] For Nietzsche, the system betrays itself—its educational mission—because philological education does not train "young men" for "life" but for reflecting on the reflections of life: for "literature" or "learned enlightenment" (WP 38).[3] The archival deposits should not themselves be the focus of pedantic attention. They are only important for the life that they represent.

Most important of all, that call to attention is for Nietzsche a call to imitation:

> The whole feature of study lies in this: that we should study only what we feel we should like to imitate; what we gladly take up and have the desire to multiply. What is really wanted is a progressive canon of the *ideal* model, suited to boys, youths, and men. (WP 178)

Reading such passages today is disconcerting in ways that Nietzsche would not, perhaps, have expected. I set aside for the moment that premise of learning by imitating an "ideal model" in order to consider those boys, youth, and men. *Paideia* in late nineteenth-century Europe—in Friedrich Nietzsche himself—is Hellenic yet. Nietzsche's education by ideal models does (briefly) recall the distaff world, but when that happens the invidious distinction remains: "There will perhaps come a time when scientific work will be carried on by women, while the men will have to *create,* using the word in a spiritual sense: states, laws, works of art, &c." (WP 177). For the ladies, then, not *paideia* but what the Greeks termed *banausos.* To say that this thought merely reflects the prejudices of the time only underscores our problem, particularly for Nietzsche, the self-declared critic of a blinkered age. Besides, is that imagination of the science of the future just dismissive (and misogynist) Nietzschean irony? The idea of the "sovereign individual" seems doubly constrained.[4]

If we cannot track an origin of those particular constraints, we know their Western genealogies. Aphorism 177 reflects Nietzsche's memory of that special, not to say that fantastic, moment when "the Hellenic ideal . . . the true meaning of classical studies altogether" was realized in mortal Nietzschean time.[5] But in that genealogy, the moment soon passed into the decadence of "Alexandrian culture—not Hellenism" (WP 87). So he says that, in studying antiquity, "We must distinguish . . . its purely productive period [from] the entire Romano-Alexandrian culture" (WP 37).

Nietzsche decries modern philology because, in failing to make that historical distinction, it mistakes its object of imitation. It imitates not "the Hellenic ideal" of the sovereign individual but its literary derivatives built up in succeeding centuries by "Alexandrian savants" (WP 177) and their successors. Nietzsche tracks a deplorable descent that actually begins with the library of Alexandria and then marches on through medieval scriptoria to the great archives of modern Europe. The result is what Nietzsche, quoting F. A. Wolf, calls "a mere civilization and bourgeois acquirement" (WP 37). Had Nietzsche given a comprehensive account of that descent he could have called it *A Genealogy of Philology*.

The method of genealogy has two faces, one critical, one prophetic, and the two complement each other. The critical function attacks the empirical foundation of philological research, arguing that the objects of historical inquiry are not determinate *in se* but constructions established for ethical and political purposes. Critically observed from the present, history is exposed as the authority of what Byron, one of Nietzsche's touchstones, named "the dead, but sceptred sovereigns who still rule / Our spirits from their urns" (*Manfred* III. iv. 42–43). A genealogical method analyzes those sovereignties—"we are the multiplication of many pasts"[6]—so that they can be evaluated and judged. In that process "the true aim of all classical studies," the model of life that sovereign men should imitate, begins to emerge from the "chaos" of the facticities of the past. "The breeding of superior men" (WP 100) remains possible when "contemporary man" raises himself to the "superhistorical viewpoint" (UM 2) that was achieved by "the classical and rare person" of Nietzsche's "Hellenic ideal":

> Now, what purpose is served for contemporary man by the monumental
> consideration of the past, by busying himself with the classical and rare

person of earlier times? He derives from that the fact that the greatness which was once there at all events once was *possible* and therefore really will be possible once again. (UM 2)

There we see why Wagner was so crucial for Nietzsche. Wagner seemed to realize the "music of the future" in the present and thus to provide a contemporary model of the eternal return of sovereign possibility. Nietzsche then *philosophizes*—generalizes—that singular achievement. The history that we might ideally imagine is a permanent actual possibility. When he later attacked Wagner as a representative of European decadence, he was not altering his general ethical view. He was declaring that he had misjudged the true import of Wagner's position.[7]

From our vantage, the major problem with these ideas runs right through the problem we initially noted: the gendered form of Nietzsche's thinking. His view of women is a synecdoche for his view of all that seems "strange and incoherent" in quotidian life, whether past, present, or even future. The "Hellenic ideal" cannot tolerate "strange guests," whether women or barbarians, because they represent disorder: "they themselves are in conflict with one another and it seems necessary to constrain and control them if one is not to perish in their conflict" (UM 2). "The Woman Question" dramatizes Nietzsche's fear of what Matthew Arnold, thinking in much the same way a few decades earlier, called the "confused multitudinousness" of the contemporary world.[8]

> For since we are the outcome of earlier generations we are also the outcome of their aberrations, passions, and errors, and indeed of their crimes; it is not possible to wholly free oneself from this chain. If we condemn these aberrations and regard ourselves as free of them, this does not alter the fact that we originate in them. (UM 2)

If we switch our perspective from ethics to educational method ("humanities research"), the same problem appears in Nietzsche's view of philology, which he says has crippled itself by trancing on "the trivial, circumscribed, decaying and obsolete" particulars of the past (UM 2). For Nietzsche, a Hellenic ideal lies buried in those Alexandrian trivialities which, like textual corruptions, must be exposed and removed, cleansing the text to its pristine truth.

Despite philology's Hellenistic character, Nietzsche's sympathy with its antiquarian research is clear. "People in general think that philology is at an end—while I believe that it has not yet begun" (WP 24). Indeed, the critical function of historical method—and ultimately the monumental function—rests on the microscopic vantage and passion of "the antiquarian man" whose skill can "detect traces almost extinguished" of the lost Hellenic vision "no matter how intricate the palimpsest may be" (UM 2). He takes the same line in *Dawn of Day*, the first of his explicitly genealogical works. The preface to the second edition (1886) is especially pertinent:

> It is not for nothing that I have been a philologist . . . that is to say, a teacher of slow reading. . . . For philology . . . demands of its votaries one thing above all: to go aside, to take time, to become still, to go slow—it is a goldsmith's craft and connoisseurship of the *word* which has nothing but delicate, cautious work to do and achieves nothing if it does not achieve it *lento.* (*Dawn of Day* 8)[9]

Connoisseur of chaotic words, prophet of the sovereign man. If we for our part trance on such Nietzschean contradictions, the virtue of his example for humanities education can escape us. After all, the intellectual liberation Nietzsche pursued and perhaps even promised has been contested from the beginning and continues in more recent and sympathetic commentators. Reflecting on "Nietzsche's attempt to overcome the historical and political crisis of modernity," Christian Emden correctly observes that Nietzschean genealogy is a self-consuming artifact. While it is a critical method for exposing "the historical trajectory of . . . illusions . . . it does not provide us with an escape from those illusions".[10] Once again Byron's *Manfred*, a key Nietzschean text, comes to mind: "The Tree of knowledge is not that of life" (I. I. 13).[11]

Nietzsche is perhaps a worse philosopher but a better philologist than he has been made out. His philosophical interests drew him away from the close material focus that Wilamowitz and his epigones pursued, and Wilamowitz had no difficulty ridiculing Nietzsche's grand syncretic account of Greek cultural history. But as the passage I just quoted from *Dawn of Day* shows, Nietzsche never denied the importance of a philological perspective.

Since that time philology itself has retreated from the confident truth claims that Wilamowitz made for his discipline in his attack on Nietzsche. He writes about Nietzsche in a sovereign key because Nietzsche's book called the truth claims of philology to account in an impudent and, for Wilamowitz, an unphilological way. But when asked many years later to attest the glory of philological method by two of its less thoughtful practitioners, Wilamowitz made this famous remark: " 'Philological method'? There simply isn't any—any more than a method to catch fish. . . . And hunting? I suppose there is something like method there?

[But] there is a difference between hunting lions and catching fleas." And again:

> It is far more to the point that the ancient poet speak, not some modern professor. We perform our task correctly only when we don't force our own mind into every ancient book ... but rather read out of it what is already there. That is precisely the philological task of comprehending a different individual. ... In the self-sacrifice of our own individuality lies our strength. We philologists ... ought to carry something of the actor in ourselves, not of the virtuoso who sets his own idiosyncratic touches onto the role; but of the true artist, who gives life to the dead through his own heart's blood.[12]

The study of antiquities for both Wilamowitz and Nietzsche is a difficult and chastening pursuit. The remains must be read closely and *lento*. "Philology is now more desirable than ever before," Nietzsche adds in his 1886 preface to *Dawn of Day*, because of the pressure of "an age of work; that is to say, of haste, of ... 'getting things done' at once, whether old or new ... [Philology] teaches how to read *well*: i.e., slowly, profoundly, attentively" (*Dawn of Day* 8–9). That demand for careful attention to minute material particularities is for both men the heart of the matter. Nietzsche: "One very great value of antiquity consists in the fact that its writings are the only ones which modern men still read carefully" (WP 17). The argument is the same as in *Dawn of Day*, that a philological perspective is especially needed for the just-in-time condition of "Modern men."

*The Birth of Tragedy*, however, is not always a judicious weighing of the evidence, least of all a persuasive account of the meaning of the evidence. But it does try to look carefully at certain particulars, and even more the relation of those particulars, in order to achieve a better understanding of the Greek world. Nietzsche's philosophical (ethical, institutional, and political) interests led him "to force [his] own mind" into the evidence rather than "read what is already there." That would be, for the ideal philologist of *our* time, *everything* that is already there, not setting aside or discounting what the inquirer's mind might judge "trivial" or "obsolete."[13] But for Nietzsche, recovering the past meant "forgetting" things that distract one from what his political and ethical commitments determine to be the *significant* relations.[14] Pedantic scholars lose the forest of ancient Hellas when they muse on Alexandrian trees.

For all their differences, however, Wilamowitz and Nietzsche share a faith that the past can speak reliably to the present *from the past*. When

Wilamowitz says that the philologist must "read what is already there" in the deposits and not intrude his own views, he is expressing an act of faith that Nietzsche shares: "Antiquity speaks to us when it feels a desire to do so, not when we do" (WP 88). Because a post-humanist ethos does not inherit that faith, scholarship has come to approach the historical record with greater freedom and greater skepticism even than Nietzsche's. For we now see, more clearly than either Nietzsche or Wilamowitz, that the facticities of material culture are not self-transparent in their facticities. For Wilamowitz to say, dismissing Nietzsche's history of Greek music, that "I thought Plato had spoken clearly enough: . . . 'Harmony and rhythm should follow the language' "—well, this way of thinking is clearly no longer enough.[15] If we depend upon those received *ipsa verba* (whoever may have authored them), we also know that an extensive genealogy pervades the words so that their significance is always multiple.

Trying to decipher even apparently simple statements, like the one Wilamowitz cites from Plato, can be as difficult—more difficult surely—than trying to catch fish or fleas. Too many variables impinge. "Method," in fishing and philology, can reduce the variables, but in that move there is necessarily both gain and loss since some things will be set aside a priori. From that fundamental constraint postmodern philosophy fashioned its notorious *mise en abyme,* the final resting place of the Enlightenment *superbia* that was the ground of philology and historical method itself. But the problem here is not in the constraint, it is in the *superbia.* In face of such constraints—really, in the midst of them—fishermen and philologists both will count on experience, long acquaintance, and learned habits of attention. These not only increase the odds of some kind of success, they open a field of unanticipated possibilities. No more than that, but also no less than that. And if we are trying to succeed in making rapprochement with so vast and complex a world whose remains will always be for us so few and fractured, we will want to be more cautious and catholic than either Wilamowitz or Nietzsche were prepared to be.


## II


Few and fractured. The study of antiquities, Western or not, will always face problems that students of more recent history and culture do not. The difference is plain when we reflect on that foundational act of literary and cultural studies: establishing the authority of the texts and other material artifacts. The further we retreat in time from any present, the fewer and more problematic seem the remains. We have Byron's and

Poe's autograph manuscripts, often multiple manuscripts, as well as large corpora of related compositional and publication materials. And we have as well great quantities of contemporary contextual materials of every kind that fill out the details of their worlds. But we read Sappho and Aeschylus through a glass darkly because the earliest texts that we have—fractured or not—are copies of copies, far removed from their authorial source. And the contextual materials that could illuminate their circumstances for us are impoverished by comparison with recent cultural heritage.

But even when the resources are so rich, the darkness is clearly visible still. For all history comes to us in few and fractured forms. Indeed, the extent of more recent surviving records only clarifies the presence, and the absence, of multiple witnesses and agents in whatever field is holding our attention. I cite Byron and Poe exactly because their work—the records that remain of it and that keep augmenting—so dramatically illustrates the problem of understanding it. The same is true for the American Constitution, the Salem Witch Trials, George Washington, as well as for documents, persons, and events of much less moment. The records we have expose the absence of the records we don't have, or records that never passed beyond an immediate (perhaps oral, in any case ephemeral) experience. Our problems with the meanings of the extant records are bound up, are sealed with, those that are not extant. They tell of relationships that, as we glimpse their absent presences, now reveal the presence of a dizzying network of further relations. Nietzschean genealogy was a move to penetrate the mysteries of a textual condition that most of his philological colleagues, riding the success of their historical methods, were not addressing. Even Wilamowitz, who understood, did not.

Here the example of twentieth-century Anglo-American textual criticism is instructive, and especially the work of its greatest practitioner, Fredson Bowers. Faced with the task of editing works for which we have a plethora of witnesses, all authoritative in one way or another, Bowers worked out "eclectic" critical procedures for extracting from the witnesses a set of readings that would most reliably represent the author's intentions. As we know, this plays a variation on traditional philological methods for clearing historical documents of accumulated historical error. And while the rigor and logical procedures of Bowers's model are fundamental to a slow and attentive reading of the documentary record, they represent as well, paradoxically, a curious example of Nietzschean "forgetting." The object of the exercise is not to elucidate the truth of a documentary record, a comprehensive genealogy of a complex discourse field. It is to analyze and ultimately shape the field in such a way that we get a map of it drawn from a single perspective. The remains of a larger truth are secreted away in an *apparatus criticus* and lists of "rejected readings" and "historical colations," editorially compiled.

But traditional philology reminds us to be wary of its own ways, as Wilamowitz's remarks about hunting and fishing reminded his colleagues. In fact, the pursuit of a single correct text is quixotic. Like the quests of Cervantes's knight errant, it is also illuminating. There is no single "correct" work that history has come to call *Don Quixote*. Nevertheless, to imagine that impossible object in a factive world is highly instructive, especially if you are aware of the heuristic character of your imagining. And the Cervantes example is exemplary. The idea that there is one ring to rule all the documents will only bind us in their darkness. We can and should distinguish a British *Moby-Dick* and an American *Moby-Dick*— again, nothing special, a common case. Melville's work is differently mapped in each and the textual variations are only one index of the differences. After all, British maps of the nineteenth-century world are not the same as American maps. The significance of these bibliographical differences gets underscored in a publication scene, like antebellum America, dominated by a conflict of periodicals that are themselves internally diverse, offering poetry and prose, fiction and fact (contemporary and historical), essays and stories. As we know, Poe had a deep understanding of the dynamics of this periodical scene.[16] Because the antebellum map of America could be and was variously drawn, Poe worked to exploit its resources. Of course, these are only focused textual cases—philological in the most restricted sense. But they illustrate the genealogical condition of all discourse fields.

For almost a century now humanists have been taking philosophical approaches toward these complex discursive formations. Rigor of theory rather than rigor of method would, it was hoped, help to solve the historical riddles and labyrinths in which literary works were involved. Consider Kenneth Burke's *The Philosophy of Literary Form* (1941), an early and influential effort to give a comprehensive philosophical account of discourse fields. His central idea is that these fields are organized by "associational clusters" of differential textual relations that pervade multiple contextual frameworks: economic, religious, political, and so forth. He seems to have perceived discursive formations as a set of field equations.

By inspection of the work, you propose your description of this equational structure. Your propositions are open to discussion, as you offer evidence

for them and show how much of the plot's development your description
would account for. "Closer approximations" are possible, accounting for
more.[17]

To speak of the field measurements as "open to discussion" and revision implicitly specifies the socioinstitutional context his model assumes.
But while the field's "symbolic action" is thus enriched in both its subject
and object ranges, it has not yet become the *aporia* that it forecasts.
Burke's reference to "closer approximations" shows the difference between his empirical orientation and the "readerly" orientation of later,
broadly "deconstructive," methodologies that yet adopt the same philosophical vantage.

Nonetheless, both Burke and, say, Paul de Man, "control" their interpretive horizons by generalizing the target object: "The Rime of the Ancient Mariner" rather than any or many of its documentary instances.
Burke's interpretive object is an empirical abstraction whereas de Man's is
typically a conceptual abstraction. But in neither case is the object philological because in neither case is the documentary situation part of the
interpretive issue. In these approaches, the documents are not variables
put under investigation but constants hypothetically gathered: "The Rime
of the Ancient Mariner."[18] This is not to deny the usefulness of a Burkian
or DeManian reading. It *is* to suggest that such readings limit their interpretive range by seeking to control important expressive variables.

Nietzschean genealogy is a philological effort to recover "the greatness [of ancient Greece] which was once there at all events."[19] "At all
events"—*jedenfalls*—is not a casual usage. It reflects Nietzsche's double
commitment: on the one hand to break up the carapace of positivist facticities that have buried Hellenic greatness, on the other to recover a hypothetically true Hellenic order pervading the historical events. Later
critics of Nietzsche—Geuss and Williams for example[20]—correctly point
out that the procedure is "fact-deficient," which is fundamentally the
same criticism that Wilamowitz originally raised against *The Birth of
Tragedy*. But if it is indeed—and deliberately—fact-deficient, genealogy is
not therefore "conjectural history," for it is shaped *jedenfalls*: by remembering certain things and forgetting others.[21] Furthermore, note what
this indicates about the meaning of *jedenfalls* in the particular event of
Nietzsche: every event is taken into account, but some are counted *out*
of the accounting, as a textual scholar might draw up his list of "rejected
readings."

For an empiricist like Wilamowitz, this will never do. But it will never
do *not* because Nietzsche finessed inconvenient and apparently irrelevant
facts about the ancient world, and certainly not because he abandoned

the obligation to preserve the Hellenic Ideal. Nietzsche is cast out because his critical method calls facticity itself into question. His move gives an entirely different view not of the ancient but of the modern world. When Wilamowitz coolly declared that "Plato had spoken clearly enough," he tells us, clearly enough, about his confidence in a *fact sufficient* view of the past.

Nietzsche's fact deficient history is the reflex of Wilamowitz's fact-sufficient history. They share the fault line that Nietzsche's genealogical method exposed: that historical events and data are ex post facto constructions. The Hellenic Ideal does not depend upon facticities but upon imperative interpretations that are applied to whatever facts are taken as ready-to-hand *(zuhanden)*. For Nietzsche, it is not that Wilamowitz has erred in his commitment to the Hellenic Ideal; he has erred in thinking his research methods justify that commitment. In this view, facts can never be sufficient to the truth of history. For Nietzsche, however, their necessary deficiency becomes an index of a truth that supervenes facticity and its empirical procedures. This is the truth Nietzsche defines as *für das Leben*. But having mounted his genealogical critique of *Historismus,* Nietzsche can only sustain the truth of any Ideal as an impossible historical condition beyond the good and evil of living history and *das Leben.*

In mounting his critique of traditional philology, Nietzsche, like his contemporaries, reads only part of the historical record *lento*. The correspondence that Nietzsche wants to realize between ancient Hellas and modern Europe reflects his desire and pursuit of the Hellenic Whole. Schiller would have called it sentimental scholarship replying to naive history:

> There were centuries in which the Greeks found themselves in a danger similar to the one in which we find ourselves, that is, the danger of destruction from being swamped by what is foreign and past, from "history." The Greeks never lived in proud isolation; their "culture" was for a long time much more a chaos of foreign, Semitic, Babylonian, Lydian, and Egyptian forms and ideas, and their religion a real divine struggle of the entire Orient, something similar to the way "German culture" and religion are inherently now a struggling chaos of all foreign lands and all previous ages. Nevertheless Hellenic culture did not become an aggregate, thanks to that Apollonian saying [i.e., "know thyself']. The Greeks learned gradually *to organize the chaos* because, in accordance with the Delphic teaching, they directed their thoughts back to themselves, that is, to their real needs, and let the apparent needs die off. (UM 2)

Such a passage underscores the importance of what it has thrown away: precise facticities, sharp distinctions, clear relationships. Wilamowitz was appalled, yes, but not because Nietzsche had neglected to deal with all the minute particulars. He was appalled because Nietzsche's work threatened to undermine Enlightenment itself.

But there is more to learn from this passage than how to catalogue its errors. The prose is a vivid drama of Nietzsche's mind—what Emerson, a similar mind, called "man thinking." Thinking in response, Wilamowitz would mark its iniquities. But he would not say much about Nietzsche's principal subject, which is far less an Ideal Greece than his anxiety about accessing such an ideal in face of his own philological training. Nietzsche is expressing the need we all have of the loved and the lost, and the fear that they will escape us forever in the press of what the poet called "circumstance, that unspiritual god"[22] and what Nietzsche, more melodramatically, calls "chaos." This is an ancient Alexandrian chaos that he recognizes through its contemporary repetitions. Reading the passage *lento* we may begin to think again about promiscuous culture, about real and apparent needs, about the significance of "that Apollonian saying." We may even wonder: may people forget too quickly their apparent needs and imagine too narrowly their real ones?

I remarked earlier that Nietzsche seems a better philologist than a philosopher. He is better because he did not think that "Plato had spoken clearly enough." But because he is a better rhetorical poet than a philologist, his philological virtues become obscured—as time passes, increasingly obscured—by his demonic pursuit of philosophy, the *agon* of his struggle in the coils of what he called "Critical History." *Beyond Good and Evil, The Antichrist,* and especially *The Genealogy of Morals* are masterpieces of a tormented ethical polemic.

*The Birth of Tragedy* certainly left out much in its effort to give a new monumental account of Greek tragedy. The narrative was only possible because Nietzsche deliberately chose to forget much of what he had learned through his philological training. Wilamowitz had no difficulty exposing the flaws in Nietzsche's account. But that dismissal misunderstood the deeper import of Nietzsche's book. To Wilamowitz it looked like a new master narrative written to displace received historical truth, and this may even have been Nietzsche's own belief or hope at the time. But Wilamowitz's attack forced Nietzsche to reflect critically on his own work. The event led him to his famous investigation of the three modes of historical method: Monumental, Antiquarian, and Critical. It is now a truth universally (or academically) acknowledged that *The Birth of Tragedy* is a work of Critical, not Monumental (and least of all Antiquarian), history.

In *The Birth of Tragedy* Nietzsche was responding to the limitations of the historical method he had been trained in. If empirical thoroughness could not reveal the truth of ancient Greece, it could reveal how such a truth had grown obscure even to itself. "I thought Plato had spoken clearly enough," Wilamowitz dryly remarked. If Plato's words were self-transparent, as Nietzsche himself clearly believed they were, they nonetheless acquired many strange defeatures in their reception and subsequent transmission. Like ancient Greece herself, they were self-transparent only in that *once upon a time* of an Ideal Greece. Nietzsche harangues against Alexandrian Hellas because in it he believed he saw the truth of Greece being infected with alien cultures. And Nietzsche was right. Our knowledge is marked and constantly reshaped by the agents of its transmission, including of course Nietzsche and ourselves. Who should be able to see this more clearly than the philologist? Every text that comes down to us—every expressive object, whatever its material form—bears within itself "the record of its own making."

But for Nietzsche, a defeatured Greece passed on to contemporary persons an intolerable legacy. It showed that we all work from an ambiguous inheritance of barbarity and civilization. (His own inheritors would deepen his critical thought by showing that barbarity and civilization are themselves ambiguous categories.) The first form of Nietzschean forgetting, then, was "an attempt to give oneself, as it were, a past *a posteriori*," a new past, a "second nature" free of the corrupted "one from which we are descended" (UM 2). This move shapes his thinking in the immediate aftermath of the attack by Wilamowitz. It was a move to escape, if only in the philosophical imagination, the "aberrations, passions . . . errors, and . . . crimes" that are mixed in our inheritance. But the philosophical weakness of this move was already clear to Nietzsche's philological conscience, which could see only too clearly how "impossible [it would be] to loose oneself from this chain entirely." So in his later work he moved to a more decisive mode of forgetting. As a legacy of illusions, some attractive, some repellent, history was to be remembered so that it could finally be forgotten. He would take his stand in a region he located outside of history, Beyond Good and Evil.

## III

The Nietzsche-Wilamowitz controversy thus exposes in dramatic fashion that a supreme achievement of secular enlightenment—the historicist method of German scholarship—was internally unstable. The twentieth century's project of *L'histoire des mentalités* inherits and then tracks both the significance and the long afterlife of their original dispute.[23]

Two exemplary contemporary inheritors, Pierre Nora and Paul Ricoeur, help us define the shape of that afterlife as we have received it. I take them up here because both of their approaches—the one historical, the other philosophical—set aside the question of (so to say) facticities for life—Stiegler's "inorganic organization of memory."

"To interrogate a tradition, venerable though it may be, is no longer to pass it on intact."[24] Pierre Nora's observation certainly recognizes itself as carrying on the foundational Wilamowitz-Nietzsche dispute, indeed, as establishing it as foundational to the tradition of *Historismus* itself. His comment is thus broadly Modern, as applicable to Voltaire and Diderot as to himself and Paul Ricoeur. But the double meaning in Nora's misrecognition—it knows how blind are its own critical insights—has made a postmodern critical turn on Nietzsche's original critique of historical method.

Raphael Samuel criticizes Nora's understanding of historical memory, ironically and paradoxically, as a postmodern form of what Nietzsche called Monumental or Enlightenment history.[25] Because fragmented memory is such a distinctive feature of Nora's project, Samuel's criticism might appear wildly off the mark. But its force lies in his clear view that Nora's radical pluralism—"all lieux de mémoire are objects mises en abyme" (Nora 1989, 20)—moves him to postulate a categorical imperative for historical order:

> For the very possibility of a history of *lieux de mémoire* demonstrates the existence of an invisible thread linking apparently unconnected objects. It suggests that the comparison of the cemetery of Pere-Lachaise and the Statistique generale de la France is not the same as the surrealist encounter of the umbrella and the sewing machine. There is a differentiated network to which all of these separate identities belong, an unconscious organization of collective memory that it is our responsibility to bring to consciousness. The national history of France today traverses this network. (23)

For Samuel, to speak in this way is to miss the most distinctive quality of human memory and human history: its fragility. As massively learned as Nora's, Samuel's work is inflected with a personal style that echoes his sense of human subjects. By contrast, Nora's prose, like his project, is magisterial. Bertrand Taithe succinctly draws the difference when he says that "Samuel was fascinated with the vernacular and the self whereas Nora celebrates the intellectual, the elite, the ethnocentric and the grand narrative."[26] From that vantage, Nora's project is what Andreas Huyssen would call a "Monumental Seduction": "a monumentality that can do

without permanence and without destruction, that is fundamentally in-
formed by the modernist spirit of a fleeting and transitory epiphany, but
which is no less memorable or monumental for that."[27]

Nora's project is plainly monumental. Its seven large volumes and 130
eclectic essays form an imposing collage that resembles nothing so much
as what we now call an indefinitely extensible social software network—in
Peter Carrier's words, "an 'a la carte' France . . . from which each individual may construct a personal 'menu' of memories" (53). Monumentality
here comes as "a *third* degree of memory"—a "pluralist and unitary . . .
*idea* of France" (51) that we may individually extrude from the work.
Its bulk and its flaunted fractures are codependent operators whose function is to index the unimaginably large corpus of events and archival records of which *Les Lieux* is the merest trace ("*lieux de mémoire* only exist
because of their capacity for metamorphosis, an endless recycling of their
meanings and an unpredictable proliferation of their ramifications"
(Nora 1989, 19).

But in another sense, modesty rather than monumentality may be the
great if secret virtue of Nora's project. It can be seen as a self-conscious
recovery of the system of antiquarian history—implicitly, an argument
for the meaning and importance of antiquarian history in a world still
dominated by Enlightenment models of knowledge.[28] The project presents a classically dialectical shape that moves from *La République* and *La
Nation* to *Les France*. Those headings are notable. The "idea of France" is
generated from a pair of great cultural singularities to a third person plu-
ral, a grammatical figure for a "pluralist and unitary . . . *idea* of France."
The result does not tell us what this idea of France is, it does not even tell
us what Nora's idea of the idea is. The result tells us what Demogorgon
told Asia in Shelley's *Prometheus Unbound:* "Each to itself must be the
oracle."

This would be antiquarian history executed by scholars trained in the
schools of Enlightenment. Rather than moving to organize fractured human memory into an historical order, Nora's work marks all historicalities as acts of memory. The "places" raised up in the project are what topologists would call basins of order where human memories gather and
swirl through various morphogenetic transformations. "As history has
entered its epistemological age, with memory ineluctably engulfed by history, the historian has become no longer a memory-individual but, in
himself, a lieu de memoire," and as such "ready to confess the intimate
[and disintegrated] relation he maintains to his subject" (Nora 1989, 18).
The individual essays in Nora's volumes thereby get marked as data at
a second order: documentary records carrying a Dublin Core of their

essential metadata. The organizational structure of Nora's project marks the documentary status of the essays, thereby defining them as local histories, on one hand, and particular field reports on the other. The consequence is that the essays have the same evidentiary status as the materials they place under examination.

In that perspective, everything about *Les Lieux* bespeaks the evidence of things not seen. "There is a differentiated network to which all of these separate identities belong, an unconscious organization of collective memory that it is our responsibility to bring to consciousness. The national history of France today traverses this network." (23). What goes unseen is not *La* France, however. La France is everywhere apparent, it is the place of all the places, an atomized scholar's topic no more and no less important than any of the 130 topics enlisted for the project. What goes missing—is this the very *point* of the project?—is "traditional narrative, with its syncopated parts and formal closure" (17): "for it is difference we are seeking, and in the image of this difference, the ephemeral spectacle of an unrecoverable identity. It is no longer genesis that we seek but instead the decipherment of what we are in the light of what we are no longer" (17–18). So the collage of essays becomes a representative report on what Lyotard famously called "the postmodern condition."

But a difficulty arises from the idiosyncratic character of the individual essays. Do we care that certain topics are addressed and others not? Does *Les Lieux* even let it matter whether anyone does or doesn't care? The machinery of *Les Lieux de Mémoire* generates those kinds of anxious ethical questions. Of course Nora does implicitly respond to such questions. For him the essays are so to speak meta-representative: i.e., they represent the *mise en abyme* of contemporary Everyman. *Les Lieux* is a kind of index or postmodern allegory, a mirror in which every reader can see his or her reflection:

> Every previous historical or scientific approach to memory, whether national or social, has concerned itself with *realia,* with things in themselves and in their immediate reality. Contrary to historical objects, however, *lieux de memoire* have no referent in reality; or, rather, they are their own referent: pure, exclusively self-referential signs. This is not to say that they are without content, physical presence, or history; it is to suggest that what makes them *lieux de memoire* is precisely that by which they escape from history. (Nora 1989, 23–24)

This is a distinctly Nietzschean escape licensed by Nora's genealogical sense of history. "All lieux de memoire are objects mises en abyme" because of what he calls their "double identity": "[their] original intention and [their] return in the cycles of memory" (20). The return comes as the particular need of particular individuals in the present, when "society [is] entirely absorbed in its own historicity. . . . Living entirely under the sign of the future, it would satisfy itself with automatic self-recording processes and auto-inventory machines, postponing indefinitely the task of understanding itself (18)." *Les Lieux* is his effort to move postmodern society to its special self-understanding: to preserve and archive the past in such a way that the vast network of possible connections between the past and the future can be seen as a personal responsibility. For "in the last analysis, it is upon the individual and upon the individual alone that the constraint of memory weighs insistently" (16). The virtue of *Les Lieux* is thus that it is itself a *lieu de memoire* reflecting the *abyme* into which Nora's project understands itself to have been thrown.

Paul Ricoeur resumes the legacy of the Nietzsche-Wilamowitz controversy in a philosophical rather than in Nora's historical frame of reference. His critical and sympathetic mind pursues a systematic coherence in history and historical consciousness. Unlike Nora, Ricoeur approaches the problem of fractured history and atomized memory through a study of the ethical power of plotted narrative.[29] Thus, Nora's monumental antiquarianism is more or less precisely what Ricoeur's studies of temporality stand against. So *Time and Narrative* reflects mordantly on "the death of narrative" (70) in various postmodern fictional forms "and the disorganized experiences they finally end up imitating" (73). In Ricoeur's perspective, the spatial, nonnarrative form of *Les Lieux* has misunderstood Nietzsche's call to forget. Narrative emplotment in fictional or historical works arranges selective representations in order to create ordered forms of temporality. Unremembering the multiple particulars that might be exposed in any given set of events allows the narrative to realize a form of fundamental order that might otherwise be obscured or even blocked by distracting or irrelevant detail.

Ricoeur's ethical point becomes especially clear in the "Epilogue" to *Memory, History, Forgetting*,[30] where he proposes a categorical imperative of forget-and-forgive to counter the burdens of personal and historical guilt: what Nietzsche calls "chaos" and Nora "the repayment of an impossible debt" (Nora 1989, 16). Ricoeur's determining move comes as a philosophical meditation (Ricoeur 2004, 505) on the act of forgetfulness described in Matthew 6:25–34 ("Consider the lilies of the field," etc.), where he sees a primal form of Happy Forgetting to balance the forms of Happy Memory that have long been the basis of his theories of narrative, with their implicit or explicit "wish for a happy and peaceful" ending (Ricoeur 2004, 459). Ricoeur's forgetting throws us not into an abyss where our fractured selves are fully exposed, but into the loving embrace of a benevolent and nonsubjective ministry.

Both Nora and Ricoeur insist on the importance of an orderly approach to the problem of the breakdown of historical consciousness. "Representation proceeds by strategic highlighting, selecting samples and multiplying examples," (Nora 1989, 17) Nora says, and he lays out (18–23) the rules controlling the organization of *Les Lieux*. His organization means to dramatize the crisis of orderly representation, a burden less of the past than of the present, with its frenetic just-in-time ethos. By contrast, Ricoeur loves and meditates narrative forms that sublimate the *agon* Nora's project puts on display. An ending is "happy" for Ricoeur when, to recall Keats, it seems to "come as naturally as the leaves to a tree," when the plot-maker appears to work without "a palpable design upon us" or any troubled "reaching after fact & reason."[31] That mode operates a grammar of assent to the presence of an objective and transhuman ethical order. The order need not be religious in any traditional sense, as is clear enough from one of Ricoeur's favorite examples, Proust.

Philology is as interested in *Memory, History, Forgetting* as Ricoeur has been. But the philologian's focus is material culture—the documentary records that, fashioned and refashioned over time, get remembered, maimed, forgotten, and re-remembered. Because philology cannot escape the attention of those particulars, which are always exceptional at whatever scale of attention, systematic and ethical coherence are a priori secondary concerns. Philology's notorious passion for facticities marks it as a provocative science, even "a science of exceptions."[32] To a theoretical mind, these defeatures mark it as a disreputable science—indeed, from a certain point of view it is hardly a science at all, as Wilamowitz himself suggested to his method-obsessed colleagues. It is more a set of disciplinary procedures—what Astrid Erll, speaking of her hopes for "cultural memory studies," called "a conceptual toolbox [for] an array of different disciplines and national academic cultures . . . with their own vocabularies, methods, and traditions"[33] Where the meanings of its studies are concerned, philology can only be pursued with a skepticism crowned by a resolve—I think of Tennyson—"to strive, to seek, to find, and not to yield" before the inevitable uncertainty of the effort.

Philology is thus a true science because it acknowledges the priority of the material world—what William Wordsworth called "rocks and stones and trees"—to our conscious acts of reflection. For the philosopher this is an epistemological priority, for the scientist—in this case, the philologist—it is a methodological requirement. So the immediate concern of the philologist, our inorganic organizations of memory, have the same empirical status as rocks and stones and trees; and—crucially—vice versa. For the natural world has been cast by science to an inorganic organization that it might be better understood. Of course, not all transmitters of culture are concerned with a memorial reorganization of the geophysical world. Wordsworth and James Fenimore Cooper are notable in this respect, and their orientation helps philology push its inquiries from words to things, including the thingness of discursive fields themselves. Then again, philology can be driven by writers and artists of a very different kind—for instance, by William Blake, an urban poet and artist who regarded the natural world as "a Delusion / Of Ulro: & a ratio of the perishing Vegetable Memory" (*Milton* 26: 45). His illuminated books, however, which insist on their materialities, are clear indices that memorialization demands inorganic organization. So is the work of Emily Dickinson. From such work scholars discover their mission to investigate its many second-order inorganic reorganizations.

Those investigations bring a set of recognized commitments: to instrumental reason and knowledge/research shaped in a social process of education; to institutional obligations and requirements; and to the investigation of the particular and complex ways people go about constructing a sense of the past. Because those ways are so many and diverse, "a certain anarchic quality" pervades philological work, which can therefore seem, as Alon Confino remarks, "more practiced than theorized."[34] But that emphasis on specific practice indexes the conceptual strength of the method.[35] For when we reflect on the anarchic multiplicities exposed in Memory Studies, we realize that the imbalance between practice and theory represents a fundamental disciplinary adequacy: as a similar imbalance between (say) liturgical practice and theological speculation would reflect the strength of that most powerful of Memory Machines, religion.

I bring that example forward as a *theoretical* move in this discussion. For what we call Memory Studies today is a set of highly developed philological practices. We now trace their microhistory from the work of Maurice Halbwachs and Marc Bloch to Pierre Nora and Paul Ricoeur. That special disciplinary emergence has itself been a response to the crisis in Cultural Memory precipitated by Nietzsche and dramatized in the philological struggles of Nietzsche and Wilamowitz, as so many scholars of Memory Studies have emphasized. Beyond and behind those struggles stands the widely recognized critical effort of Enlightenment to exorcise contemporary society from the demons of religious illusion. Our touchstone for that effort has been *The Genealogy of Morals*.

The problematic victory of those secular forces has been told many times, not least of all in the Nietzsche-Wilamowitz controversy itself. But Danièle Hervieu-Legér's *Religion as a Chain of Memory* [36] is especially important for its sure grasp of how deeply the afterlife of religious needs has compromised the pretensions of Modernity's secular humanism. The common secular view that "religion is structurally alien to modernity and that it survives only as a residue of a bygone world" (93) is not only belied by the global facts of our own contemporary history, it is nothing more than a corollary of Enlightenment progressivist self-conception. Far from having cast out the devils of religion, modern Enlightenment "produces what is of essence contrary to it." Drawing on Louis Dumont and Karl Polanyi, Hervieu-Legér lays out the process by which "the very development of individualistic values set off a complex dialectic" whereby those values are, in several senses, magically transformed to their opposite (93). With Enlightenment, religion metastasizes. It is as if Modernity itself realized a secular version of the parable of the seven devils turned to seventy. Enlightenment's "tendency towards the individualization and atomization of belief has often been stressed," Hervieu-Legér observes, "but that it inevitably encounters a limit has been less often remarked on." The problem here is culturally radical. It is not merely a question "of what the philosopher Paul Ricoeur has called the available scope for belief . . . at any one time," but of "an internal limitation to the process of producing meaning." For meaning cannot even be a personal achievement if it is not also a social function: "there must be at a given point the effect of meaning shared; meaning that is individually constructed must be attested by others; it must be given social confirmation (94)." In short, a personal experience of meaningfulness requires networks of social interaction whose behavior is monitored by an authorized social institution. Enlightenment worked to replace Church institutions by a secular network of public instruments of education, with the model of the German university gradually arrogating to itself ever more authority for validating the production of knowledge.[37]

The Nietzsche-Wilamowitz controversy thus forecast the coming of Pierre Nora and Paul Ricoeur. With Nora, the internal crisis in the program of historicist philology precipitates as a fractured empiricism; with Ricoeur, as a plangent hermeneutics of desire. In each case, fragments are shored against the ruins of cultures judged unstable both in the sphere of common life and the green zones of protected knowledge. Furthermore, the most significant outcome of their dispute, Nietzschean genealogy, proved to harbor an ambiguous legacy. Its conceptual brilliance eventually worked to transform philology from a pragmatistic to a theoretical discipline. It shifted the disciplinary foundation of literary studies from procedural thoroughness to conceptual integrity. For Nietzschean geneal-ogy is doubly conceptual. It invokes a conception of a Hellenic ideal wor-thy of imitation because uninfected by the heteroglot cultural world in which it grew, like wheat among the tares of its age. Correspondingly, it deploys a critical method, genealogy itself, which supplies the scholar with a presumptively "superhistorical" view of incoherent historicalities. Genealogy mirrors in its idea the naïve perfection of a sentimental schol-arship, a "Monumental Seduction."

## IV

Not long after the Nietzsche and Wilamowitz controversy, Mark Twain gave his own view about truth, remembering, and forgetting in a note-book entry of 1894: "If you tell the truth you don't have to remember anything."[38] Much quoted and admired, the statement would seem pre-posterous if the issue for him were the objective reliability of a report or a document. But that isn't his concern. Twain is talking about troth, not truth, and he has in mind a person like Melville's Confidence Man. The comment reflects critically on an ethos famously struck off many years before by—of all people, considering Twain's view of the man—Walter Scott:

O what a tangled web we weave
When first we practice to deceive. (*Marmion* VI. 17)

Although Twain and Scott were thinking in a discourse of practical ethics and everyday life, their perspective is yet deeply pertinent to the everyday life of scholarship and education. No one, least of all a scholar or educator, can neglect the obligation to a disciplinary address that is candid and honest. But accepting those demands, the scholar's vocation forces him to confront a further range of truth: thoroughness, "the whole truth, and nothing but the truth." In that confrontation scholars lay them-selves under an even more demanding obligation: "If you want to tell the truth, you have to remember everything."

The impossibility of meeting that obligation does not make it any less the primary commitment of scholarship. Here the truth that is the whole truth and nothing but the truth is not simply an honest report, though that expectation is a given. It is equally a pledge of faith to *Die Erkennt-nis des Erkannten*—the archive of documentary representations, now including your own, that time and circumstance expose to perpetual loss, revision, and disconfirmation. Because error, even deceit, pervades these truth-representations, philology marks its judgments about them as relative. They require constant monitoring and revision. So taking their marching orders from the poets, philologists try to understand (for instance) that if the whole truth of the story of Othello's world were known, the tragedy might well appear as Iago's. So it happens that Satan may turn out the hero of *Paradise Lost* and Milton's God, Blake's Nobodaddy.

Because a philological consciousness pervades Thomas Hardy's work, his perspective on these human matters is less severe than Blake's. Hardy's God, redeemed in the trials of time, returns as the forgetful if well-meaning artificer of Hardy's "God-Forgotten":

> —"The Earth, say'st thou? The Human race?
>   By Me created? Sad its lot?
> Nay: I have no remembrance of such place:
>   Such world I fashioned not."—
>   —"O Lord, forgive me when I say
>   Thou spak'st the word, and mad'st it all."—
> "The Earth of men—let me bethink me . . . Yea!
>   I dimly do recall
>
>   "Some tiny sphere I built long back
>   (Mid millions of such shapes of mine)
> So named . . . It perished, surely—not a wrack
>   Remaining, or a sign?
>
>   "It lost my interest from the first,
>   My aims therefor succeeding ill;
> Haply it died of doing as it durst?"—
>   "Lord, it existeth still."—

Eternity has played havoc with God's memory, so Hardy keeps sending Him back to school to brush up on a subject twenty centuries of stony sleep taught him to forget: human life in mortal time. "God's Education" starts when He finally understands that "Forsooth, though I men's master be, / Theirs is the teaching mind."

"Forsooth": Hardy has chosen exactly the right (antique) word for God to speak in 1909.[39] We know that God is telling the truth because, had He said (had he been made to say) "In truth" instead of "Forsooth," he would have been out of dialect. Equally jarring, though at the other end of the history being exposed here, would have been "forsoð." "In truth" is too naïve for Hardy's God, "forsoð" is too sophisticated. We believe in this God because Hardy has learned an elementary lesson of philology, the lesson of Sir James Murray's *New English Dictionary on Historical Principles*.[40] So do we watch God, like Hardy, fallen into the truths of time and history.

These are specifically philological truths and, as such, very different from the truths that preside over philosophy or the natural sciences. No more succinct or trenchant account of philological Truth and Method exists than Milman Parry's three-paragraph discussion of a brief passage in Book XII of the *Iliad:* Sarpedon's call to "his friend Glaucus to follow him to the assault on the Greek wall."[41] Parry's account shows that the horizon for a philological truth-telling must recover the particulars of the entire composition and reception history of the work being studied, from its *fons et origo* down to the present (every present) moment. So *of course* "The work upon it will never be done" (409), as Parry remarks. But it is work that, truth to tell, must proceed nonetheless. And so Parry summarizes in nine brilliant words philology's *Wahrheit und Methode:* "I make for myself a picture of great detail" (411).

Which is to say: even if it comes as a text, it must be read as a picture (so that the picture, though a *gestalt,* flaunts its negative space); the picture will be as detailed as I can make it (on the understanding that it could never be *made* detailed enough); the picture is my particular, date-stamped construction (understanding that it can, now and henceforth, be read by others who will have their own pictures to make, including a picture—it could never be made detailed enough—of the picture I have made); and finally, it is therefore a picture in fractal dimensions (so that Parry's sentences, understood as making "a picture of great detail," resemble what mathematicians conceive as a one-dimensional line with the functional character of a surface).

PRINTER'S DEVIL. Huh? Are there actually *people* who will read and understand any of this? Who will even *care* to?

FOOTNOTE. Some, not many. Scholars.

PRINTER'S DEVIL. Pedants.

FOONOTE. That's what Parry himself feared and why he gave this work as a lecture in 1934 to a nonscholarly audience—to the Board of Overseers of Harvard College.[42]

PRINTER'S DEVIL. Now that's what I call reaching out to the man in the street! I don't suppose it was reprinted in *Reader's Digest.*

FOOTNOTE. Suppose it *had* been. Would you have read it?

PRINTER'S DEVIL. Be real. I just clean up the mess around this place.

FOOTNOTE. Odd you should say that. Because Parry wanted his lecture to help clear up the mess around here as well. He worried that his meticulous philological quest for truth was only straining "the flimsiness of the hold which our past literature" (410) has *für das Leben*. For while the scholar "perfects [his] method and learns more about the past, the true understanding of what knowledge [s/he] has or gains is limited to a smaller and smaller number":

> and from the standpoint of people in general [scholarly truth] is probably now having a greater influence as a source of material for propaganda than as a source of real understanding of what is and has been. . . . In times of social changes and confusion, a bewildered people will . . . create a past for itself without bothering about the verity of the details. (412)

Remember—do you see why we now *should* remember?—that Parry was speaking in 1934, in full awareness of the "propaganda . . . social changes and confusion" that were then taking hold of bewildered people throughout Europe and America.

> The chief emotional ideas to which men seem to be turning at present . . . are those of nationality—for which they exploit race—and class. . . . Anyone who has followed the history of the use of propaganda for political purposes, with its extraordinary development of intensity and technique in the past fifty years [recognizes how] those who were directing that propaganda expressed their lack of concern, or even contempt, for what actually was so, or actually had been so. (Ibid.)

A bewildered people of 1934 . . . or of 2013? And what do "men at present"—when *would* that be?—learn, or fear, from the fifty years of intense and cynical propaganda that frightened Milman Parry?

Because people "must, as they always have, attach their action to some emotional body of ideas [and] moral code" (412), Parry urges his audience—the Harvard College Board of Overseers and the Harvard alumni—to make a moral commitment to the "belief that there is nothing at the same time finer and more practical than the truth" (ibid.). Parry inflects that truth very particularly as "the European humanistic tradition" which, he rightly says, "is no inglorious thing" (413). How fine a thought is held out in that double negative. For the truth, the whole truth, and nothing but the truth of his tradition is, as he knows, more than he knows or will ever know. Certainly more than the not-inglorious European humanistic tradition.

To follow knowledge like a sinking star
Beyond the utmost bounds of human thought. (Tennyson, "Ulysses" 31–32)

PRINTER'S DEVIL. Before you go on that not-inglorious journey, don't forget to put out the trash.

FOOTNOTE. Around here we recycle. Don't you?

# II

## FROM THEORY TO METHOD

# 4

# The Documented World

I N THE NEED FOR ROOTS, Simone Weil criticizes historical thinking and its search for documentary foundations. "There are holes
in documents," Weil points out, so that when we read them we want to
ensure that "unfounded hypotheses be present to the mind." Reading
documents requires "reading between the lines, to transport oneself fully,
with complete self-forgetfulness, into the events evoked there. . . . The so-
called historical mind does not pass through the paper to flesh and blood;
it consists of a subordination of thought to the document."[1]

Weil always saw reading as a spiritual emergency. Readings which "pass
through the paper to flesh and blood" can take many forms—readings like,
for instance, Weil's reading of *The Iliad,* Lautréamont's of gothic fiction, or
Kathy Acker's outrageous travesty of *The Scarlet Letter* and other classic
nineteenth-century novels. For Weil, the best reader experiences a kind of
transport and self-extinction, a passage to a human encounter "that is not
me in any sense," as D. H. Lawrence once put the matter in his poem
"Manifesto."

"To find flesh and blood" is the ultimate purpose of reading and its sophisticated partner, interpretation. So to achieve that engagement, it helps
to begin with Weil's documents rather than with that immaterial reading
matter called "texts." For unlike texts, documents in fact do often have real
holes in them, or are otherwise marked by marks of their historical passage.
The physical object—the specific manuscript, the particular edition or
printed object we read (like this very object you are reading now)—is coded
and scored with human activity. An awareness of this is the premise for interpreting material culture, and the awareness is particularly imperative for
literary interpretation, where linguistic "message" regularly invisibilizes the
codependent and equally meaningful "medium" that codes all messages.

The power of D. F. McKenzie's "sociology of texts" project rests in the
thoroughness of his understanding of "the primacy of the physical artifact

(and the evidence it bears of its own making)."[2] As the literary work passes on through time and other hands, to other readers besides ourselves, it bears along with and *as* itself the gathered history of all its engagements. Sometimes some of these codes appear explicitly in the documents—as inscriptions, for instance, or marginalia, or bookplates or labels or other physical transformations, like book damage or ornamental additions. Secret and multiplying histories lie concealed in those tracings. Often, perhaps even more often, those multiplying histories have to be pursued in other, less direct ways: who were its readers, when was it read, when wasn't it read, where is/was it located, how was it produced, why and how has it survived?

Those flesh-and-blood questions need flesh and blood answers. Why? Because interpretation is a social act—a specific deed of critical reflection made in a concert of related moves and frames of reference (social, political, institutional) that constitute the present as an interpreted inheritance from a past that has been fashioned by other interpreting agents. All these multiple agencies leave the documents marked with their diverse intentions and purposes, many of which were unapparent even to those who executed those purposes. Those three governing temporalities (past, present, future) are subject to an unlimited number of redeterminations, and every interpretational move is an instance of such a redetermination (itself subject to interpretation within the ancient idea of "the hermeneutic circle," reinvigorated more recently by Gadamer and Heidegger and their legacy). Herself imbedded within the circle (at "an inner standing point," as D. G. Rossetti called it), the interpreting agent can be at most partially aware of this impinging and dynamic concert of reflection.[3] The ideal interpreting agent can know the presence of the whole but never the sum of the parts.

I

Within that general field of dynamic reflection we may usefully distinguish two kinds of interpretive action: a mode oriented in performative models, of which translation and parody are perhaps the master types; and a mode oriented in scholarship, which is our customary exemplar of interpretation. Although this essay will focus chiefly on scholarly interpretive models, we shall want to give close attention to performative models for a couple of important reasons.

Scholarly models regularly operate under a horizon of truth and the idea of its accessibility. This truth may be either normative (like Aristotle's rules) or positive ("scientific method" for determining facts) or some combination of both. The most advanced forms of interpretive scholarship—the production of scholarly editions—exhibit this hankering for truth in their common attachment to the idea of what has been called the "definitive edition": the edition that, if properly done, would obviate the need for further scholarly editions. When we speak of "the meaning" of a work (*the* meaning!) we are invoking the same fundamental ideological commitment. The spell of that (literally charming) ideal gets broken when one realizes (1) that scholarship is itself an historical performance executed within the framework of a certain limited (and limiting) set of protocols; and (2) that the scholar's interpretive intervention alters the object of interpretation and the fields that organize those objects. Scholarship, in short, is itself performative. Like science, its basic commitment is not to "Truth" but to rigor (as to method), thoroughness (as to empirical evidence), and accuracy (in the treatment of its facts and data).

Scholarship and interpretation, therefore, are too narrowly conceived when they are imagined as being *about* something—as one might say that this essay is "about" interpretive method, or that one over there is about *Don Juan*. Rather, scholarship and interpretation are procedures that *do something about something*. The significance of that fact may become more clear if we shift our attention briefly to performative modes of interpretation per se.

In the nineteenth century, for example, the appreciation and study of literature was intimately tied to recitation. "Readers" (like the famous McGuffey series of school books) compiled prose and poetic works for training people in oral performance and articulation. This ancient interpretive model lost nearly all of its authority during the last century, an unfortunate cultural lapse (we can now see). More rationalist procedures, thematically focused, worked to unhinge us from the physique of the literary experience that comes through so much more clearly in performative recitation.

Literary works can be, have been, "performed" in a variety of interpretive ways. "Did you ever read one of her Poems backwards . . . ? A something overtakes the Mind."[4] That is Emily Dickinson's remarkable proposal for a recitation-based method of radical reinterpretation. William Morris's Kelmscott Press editions—for example of Chaucer, Keats, Rossetti, and of his own works, perhaps especially *The Earthly Paradise*—are acts of reinterpretation executed as bibliographical performances. Johanna Drucker's analysis of the different types of white space that function on a single page of the Kelmscott Chaucer—she distinguishes some twenty kinds—is a dramatic demonstration of the critical/interpretive potentials of bibliographical coding.[5]

Such work bears a close functional resemblance to the interpretive per-formance of linguistic translation as such. In each case a target work is re-cast into another medium. If literary works were fundamentally data and information corpora, then translation—bibliographical or linguistic—would aspire to as much literal transparency as possible. This is the work-ing assumption guiding the practice of most information-technology approaches to literary works, such as TEI. But literary works covet a precision of heteronomy: they are machines that aspire to the multiplica-tion of particular meaning, and adequate translations are obliged to re-flect that quality.

One of the great acts of English language translation, Sir Thomas Urquhart's 1653 *The Works of Mr. Francis Rabelais,* illustrates what is called for. Rabelais is "now faithfully translated into English," we are in-formed on Urquhart's title page. But to be faithful in such a case is not to be literal, and if one compares Urquhart's work with his Rabelais origi-nal, one is struck by the astonishing freedom of his translation consid-ered in a literal sense. Indeed, Urquhart's work often resembles a jazz performance in the riffs it plays off the Rabelaisian riffs it is responding to. Swinburne's translations of the "Dies Irae" or of Villon, like Rossetti's of Dante's *La Vita Nuova,* are great translations because they exhibit the quality of "original works." All are also "critical" and interpretive acts, as we see, for example, in T. S. Eliot's recoil from Rossetti's work, which ap-proaches Dante in a spirit utterly inimical to Eliot's twentieth-century Anglo-Catholicism.

Like Swinburne, Rossetti was well aware of the critical function his work was undertaking: "a translation," he observes in his Introduction to his book of translations, *The Early Italian Poets* (1861), "involving as it does the necessity of settling many points [of interpretation] without discussion . . . , remains perhaps the most direct form of commentary."[6] We would add only that bibliographical design and literary recitation are equally "direct forms of commentary," as are pastiche, hoax, and parody. Brilliant examples of the critical use of such forms are plentiful, from Poe and Wilde through Jarry and Borges. So far as scholarly inter-pretation is concerned, we have good recent examples of the critical po-tential of such models. The vigorous discussion that followed the hoax essay published in 1998 by Alan Sokal in *Social Text*[7] is a succinct illus-tration of the critical power of the hoax form, as are the two books of Pooh parodies issued by Frederick Crews (in 1963 and 2001).

Those kinds of critical acts are humane and unnatural. That is why they are so common in the humanities, and so rare in the objective sci-ences, which focus on what is normative and what is natural (natural:

that is to say "non-human," including the nonhuman aspects of human being). Acts of interpretation get invested with ludic elements in order to raise their level of self-critical awareness, on one hand, and on the other to dramatize how and why meanings are *made*. Philology's nineteenth-century turn to science for procedural models often obscures the subjectivity that is essential for literary and aesthetic interpretation. In science per se, objective norms are functional requirements. This is not the case in the arena of humanistic inquiries. Even aggressively normative modes of humanistic interpretation—for instance, Dr. Johnson's or Laura Riding's—are proposed and argued, and are therefore always in question and at issue, Riding's explicitly so. Johnson would have thought Blake's interpretation of Milton and *Paradise Lost* reprehensible, perhaps even mad, and certainly not *true*. We may read Johnson with a similar critical freedom and construct (let us say) a Pooh parody of Johnson. That could be a useful interpretive act. It could not be done well, however, without bringing into play a fair amount of scholarly expertise, both procedural and informational. You can't parody what you haven't closely studied.

## II

We commonly associate the study of the documents of cultural memory with institutional apparatuses that develop and maintain certain rules and standards—the church, the university and its educational affiliates, professional organizations that monitor the literary law (that is to say, the arts and procedures for the accurate preservation of the works of culture). These social formations comprise what Stanley Fish called "interpretive communities." Subcommunities are continually emerging and further subdividing, within those larger "ideological apparatuses," as they were famously named by Louis Althusser. The evolution of psychoanalytic or historicist studies—their rich, not to say wild, proliferation of distinct microgroups—perfectly illustrates the special character of interpretive communities in the twentieth century.

Within those institutional orbits—where this book, myself, and yourself are located—a host of "interpretational" activities are sanctioned and executed, and in recent years have proliferated at a rate that many find alarming. These procedures are most familiar when they coalesce under specialized headings that stand for methods of reading and critical exegesis: New Criticism, Hermeneutics (various kinds), Historicism (again, in various forms), Theory (which develops in many meta-theoretical and interpretive subspecies like Feminist, Narrative, Queer, Psychoanalytic, etc.),

Narratology, Cognitive Poetics, Marxist Criticism, Literary Pragmatics, and so forth. Observed from within their professional frame of reference, these activities fairly represent, so to speak, the varieties of current interpretational experience. The phenomena of interpretation, so to say.

In the heavens of interpretation are many mansions. Because all of those superstructures are "of the earth, earthy," we pursue their readerly devotions on the common ground they share with each other: the sociohistorical environment that licenses and shapes their interpretive possibilities.

So the scholar urges his friend the reader to begin the quest of interpretation "in the foul rag and boneshop of the heart." Yeats's line reminds us that all of literature's ladders start with the materials, means, and modes of textual production. If you are after flesh and blood in interpretation, if you mean to be serious, you begin with what the scholar calls "the history of a work's production" on one hand, and "the history of a work's reception" on the other. Those two historical strands together comprise the double helix from which the many forms of culture develop. Acts of interpretation, themselves coded through this double helix, typically select a particular aspect or view of our cultural inheritance for investigation. Whatever our governing interpretive specialization, we necessarily pursue our studies under the horizon of this double and codependent set of sociohistorical determinations.

One caveat should be kept in mind, however. Certain interpreters focus their work on such technical issues—metrical and prosodic studies, for instance, or analytic and descriptive bibliography—that they often deliberately avoid engaging their foundational interpretive frames of reference and agencies. Interpretation always negotiates a compromise between the demands of procedural rigor and the call for critical reflection. These kinds of technical studies remind us that an engineer and a theologian live and work inside even the most nuanced reflexive interpreter—Roland Barthes, say, or Umberto Eco. There is a foul rag and boneshop of the brain too, after all. To the degree that an interpretive procedure makes an ideological engagement with its subject, to that degree it will be forced to study the codependent pair of historical determinants (production history and reception history) and to reflect critically upon its own place within those histories.

Given those considerations, we can construct a general model for works of cultural interpretation, which have a genetic code whose general form we understand. Like the biological code, it is a double helix with one strand comprised of a work's production history and the other of its reception history. From this model we may elaborate—as in the example given just below—an analytic outline of interpretation's essential subjects and topics. The specific subjects and topics placed under each of the categorical headings call us to clarify their circumstantial character, i.e., call us to a sociohistorical analysis of each element in the heading. These specific analyses, related together, constitute an analytic presentation of the category, and the adequacy of any interpretive act within that category will be a function of the range of discourse materials which are brought out for critical examination.

An interpretive investigation ranged under categories A and B comprises a theoretically finished sociohistorical program. Such a program gains a properly critical character when the material ranged under category C gets incorporated into the analysis.[8]

### A. The Originary Discursive Moment

1. Author
2. Other persons, groups, and agents invested in the initial process of cultural production
3. The institutional frameworks of cultural production (ideological and material)
4. The material and cultural inheritances that can be shown to shape, positively or otherwise, these three factors
5. The temporal phases that supply a coherent expository organization for analyzing each of those four factors

### B. Secondary Moments of Discursive Production and Reproduction (Individual and Related Sequences)

Discursive fields (or any portion of those fields) are dynamic and pass through processes of transformation engineered by the agencies that act within and upon those fields. These fields are what Humberto Maturana and Francesco Varela have called "autopoietic systems," i.e., systems devoted to self-maintenance through processes of self-transformation. So the five dimensions comprising the "originary discursive moment" all undergo a continual process of dynamic transformation and reconstruction. An "author" for example, will get re-viewed and reshaped over time by different people operating in the framework, material as well as ideological, of different classes, institutions, and groups. The number of Byron biographies illustrates the point, as it also shows that different cultural materials exert different levels of influence. Those reconstructive agencies themselves have to be studied and analyzed in terms of the five dimensions that characterize the originary discursive moment.

Discourse fields comprise specifiable works that emerge in certain concrete and specific forms along a series of equally concrete and specific avenues. Specifying the dynamic interplay of the field elements comprises the interpretational event. In an interpretive move, one can take as one's object of interest either some work or set of works in the field, or the discourse field itself (or some part or aspect of it). Forrest-Thomson's readings of various poems from Shakespeare to the present exemplify a move of the first kind, Friedrich Kittler's Foucauldian work is a move of the second kind.

The example of documentary transmission illustrates the general dynamical character of discourse fields. Literary documents bear within themselves the evidence of their own making, as McKenzie and others have shown, and those evidentiary marks solicit an interpretation of their meaning and significance. Historical patterns are literalized in the interpretation of a transmission history's documentary record.

Categories A and B are to be studied under interpretation's milder (and preliminary) rubric: "What does this mean?" Value judgments—political, ethical, aesthetic—remain after such a question is posed. Indeed, the question of the meaning of some feature of a discursive field must itself be ready for judgment, for the significance of an interpreter's questions cannot be taken for granted.

### C. The Immediate Moment of Interpretation

This category proposes an analysis of the interpreter's own critical purposes. This is probably the most demanding of all interpretive tasks since it involves a critical reflection on acts of interpretation that remain in process of development.

This moment appears as a specific interpretive action that may get located in a particular essay or book, imaginative or otherwise, or in a particular constellation of such works. What is important to realize is that an interpreter may approach his subject matter critically (categories A and B) without ever subjecting his own critical work to interpretive reflection. The heuristic model for such an event (i.e., for reflection only at levels A and B) would be, for example, the production of a scholarly edition by a technically skilled editor as a set task; or the production of an interpretive essay or book from a standing point assumed to be objective or in some fashion privileged with "enlightenment." Paul de Man's importance in the recent history of literary studies was a function of his acute critical sympathy with the blindness that accompanies the insight of most critical and interpretive acts.

Models for an interpretive action that positively seeks to approach a task from an inner standing point—i.e., models that solicit level C—would be either Thucydides *History of the Peloponnesian War* or Trotsky's *History of the Russian Revolution*. Models from current literary studies would be Susan Howe's *My Emily Dickinson* (1985) or Charles Bernstein's *My Way* (1999), in particular (say) his remarkable essay "The Revenge of the Poet-Critic; or, The Parts are Greater than the Sum of the Whole."[9]

Works that exhibit a high degree of expertise in this third world of interpretation will almost inevitably assume a controversial position. Such works will also exhibit—probably by necessity—more or less serious deficiencies in their interpretive grasp of their given subjects (categories A and B). This interpretive *felix culpa* follows from the decision to lay the act of interpretation open to question as the act is going on. Such interpretations succeed by exposing their own interpretive limits.

Professional interpretive essays customarily organize their evidence in order to make a case for the interpretations they advance. They wait upon other acts of interpretation for quality control. To that extent, such works can never themselves seriously address questions of value: is this interpretive understanding good or bad, is it right or wrong, and why does one arrive at such judgments?

## III

Those are the questions that Simone Weil regarded as essential, and they haunt every interpretive act whether the act deliberately seeks to raise those questions or not. They are questions that can only be addressed (and readdressed), for they are open questions, they do not have "answers." The touchstone of critical and interpretive adequacy, then, follows from this question: how much has the subject or problem been opened out by the critic's intervention?

Such a question can't be usefully engaged—it too can never be closed—if the scholar or critic does not begin with a clear understanding that *every* interpretation is an abstract reduction drawn out of the original work or object of attention. Scholars murder to dissect when their interpretations come to occupy the center of interest, rather than the works they are seeking out. Every critical performance is in this sense a *deformance*. But a useful deformance if self-consciously undertaken.

The great Italian scholar Galvano della Volpe developed a lucid explanation of how this critical procedure functions. He gives a practical demonstration of his ideas in his *Critique of Taste,* which develops what he calls a "realist" view of interpretation.[10] Because Della Volpe's ideas were shaped in a period dominated by the ideas of New Critics like Cleanth Brooks, his interpretive demonstrations typically focus on a single work, As is very clear even from René Wellek and Austin Warren's influential handbook of New Critical theory and method,[11] della Volpe's procedures are applicable to any kind of discursive formation, from the localized poem or story up to complex discourse fields like those studied by Foucault and his many followers.

Like Dante, and in contrast to, say, Coleridge or Schlegel, della Volpe sees imaginative literature as a type of "discourse" whose rationality—ragionamento—consists in its exploitation of the "polysemous" dimensions of language, whose structures are no more (and no less) difficult or even "mysterious" than processes of logical deduction and induction. For della Volpe, "intelligibility" is as much a feature of poiesis as of scientia.

Interpretation is the application of scientia to poiesis, or the effort to elucidate one discourse form in terms of another. Furthermore, the effort is not directed toward establishing general rules or laws but toward explaining a unitary, indeed a unique, phenomenon. A doubled gap thus emerges through the interpretive process itself, and it is the necessary presence of this gap that shapes della Volpe's critical thought. We may usefully recall here that when poets and artists use imaginative forms to interpret other such forms, they pay homage to this gap by throwing it into relief. Rossetti's sonnets for pictures, like all ecphrastic works, from Cavalcante de Cavalcanti to John Ashbery, do not so much translate the originary works as construct imaginative paraphrases. Rossetti's theory of translation, as we see in The Early Italian Poets (1861), follows a similar paraphrastic procedure.

Della Volpe's theory of interpretation runs along the same intellectual salient. When he argued that "critical paraphrase" should ground interpretive method, he was consciously installing a non-Hegelian form of dialectical criticism. In place of "a circular movement of negation and conservation of an original meta-historical unity of opposites," della Volpe offers what he calls "a dialectic of expressive facts"—in his case, the facts of the discrete poem and its discrete paraphrase—in which "neither of the elements of the relation can be reduced absolutely to the other . . . for . . . they . . . circulate only relatively within each other, in the diversified unity of an historical movement" (200). Interpretation for della Volpe, whatever its pretensions, always displays a gap between the work being examined and the student. But this gap does not represent a failure of criticism, or even a mysticism of poiesis. It locates the source and end and test of the art being examined. Della Volpe calls the gap a "quid," which comes into play as soon as the critic develops some "philosophical or so-ciological or historical equivalent of the poetic text," that is to say the "paraphrase . . . of the poetic thought or . . . content." Because this para-phrase constitutes "a reduction" of the original, "a comparison will neces-sarily be instituted between this paraphrase and the poetic thought or "content' which it paraphrases" (193).

Critical interpretation develops out of an initial moment of the origi-nary work's "degradation" via "uncritical paraphrase": "for in the case of the poetic, polysemic text, paraphrase—the *regression* to current lin-guistic use . . . constitutes the premise of an internal *progression* of thought . . . , an internal variation and development of meanings, which is disclosed . . . in a . . . philological comparison . . . of the paraphrase with that which is paraphrased" (133). Interpretation, then, is a constellation of paraphrases that evolve dialectically from an uncritical to a critical mo-ment, from "regression" to "progression." The interpretive constellation develops as the "uncritical" features of each critical turn get exposed—as new turns are taken, as the paraphrase is successively rephrased. One moves so to speak from "degradation" to "degradation," or, as we would say, from deformance to deformance. Thus paraphrastics becomes "the *beginning* and *end* of a whole process" of comparative explorations that get executed across the "quid" or gap that a process of interpretation brings into being. Again, the process is open-ended not because the "poem itself" possesses some mysterious, inexhaustible "meaning" but because its originary semiotic determinations must be repeatedly discovered within the historical space defined by the della Volpean "quid," where distantiation licenses "the method . . . of experimental analysis" (199).

Della Volpe carefully separates his theory of interpretation from the dialectics we associate with Hegel and especially Heidegger. The latter involves a process of thought refinement: through conversation or inter-nal dialogue, we clarify our ideas to ourselves. We come to realize what we didn't know we knew. This kind of reflection traces itself back to the idea of Platonic anamnesis. Della Volpe, by contrast, follows an Aristotelian line of thought, a "method . . . of experimental analysis." This method devel-ops a process of non-Hegelian historical reflection. Interpretive moments stand in nonuniform relations with each other so that the interpretation unfolds in fractal patterns of continuities and discontinuities. Besides re-alizing, perhaps, what we didn't know we knew, we are also led into imaginations of what we hadn't known at all.

The deformative examples set forth in the previous section are con-ceived as types of a della Volpean "experimental analysis." Being a phi-lologist, della Volpe pursues this kind of analysis through a series of searching historicist paraphrases of the texts he chooses to consider. To attempt a sociohistorical paraphrase is to experiment with the poetical work, to subject it to an hypothesis of its meanings. As in any scientific experiment with natural phenomena, the engagement with the originary phenomenon inevitably exposes the limits of the hypothesis, and ultimately returns us to an even more acute sense of the phenomena we desire to understand. So it is with della Volpe's paraphrases. By contrast, our "experimental analyses" place primary emphasis on the preconceptual elements of text. We do this because social and historical formations seem to us far less determinate, far more open to arbitrary and imaginative construction, than they appear in della Volpe's Marxist frame of reference.

If we follow della Volpe's method, then, we feel ourselves closer in spirit to the thought of, say, Blake when he remarks on the difference between the intelligence of art and the intelligence of philosophy: "Cunning & Morality are not Poetry but Philosophy the Poet is Independent & Wicked the Philosopher is Dependent & Good."[12] That is Blake's version of what Poe would soon call "the heresy of *The Didactic.*"[13] Our deformations do not flee from the question, or the generation, of "meaning." Rather, they try to demonstrate—the way one demonstrates how to make something, or do something—what Blake here assertively proposes: that "meaning" in imaginative work is a secondary phenomenon, a kind of metadata, what Blake called a form of worship "dependent" upon some primary poetical tale.[14] This point of view explains why, in our deformative maneuvers, interpretation represents a thought experiment we play with the primary materials. In the experiment of interpretation, "Meaning" is initially important as a catalyst in the investigative action. When the experiment has (for the nonce) finished, Meaning reappears in a new form, as the residues left behind for study and analysis. Meanings emerge then not as explanations of the poem but as evidence for judging the effectiveness of the experiment we undertook.

One could do worse than to recall, even in this special aesthetic frame of reference, Marx's last thesis on Feuerbach. Only philosophers try to understand art. The point is to change it. (Editorial efforts to preserve our cultural inheritance are themselves types, perhaps arch-types, of the changes we make when we try to preserve that inheritance). Our actions on these works, our deformations, help us to understand our thinking about them. To essay a more direct application of "interpretation" to imaginative work runs the risk of suggesting that interpretation can be adequate to poiesis. It cannot; it can only run a thematic experiment with the work, enlightening it by inadequacy and indirection.

In a Hellenistic age like ours, illusions about the sufficiency of interpretive meaning are especially strong. At such an historical moment one might rather look for interpretations that flaunt their subjectivity and arbitrariness, interpretations that increase their value by offering themselves at a clear discount.

To deliberately accept the inevitable failure of interpretive "adequacy" is to work toward discovering new interpretive virtues, somewhat as Lyn Hejinian claims that the

> Interpretive works that parody or ironize themselves are especially useful—works like Derrida's *The Post Card* (1980), Charles Bernstein's *My Way* (1999), or Laura Riding's remarkable *Anarchism Is Not Enough* (1928). Riding's attitude toward the process of critical thinking is helpful: "our minds are still moving, and *backward* as well as *forward;* the nearest we get to truth at any given moment is, perhaps, only an idea—a dash of truth somewhat flavouring the indeterminate substance of our minds.[15]

This thought calls for a critical method intent upon baring its own devices. We take it seriously because it makes sure that we do not take it too seriously. Examples of such critical approaches are legion: we just need to remember to look for them, and perhaps how to look for them.

# 5

## Marking Texts in Many Dimensions

I

Although "text" has been a "Keyword" in clerical and even popular discourse for well over fifty years, it did not find a place in Raymond Williams's important book *Keywords* (1976). This strange omission may perhaps be explained by the word's cultural ubiquity and power. In that lexicon of modernity Williams called the "Vocabulary of Culture and Society," "text" has been the "one word to rule them all." Indeed, the word "text" became so shape-shifting and meaning-malleable that we should probably label it with Tolkien's full rubrication: "text" has been, and still is, the "one word to rule them all and in the darkness bind them."

We want to keep in mind that general context when we address the issues of digitized texts, text markup, and electronic editing. Although these are the specialized concerns of this chapter, they have important bearings on all aspects of literary and philological studies. As we lay foundations for translating our inherited archive of cultural materials, including vast corpora of paper-based materials, into digital depositories and forms, we are called to a clarity of thought about textuality that most people, even most scholars, rarely undertake.

Consider the phrase "marked text," for instance. How many recognize it as a redundancy? All text is marked text, as you may see by reflecting on the very text you are now reading. As you follow this conceptual exposition, watch the physical embodiments that shape the ideas and the process of thought. Do you see the typeface, do you recognize it? Does it *mean* anything to you, and if not, why not? Now scan away (as you keep reading) and take a quick measure of the general page layout: the font sizes, the characters per line, the lines per page, the leading, the headers, footers, margins. And there is so much more to be seen, registered, and understood simply at the documentary level of your reading: paper, ink, book design, or the markup that controls not the documentary status of the text but its linguistic status. What would you be seeing and reading if I were addressing you in Chinese, Arabic, Hebrew—even Spanish or German? What would you be seeing and reading if this text had been printed, like Shakespeare's sonnets, in 1609?

We all know the ideal reader of these kinds of traditional documents. She is an actual person, like the texts this person reads and studies. He writes about her readings and studies under different names, including Randall McLeod, Randy Clod, Random Cloud, etc. She is the Dupin of the textual mysteries of our exquisite and sophisticated bibliographical age.

Most important to realize, for this book's present purposes, is that digital markup schemes do not easily—perhaps do not even *naturally*—map to the markup that pervades paper-based texts. Certainly this is the case for every kind of electronic markup currently in use: from simple ASCII to any inline SGML derivatives, to the recent approaches of stand-off markup.[1] The symptoms of this discrepancy are exemplified in the Artificial Intelligence community's struggles to simulate the complex processes of natural language and communicative exchange. Stymied of success in achieving that goal, these efforts have nonetheless been singularly fruitful for giving us a clearer view of the richness and flexibility of traditional textual machineries.

How, then, are traditional texts marked? If we could give an exhaustive answer to that question we would be able to simulate them in digital forms. We cannot complete an answer for two related reasons: first, the answer would have to be framed from within the discourse field of textuality itself; and second, that framework is dynamic, a continually emerging function of its own operations, including its explicitly self-reflexive operations. This is not to say that markup and theories of markup must be "subjective." (It is also not to say—see below—that they must *not be* subjective.) It *is* to say that they are and must be social, historical, and dialectical, and that some forms have greater range and power than others, and that some are useful exactly because they seek to limit and restrict their range for certain special purposes.

## II

Describing the problems of electronic texts in her book on humanities computing, Susan Hockey laconically observes that "There is no obvious unit of language."[2] Hockey is reflecting critically on the ordinary assumption that this unit is the word. Language scholars know better. Words can

be usefully broken down into more primitive parts and therefore understood as constructs of a second or even higher order. The view is not unlike the one continually encountered by physicists who search out basic
units of matter. Our analytic tradition inclines us to understand that forms
of all kinds are "built up" from "smaller" and more primitive units, and
hence to take the self-identity and integrity of these parts, and the whole
that they comprise, for objective reality.

Hockey glances at this problem of the text-unit in order to clarify the
difficulties of creating electronic texts. To achieve that, we instruct the
computer to identify (the) basic elements of natural language text and we
try to ensure that the identification has no ambiguities. In natural language, however, the basic unit—indeed, all divisioning of any kind—is
only procedurally determinate. The units are arbitrary. More, the arbitrary units themselves can have no absolute self-identity. Natural language is rife with redundancy and ambiguity at every unit and level and
throughout its operating relations. A long history of analytic procedures
has evolved certain sets of best practices in the study of language and communicative action, but even in a short run, terms and relations of analysis
have changed.

Print and manuscript technology represents efforts to mark natural
language so that it can be preserved and transmitted. It is a technology
that constrains the shapeshiftings of language, which is itself a special-
purpose system for coding human communication. Exactly the same can
be said of electronic encoding systems. In each case constraints are in-
stalled in order to facilitate operations that would otherwise be difficult
or impossible. In the case of a system like TEI, the system is designed to
"disambiguate" entirely the materials to be encoded.

The output of TEI's markup constraints differs radically from the output generated by the constraints of manuscript and print technology.
Whereas redundancy and ambiguity are expelled from TEI, they are
preserved—are *marked*—in manuscript and print. While print and manuscript markups don't "copy" the redundancies of natural language, they
do construct systems that are sufficiently robust to develop and generate
equivalent types of redundancy. This capacity is what makes manuscript
and print encoding systems so much more resourceful than any electronic encoding systems currently in use. ("Natural language" is the most
complex and powerful reflexive coding system that we know of.)[3]

Like biological forms and all living systems, not least of all language
itself, print and manuscript encoding systems are organized under a horizon of codependent relations. That is to say, print technology—I will
henceforth use that term as shorthand for both print and manuscript

technologies—is a system that codes (or simulates) what are known as autopoietic systems. These are classically described by Humberto Maturana and Francisco Varela (1980) in the following terms:

> If one says that there is a machine $M$ in which there is a feedback loop through the environment so that the effects of its output affect its input, one is in fact talking about a larger machine $M^1$ which includes the environment and the feedback loop in its defining organization.[4]

Such a system constitutes a closed topological space that "continuously generates and specifies its own organization through its operation as a system of production of its own components, and does this in an endless turnover of components" (79). Autopoietic systems are thus distinguished from allopoietic systems, which are Cartesian and which "have as the product of their functioning something different from themselves" (80).

In this context, all coding systems appear to occupy a peculiar position. Because "coding . . . represents the interactions of [an] observer" with a given system, the mapping stands apart from "the observed domain" (135). Coding is a function of "the space of human design" operations, or what is classically called "heteropoietic" space. Positioned thus, coding and markup appear allopoietic.

As machines of simulation, however, coding and markup (print or electronic) are not like most allopoietic systems (cars, flashlights, a road network, economics). Coding functions emerge *as code* only within an autopoietic system that has evolved those functions as essential to the maintenance of its life (its dynamic operations). Language and print technology (and electronic technology) are second- and third-order autopoietic systems—what Marshall McLuhan famously, expressively, if also somewhat misleadingly, called "extensions of man." Coding mechanisms—proteins, print technology—are generative components of the topological space they serve to maintain. They are folded within the autopoietic system like membranes in living organisms, where distinct components realize and execute their extensions of themselves.

This general frame of reference is what makes Maturana and Varela equate the "origin" of such systems with their "constitution" (95). This equation means that codependency pervades an autopoietic structure of relations. All components of the system arise (so to speak) simultaneously and they perform integrated functions. The system's life is a morphogenetic passage characterized by various dynamic mutations and transformations of the local system components. The purpose or goal of these

processes is autopoietic—self-maintenance through self-transformation—
and their basic element is not a system component but the relation (codependence) that holds the mutating components in changing states of dynamic stability. The states generate measurable codependency functions
both in their periods (or basins) of stability and in their unique moments
of catastrophic change.


## III

At the 2002 Extreme Markup Conference, Michael Sperberg-McQueen
offered these observations on the problem of overlapping structures for
SGML-based markup systems.

> It is an interesting problem because it is the biggest problem remaining in
> the residue. If we have a set of quantitative observations, and we try to fit a
> line to them, it is good practice to look systematically at the difference be-
> tween the values predicted by our equation (our theory) and the values ac-
> tually observed; the set of these differences is the residue. . . . In the context
> of SGML and XML, overlap is a residual problem.[5]

But in any context *other than* SGML and XML, this formulation is a
play of wit, a kind of joke—as if one were now to say that the statistical
deviations produced by Newtonian mathematical calculations left a "residue" of "interesting" matters to be cleared up by further, deeper calculations. But those matters are not *residual,* they are the hem of a quantum
garment.

My own comparison is itself a kind of joke, of course, for an SGML/
TEI model of the world of textualities pales in comprehensiveness before
the Newtonian model of the physical world. But the outrageousness of
the comparison in each case helps to clarify the situation. No autopoietic
process or form can be simulated under the horizon of a structural model
like SGML, not even topic maps. We see this very clearly when we observe the inability of a derivative model like TEI to render the forms and
functions of traditional textual documents. The latter, which deploy
markup codes themselves, supply us with simulations of language as well
as of many other kinds of semeiotic processes, as Charles Sanders Peirce
called them. Textualized documents restrict and modify, for various kinds
of reflexive purposes, the larger semeiotic field in which they participate.
Nonetheless, the procedural constraints that traditional textualities lay
upon the larger semeiotic field that they model and simulate are far more

pragmatic, in a full Peircean sense, than the electronic models that we are currently deploying.

Understanding how traditional textual devices function is especially important now when we are trying to imagine how to optimize our new digital tools. Manuscript and print technologies—graphical design in general—provide arresting models for information technology tools, especially in the context of traditional humanities research and education needs. To that end we may usefully begin by making an elementary distinction between the archiving and the simulating functions of textual (and, in general, semeiotic) systems. Like gene codes, traditional textualities possess the following as one of their essential characteristics: that as part of their simulation and generative processes, they make (of) themselves a record of those processes. Simulating and record keeping, which are codependent features of any autopoietic or semeiotic system, can be distinguished for various reasons and purposes. A library processes traditional texts by treating them strictly as records. It saves things and makes them accessible. A poem, by contrast, processes textual records as a field of dynamic simulations. The one is a machine of information, the other a machine of reflection. Each may be taken as an index of a polarity that characterizes all semeoitic or autopoietic systems. Most texts—for instance, this essay you are reading now—are fields that draw upon the influence of both of those polarities.

The power of traditional textualities lies exactly in their ability to integrate those different functions within the same set of coding elements and procedures.

SGML and its derivatives are largely, if not strictly, coding systems for storing and accessing records. They possess as well certain analytic functions that are based in the premise that text is an "ordered hierarchy of context objects."[6] This conception of textuality is plainly noncomprehensive. Indeed, its specialized understanding of "text" reflects the pragmatic goal of such a markup code: to store objects (in the case of TEI, textual objects) so that they can be quickly accessed and searched for their informational content—or more strictly, for certain parts of that informational content (the parts that fall into a hierarchical order modeled on a linguistic analysis of the structure of a book).

These limitations of electronic markup codes are not to be lamented, but for humanist scholars they are to be clearly understood. A markup code like TEI creates a record of a traditional text in a certain form. Especially important to see is that, unlike the textual fields it was designed to mark up, TEI is an allopoietic system. Its elements are unambiguously delimited and identified a priori, its structure of relations is precisely fixed, it is nondynamical, and it is focused on objects that stand apart from itself. Indeed, it defines what it marks not only *as* objective, but as objective in exactly the unambiguous terms of the system's a priori categories. This kind of machinery will therefore serve only certain, very specific, purposes. The autopoietic operations of textual fields—operations especially pertinent to the texts that interest humanities scholars—lie completely outside the range of an order like the TEI.

For certain archival purposes, then, structured markup will serve. It does not unduly interfere with, or forbid implementing, some of the searching and linking capacities that make digital technology so useful for different types of comparative analysis. Its strict formality is abstract enough to permit implementation within higher-order formalizations. In these respects it has greater flexibility than a stand-off approach to text markup, which is more difficult to integrate into a dispersed online network of different kinds of materials.[7] All that having been recognized and said, however, these allopoietic text-processing systems cannot access or display the autopoietic character of textual fields. Digital tools have yet to develop models for displaying and replicating the self-reflexive operations of bibliographical tools, which alone are operations for thinking and communicating—which is to say, for transforming storage into memory, and data into knowledge.

We have to design and build digital environments for those purposes. A measure of their capacity and realization will be whether they can integrate data-function mechanisms like TEI into their higher-order operations. To achieve that will entail, I believe, the deployment of dynamic, topological models for mapping the space of digital operations like those developed by René Thom.[8] But these models will have to be reconceived, as one can see by reflecting on a remark about textual interpretation that Stanley Fish liked to make years ago in his lectures about interpretation. He would point out that he was able to treat even the simplest text— road signage, for example—as a poem and thus develop from his own "response" and commentary its autopoietic potential. The remark underscores a basic and almost entirely neglected (undertheorized) feature of discourse fields: that to "read" them—to read "in" them at any point— one must regard what we call "the text" and "the reader" as codependent agents in the field. You can't have one without the other.

Fish's observation, therefore, while true, signals a widespread theoretical and methodological weakness in our conceptions of textuality, traditional or otherwise. This approach figures "text" as a heuristic abstraction drawn from the larger field of discourse. The word "text" is used in various ways by different people—Barthes' understanding is not the same as a TEI understanding—but in any case the term frames attention on the linguistic dimension of a discourse field. Books and literary works, however, organize themselves along multiple dimensions of which the linguistic is only one.

Modeling digital simulations of a discourse field requires that a formal set of dimensions be specified for the field. This is what TEI provides a priori, though the provision, as we know, is minimal. Our received scholarly traditions have in fact passed down to us an understanding of such fields that is at once far more complex as well as reasonably stable. Discourse fields, our textual condition, regularly get mapped along six dimensions (see below, and Appendix B in this chapter). Most important of all in the present context, however, are the implications of cognizing a discourse field as autopoietic. In that case the field measurements will be taken by "observers" positioned within the field itself. That intramural location of the field interpreter is in truth a logical consequence of the codependent character of the field and its components. "Interpretation" is not undertaken from a position outside the field, it is an essential part of a field's emergence and of any state that its emergence might assume.

This matter is crucial to understand when we are reaching for an adequate formalizing process for textual events like poetry or other types of orderly but discontinuous phenomena. René Thom explains very clearly why topological models are preferable to linear ones in dynamic systems:

> It must not be thought that a linear structure is necessary for storing or transmitting information (or, more precisely, significance); it is possible that a language, a semantic model, consisting of topological forms could have considerable advantages from the point of view of deduction, over the linear language that we use, although this idea is unfamiliar to us. Topological forms lend themselves to a much richer range of combinations . . . than the mere juxtaposition of two linear sequences. (145)

These comments distinctly recall Peirce's exploration of existential graphs as sites of logical thinking. But Thom's presentation of topological models does not conceive field spaces that are autopoietic, which seems to have been Peirce's view.[9] Although Thom's approach generally eschews practical considerations in favor of theoretical clarity, his models assume that they will operate on data carried into the system from some external source. If Thom's "data" comes into his studies in a theoretical form, then, it has been theorized in traditional empirical terms. The topological model of a storm may therefore be taken either as the description of the storm and/or a prediction of its future behavior. But when a model's data is taken to arise codependently with all the other components of its system, a very different "result" ensues. Imagined as applied to textual autopoiesis, a topological approach carries itself past an analytic description or prediction over to a form of demonstration or enactment.

The view taken here is that no textual field can exist as such without "including" in itself the reading or measurement of the field, which specifies the field's dataset from within. The composition of a poem is the work's first reading, which *in that event* makes a call upon others. An extrinsic analysis designed to specify or locate a poetic field's self-reflexiveness commonly begins from the vantage of the rhetorical or the social dimension of the text, where the field's human agencies (efficient causes) are most apparent. The past century's fascination with structuralist approaches to cultural phenomena produced, as we know, a host of analytic procedures that chose to begin from a consideration of formal causation, and hence from either a linguistic or a semiotic vantage. Both procedures are analytic conventions based in empirical models.

Traditional textuality provides us with autopoietic models that have been engineered as effective analytic tools. The codex is the greatest and most famous of these. Our problem is imagining ways to recode them for digital space. To do that we have to conceive formal models for autopoietic processes that can be written as computer software programs.

## IV

Let's recapitulate the differences between book markup and TEI markup. TEI defines itself as a two-dimensional generative space mapped as (1) a set of defined "content objects" (2) organized within a nested tree structure. The formality is clearly derived from an elementary structuralist model of language (a vocabulary + a syntax, or a semantic + a syntagmatic dimension). In the SGML/TEI extrusion, both dimensions are fixed and their relation to each other is defined as arbitrary rather than codependent. The output of such a system is thus necessarily symmetrical with the input. Input and output in a field of traditional textuality works differently. Even in quite restricted views, as we know, the operations of natural language and communicative exchange generate incommensurable effects. The operations exhibit behavior that topologists track as bifurcation or even generalized catastrophe, whereby an initial set of structural stabilities produces morphogenetic behaviors and conditions that are unpredictable. This essential feature of "natural language"—which is to say, of the discourse fields of communicative exchange—is what makes it so powerful, on one hand, and so difficult to model and formalize on the other.

In these circumstances, models like TEI commend themselves because they can be classically quantified for empirical—numerable—results. But as Thom observed long ago, there is no such thing as "a quantitative theory of catastrophes of a dynamical system" like natural language. To achieve such a theory, he went on to say, "it would be necessary to have a good theory of integration on function spaces" (Thom, 321), something that Thom could not conceive.

That limitation of qualitative mathematical models did not prevent Thom from vigorously recommending their study and exploration. He particularly criticized the widespread scientific habit of "tak[ing] the main divisions of science, the[ir] taxonomy . . . as given a priori" rather than trying to re-theorize taxonomics as such (322). In this frame of reference we can see (1) that textualization in print technology is a qualitative (rather than a taxonomic) function of natural language, and (2) that textualization integrates function spaces through demonstrations and enactments rather than descriptions. This crucial understanding—that print textuality is not language but an operational (praxis-based) theory of language—has stared us in the face for a long time, but seeing we have not seen. It has taken the emergence of electronic textualities, and in particular operational theories of natural language like TEI, to expose the deeper truth about print and manuscript texts. SGML and its derivatives freeze (rather than integrate) the function spaces of discourse fields by reducing the field components to abstract forms—what Coleridge in the *Biographia Literaria* called "fixities and definites." This approach will serve when the object is to mark textual fields for storage and access.

Integration of dynamic functions will not emerge through such abstract reductions, however. To develop an effective model of an autopoietic system requires an analysis that is built and executed "in the same spirit that the author writ." That formulation by Alexander Pope expresses, in an older dialect, what we have called in this century "the uncertainty principle," or the codependent relation between measurements and phenomena. An agent defines and interprets a system from within the system itself—at what Dante Gabriel Rossetti called "an inner standing point." What we call "scientific objectivity" is in one sense a mathematical function; in another, it is a useful method for controlling variables. We use it when we study texts as if they were objective things rather than dynamic autopoietic fields.

Traditional textual conditions facilitate textual study at an inner standing point because all the activities can be carried out—can be represented—
in the same field space—typically, in a bibliographical field. Subject and
object meet and interact in the same dimensional space—a situation
that gets reified for us when we read books or write about them. Digital
operations, however, introduce a new and more abstract space of relations into the study-field of textuality. This abstract space brings the
possibility of new and in certain respects greater analytic power to the
study of traditional texts. On the downside, however, digitization—at
least to date, and typically—situates the critical agent outside the field
to be mapped and re-displayed. Or—to put this crucial point more precisely (since no measurement has anything more than a relative condition of objectivity)—digitization situates the critical agent within levels
of the textual field's dimensionalities that are difficult to formalize
bibliographically.

To exploit the power of those new formalizations, a digital environment has to expose its subjective status and operation. (Like all scientific
formalities, digital procedures are "objective" only in relative terms.) In
the present case—the digital marking of textual fields—this means that
we will want to build tools that foreground the subjectivity of any measurements that are taken and displayed. Only in this way will the autopoietic character of the textual field be accurately realized. The great gain
that comes with such a tool is the ability to specify—to measure, display,
and eventually to compute and transform—an autopoietic structure at
what would be, in effect, quantum levels.

A series of related projects to explore such tools were taken up some
ten years ago at University of Virginia's Speculative Computing Laboratory (SpecLab).[10] The first of these, *IVANHOE,* was an online gamespace
built for the imaginative reconstruction of traditional texts and discourse
fields.[11] Players enter these works through a digital display space that
encourages them to alter and transform the textual field. The game rules
require that transformations be made as part of a discourse field that
emerges dynamically through the changes made to a specified initial set
of materials.

As the *IVANHOE* project was going forward, a second, related project
called *Time Modelling* was being taken up by Johanna Drucker and
Bethany Nowviskie. The project sought "to bring visualization and interface design into the early content modeling phase" of projects like *IVAN-
HOE,* which pursue interpretation through transformational and even
deformative interactions with the primary data.[12] *IVANHOE*'s computer
is designed to store the game players' performative interpretational moves

and it then produces algorithmically generated analyses of the moves after the fact. The chief critical function thus emerges after-the-fact, in a set of human reflections on the differential patterns that the computerized analyses expose. In the *Time Modeling* device, however, the performative and the critical actions are much more closely integrated because the human is actively involved in a deliberated set of digital transformations. The *Time Modelling* device gives users a set of design functions for reconstructing a given lineated timeline of events in terms that are subjective and hypothetical. The specified field of event-related data is brought forward for transformation through editing and display mechanisms that emphasize the malleability of the initial set of field relations. The project stands, conceptually, somewhere between design programs (with their sets of tools for making things) and complex websites like *The Rossetti Archive* (with their hypertextual datasets organized for on-the-fly search and analysis). It is a set of editing and display tools that allows users to design their own hypothetical (re)formulations of a given dataset.

The frankly experimental character of *Time Modelling*'s data (re)constructions led to an important reimagining of the original *IVANHOE* project. From the outset of *IVANHOE* we intended to situate the "interpreter" within the discourse field that was the subject of interpretive transformation. Our initial conception was toward what we called "Ultimate *IVANHOE*," i.e., toward a playspace that would be controlled by emergent consciousness software. With the computer an active agent in an *IVANHOE* session, players could measure and compare their own understandings of their actions against a set of computer generated views. This prospect for *IVANHOE*'s development remains, but the example of *Time Modelling* exposed another way to situate the human interpreter at an inner standing point of an autopoietic system.

If 'Pataphysics is, in the words of its originator, "the science of exceptions," the project here is to reconceive *IVANHOE* under the rubric of 'Patacriticism, or the theory of subjective interpretation. The theory is implemented through what is here called the dementianal method, which is a procedure for marking the autopoietic features of textual fields. The method works on the assumption that such features characterize what topologists call a field of general catastrophe. The dementianal method marks the dynamic changes in autopoietic fields much as Thom's topological models allow one to map forms of catastrophic behavior. The 'patacritical model differs from Thom's models because the measurements of the autopoietic field's behaviors are generated from within the field itself, which only emerges as a field through the action of the person interpreting— that is to say, marking and displaying—a specific set of elements and relations for the field. The field arises codependently with the acts that mark and measure it. In this respect we characterize its structure as demential rather than dimensional.

As the device is presently conceived, readers engage autopoietic fields along three behavior dementians: *transaction, connection,* and *resonance.* A common transaction of a page space moves diagonally down the page, with regular deviations for horizontal line transactions left to right margin, from the top or upper left to the bottom at lower right. Readers regularly violate that pattern in indefinite numbers of ways, often being called to deviance by how the field appears marked by earlier agencies. (In Chapter 9 I transact the field of a pagespace, the first edition title page of James Fenimore Cooper's *The Pioneers,* by consciously deviating from the page's original spatial argument.) Connections assume, in the same way, multiple forms. Indeed, the primal act of autopoietic connection is the identification or location of a textual element to be "read." In this sense, the transaction of an autopoietic field is a function of the marking of connections of various kinds, on one hand, and of resonances on the other. Resonances are signals that call attention to a textual element as having a field value—a potential for connectivity—that appears *and* appears unrealized.

Note that each of these behavior dementians exhibit codependent relations. The field is transacted as connections and resonances are marked; the connections and resonances are emergent functions of each other; and the marking of dementians immediately reorders the space of the field, which itself keeps reemerging under the sign of the marked alteration of the dynamic fieldspace and its various elements.

These behavioral dementians locate an autopoietic syntax, which is based in an elementary act or agenting event: G. Spencer Brown's "law of calling" which declares that a distinction can be made.[13] From that law comes the possibility that elements of identities can be defined. They emerge with the codependent emergence of the textual field's control dimensions, which are the field's autopoietic semantics. (For further discussion of these matters see Appendixes A and B in this chapter.)

## V

This 'patacritical approach to textual dementians is a meta-theory of textual fields, a pragmatistic conception of how to expose discontinuous textual behaviors ("natural language" so called, or what Habermas has better called "communicative action"). Integration of the dynamic functions begins not by abstracting the theory away from a target object—that is the method of a taxonomic methodology—but by integrating the meta-theoretical functions within the discourse space itself.

Informational discourse fields function well by working to limit redundancy and concurrent textual relations. Because poetry—or imaginative textuality broadly conceived—postulates much greater freedom of expressive exchange, it exhibits a special attraction for anyone wishing to study the dynamics of textuality. Aristotle's studies of semiotic systems preserve their foundational character because they direct their attention to autopoietic rather than allopoietic discourse fields. His studies pursue a taxonomy for the dynamic process of making and exchanging (remaking) simulations.

Plato's dialogues, by contrast, situate—or, more precisely, generate—their critical reflections at a standing point inside the textualities they are themselves unfolding. In this respect they have much in common with Wittgenstein's critical colloquies in the *Philosophical Investigations* or with Montaigne's *Les Essais*. But the dynamic play of even these textual fields remain, from the point of view of their readers, exemplary exercises. This situation prevails in all modes of critical reflection which assume to preserve the integrity and self-identity of the textual fields they study. Two forms of critical reflection regularly violate the sanctity of such self-contained textual spaces: translation and editing. The idea that an object of criticism like a textual field *is* an object can be maintained either as a heuristic procedure or as an ontological illusion. Consequently, acts of translation and editing are especially useful forms of critical reflection because they so clearly invade and change their subjects in material ways. To undertake either, you can scarcely *not* realize the performative—even the *deformative*—character of your critical agency.

At this point let me exemplify the general markup model for autopoietic textualities. This comes as the following hypothetical passage through an early poem by Robert Creeley, "The Innocence." Because imaginative textuality is, in this view, an exemplary kind of autopoietic process, any poetical work would do for a narrative demonstration. I choose "The Innocence" because it illustrates what Creeley and others called "field poetics."[14] As such, it is especially apt for clarifying the conception of the autopoietic model of textuality being offered here. "Composition by field" poetics has been much discussed, but for present purposes it suffices to say that it conceives poetry as a nonsubjective autopoietic discourse. "The poem" is the "field" of action and energy generated in the poetic transaction of the field that the poem itself exhibits. "Composition by field," whose theoretical foundations may be usefully studied through

Charles Olson's engagements with contemporary philosophy and science, comprised both a method for understanding (rethinking) the entire inheritance of poetry, and a program for contemporary and future poetic discourse (its writing and its reading).

The text chosen is taken from Donald Allen's famous anthology (first published in 1960) *The New American Poetry* in its 1999 University of California Press reprinting.

THE INNOCENCE

Looking to the sea, it is a line
of unbroken mountains.

It is the sky.
It is the ground. There
we live, on it.

It is a mist
now tangent to another
quiet. Here the leaves
come, there
is the rock in evidence

or evidence.
What I come to do
is partial, partially kept

Before tracing a model for this poetic field we want to bear two matters in mind. First, the field we are transacting is localized in relation to this documentary instance of "the text." One of the most persistent and misleading procedures in traditional hermeneutics is to take the object of study as something not only abstract and disembodied, but as something lying outside the field space—itself specific and material—of the act of critical representation. Second, the sequence of readings (below) consciously assumes a set of previous readings whereby certain elementary forms of order—by no means insignificant forms—have been integrated into the respective textual dementias. All such forms are extrusions from the elementary semiotic move, which is Spencer Brown's basic law of form: that a distinction can be drawn (*as* a dementian, or within and between dementians). Thus the readings below assume that each dementian is oriented to a set of established formal objects which get called and then crossed (transformed) in the transaction of the field.

That said, let me transact the poetic field through the initial textual model supplied above.

*A First Reading:* I mark the following elements in the first line group (and in that act I mark as well the presence of (a) lines and (b) line groups): "Looking" as a dangling participle; "it" (line 1) as ambiguously pronominal; "line" as a word play referencing (first) this line of verse I am transacting, and (second) a landscape of "unbroken mountains" (to be marked as such only with the marking of the final line in the group). All of these are defined (connected to the fieldspace) as textual elements with marked resonances (anticipations and clear if inchoate recollections) as well as several manifest, second-order connections (e.g., "sea," "line," and "mountains" as objects in a landscape).

Line group two emerges to connect a network of "it" words as well as to settle the dominance of a linguistic gravity field centered in the initially marked "landscape" (a linguistic dementian subdomain). As the third line group continues to elaborate the "landscape field," several distinctly new elements emerge and get marked. They center in the words "tangent," "quiet," "evidence," the notable enjambment at the end of the line group, and the deictics "Here" and "there." The first four resonate by the differences they make with the previous elements I had defined in my transaction of the field. The deictics connect back to the second linguistic dementian subdomain (the self-reflexive set of textual elements marked in line one as the dangling participle and the final word "line"). The fourth and last line group is itself marked as strongly resonant in itself because of the emergence within it of the unique "I" and the startling repetitions ("evidence," "partial"/"partially").

So the field transaction is marked geometrically as a complete and continuous passage from upper left to lower right and proceeding line by line left to right. That passage of the textspace marks out two control dementians, linguistic and graphical, as well as several distinct basins of order within them. In the graphical dementian we see an array of marked letters, words, lines, and line groups. In the linguistic dementian I have marked two distinct subdomains, one referential (the set of "landscape" semantics), one a subdomain of pure signifiers (proliferating from line 1 through the deictic markers "Here" and "there."

*A Second Reading.* I mark the title as strongly resonant and I find myself scanning the poem rather than reading it linearly, and marking elements unnoticed in the first reading. I re-mark the array of "it" words and connect all of them to the title, marking thereby another linguistic subdomain. I mark as resonant the striking idea of "a mist/now tangent to another/quiet," and I mark a distinction in the linguistic subdomain (of "landscape") between different sensory aspects of a "landscape." I mark as resonant the equally striking final sentence and the phrase "the rock in evidence//or evidence."

*A Third Reading.* This is a sequential transaction through the poem as in the first reading. It is largely devoted to marking connections between the various elements already marked with resonance values. The word-play in "line" is marked as a strongly resonant locus of fieldspace connections across the several linguistic subdomains. This connective fieldspace is especially resonant as the connection between the words "line" and "tangent." I mark all of the previously marked textual elements as connected to each other in a broadly dispersed semiotic dementian because I am seeing that elements in different fieldspace dementians and domains (e.g., "mist" and "quiet") are connected to each other.

*A Fourth Reading.* A sequential reading leads to marking the final sentence as a dramatic locus of a rhetorical dementian in the fieldspace. The construction of the textspace is "What I come to do." The emergence of this idea allows me to mark the poem as a deliberated sequential organization that exposes itself in certain telling (marked) moments and textual elements: "Looking," "line," "tangent," the deictic words, the previously unmarked "we" (line 5), the enjambment between the third and fourth line groups. In all these I mark a rhetorical organization tied most centrally to the phrase "What I come to do." I mark that these marks unfold as a relation that must be seen as sequenced: "I" in the present tense here is always the present tense in the linguistic dementian of this work. Marking the verb tense in that way immediately produces the first, remarkable emergence in this reading process of the work's social dementian. "I" comes to write this poem, which is marked thereby as an event in the world and as objective as any material thing (these material things, the "landscape" things, first marked in the linguistic dementian). In that rhetorical dementian I mark as well a key element of this work's social dementian first marked in the linguistic dementian: the relation between the "we" and the "I." The phrase "is partial/partially kept" is marked now as an element in the social dementian of the textspace—as if one were to say, interpretively, that the "doing" of the poem is only one event in a larger field that the poem is part of and points toward. My acts of marking the poem fall into both the local fieldspace and the larger discourse field marked by this local poetical field. And I further mark the social space by connecting the textspace to the book in which the text is printed—for that book (the polemic it made) marks this specific text in the strongest way. At this point the sixth dementian of the fieldspace begins to get marked, the material dementian. I mark three documentary features in particular: the placement of the text in the book, the organ of publication, the date of publication. I mark as well the fact that these material features of the work are, like the word "line," double-meaninged (or double dementianed), having as well a clear placement in the work's social dementian as well.

*A Fifth Reading.* I mark new elements in the six marked dementians that emerge in a widespread process of subdividing and proliferating. Elements defined in one dementian or subdomain get marked in another (for instance, "I" began in the rhetorical, reappeared in the social, and now gets marked in all the other dementians as well); unmarked textual features, like the letter "t," get marked as resonant; the shape of the textspace from word to line to word group is marked as a linked set of spare elements. These additional markings lead to other, previously unseen and unmarked relations and elements. The spare graphical dementian gets linked to the linguistic dementian ("The Innocence") and to the social and rhetorical dementians (the graphical spareness is only markable in relation to the absent/present discourse field in which this poetical work stands and declares its comparative allegiance.

*A Sixth Reading.* This is a reading that poses significant theoretical and practical issues. Time-stamped two weeks after the previous readings, this reading was negotiated in my mind as I recalled the history of my readings of the poem. It is thus a reading to be digitally marked after-the-fact. Focused on the final line group, it also marks the entirety of the autopoietic field. The reading marks the "I" as a figure in the social dementian, the poet (Creeley) who composed the poem. In that linking, however, I as reader become linked to the linguistic "I" that is also a social "I." This linkage gets enforced by marking a set of "partial" agents who "come to do" part of the continuous making of the autopoietic field. (Creeley does what he does, I do what I do, and we both inhabit a space resonant with other, as yet unspecified, agents.)

## Conclusion

What I theorize here and propose for some digital practice is a science of exceptions, a science of imaginary (subjective) solutions. The markup technology of the codex has evolved an exceedingly successful instrument for that purpose. Digital technology ought to be similarly developed. Organizing our received humanities materials as if they were simply information depositories, computer markup as currently imagined handicaps or even baffles altogether our moves to engage with the well-known dynamic functions of textual works. An alternative approach to these matters through a formal reconception of textspace as topological offers distinct advantages. Because this space is autopoietic, however, it does not have what mathematicians would normally call dimensionality. As autopoietic, the model we propose establishes and measures its own dimensions autotelically, as part of its self-generative processes. Furthermore, space defined by pervasive codependencies means that any dimension specified for the system might be formally related to any other. This metamorphic capacity is what translates the concept of a dimension into the concept of a dementian.

This model of text-processing is open-ended, discontinuous, and nonhierarchical. It takes place in a fieldspace that is exposed when it is mapped by a process of "reading." A digital processing program is to be imagined and built that allows one to mark and store these maps of the textual fields and then to study the ways they develop and unfold and how they compare with other textual mappings and transactions. Constructing textualities as field spaces of these kinds short-circuits a number of critical predilections that inhibit our received, common-sense wisdom about our textual condition. First of all, it escapes crippling interpretive dichotomies like text and reader, or textual "subjectivity" and "objectivity." Reader-response criticism, so-called, intervened in that space of problems but only succeeded in reifying even further the primary distinctions. In this view of the matter, however, one sees that the distinctions are purely heuristic. The "text" we "read" is, in this view, an autopoietic event with which we interact and to which we make our own contributions. Every textual event is an emergence imbedded in and comprising a set of complex histories, some of which individual readers each partially realize when they participate in those textual histories. Interestingly, these histories, in this view, have to be grasped as fields of action rather than as linear unfoldings. The fields are topological, with various emergent and dynamic basins of order, some of them linear and hierarchical, others not.


## APPENDIX A:
## THE 'PATAPHYSICS OF TEXT AND FIELD MARKUP

Texts and their field spaces are autopoietic scenes of codependent emergence. As such, their primal state is dynamic and has been best characterized by G. Spencer Brown's *Laws of Form,* where "the form of distinction"—the act of making indications by drawing a distinction—is taken as "given" and primal (1). This means that the elementary law is not the law of identity but the law of non-identity (so that we must say that "*a* equals *a* if and only if *a* does not equal *a*"). Identities emerge as distinctions are drawn and redrawn, and the acts of drawing out distinctions emerge as codependent responses to the field identities that the form of distinction calls to attention.

Spencer-Brown supplies a formal demonstration of what Alfred Jarry called 'pataphysics and that he and his Oulipian inheritors demonstrated in forms of traditional textual practice (i.e., in forms of "literature"). 'Pataphysics is a general theory of autopoietic systems (i.e., a general theory of what we traditionally call "imaginative literature"), and *Laws of Form* is a specifically *'pataphysical* event because it clearly gives logical priority to the unique act and practice of its own theoretical thought. The fifth "Chant" of Lautréamont's *Les Chants de Maldoror*, Jarry's *Gestes et opinions du docteur Faustroll, 'pataphysician,* and all the descendents of those self-conscious works—Laura Riding's stories are perhaps the earliest English-language examples—are the "literary" equivalents of Spencer-Brown's *Laws of Form.*

In this view of any systematics, the taxonomy of a system is a derivation of what Peirce called an initial abduction. The abduction is a hypothesis of the total semeiotic integrity of the system. The hypothesis is tested and transformed (internally as well as externally) in a dialectical process—ultimately endless—of representation and reflection.


APPENDIX B:
CONTROL DEMENTIANS FOR A 'PATACRITICISM OF TEXTUALITIES

The transaction of textual fields proceeds by a series of moves (field behaviors) that proliferate from an elementary modal distinction between what have been specified above as *connections* and *resonances*, which are the elementary behavioral forms of the textual *transaction*. These modes correspond to what traditional grammarians define as an indicative and a subjunctive verbal mood. (In this view, interrogative and interjective moods are derivatives of these two primary categories.) Emerging codependently with these behavioral dementians is an elementary taxonomy of control dementians that are called into form and then internally elaborated.

The history of textual studies has evolved a standard set of field formalities that may be usefully analyzed in six distinct parts. These correspond to an elemental set of dimensions for textual fields (or, in fields

conceived as autopoietic systems, an elemental set of six dementians).
These control dementians locate what grammarians designate as the semantics of a language.

Let it be said here that these behavioral and control dementians, like
their allopoietic dimensions, comprise a set of categories that recommend
themselves through an evolved history of previous use. Other dimensions
(and dementians) might be proposed or imagined. However, since the
proposals being advanced here are all conceived within a pragmatistic
frame of reference, the categories bring with them the strong authority of
a habitual usefulness. They comprise a history.

*The Linguistic Dimension/Dementian.*   This aspect of the textual condition has been the principal focus of attention in the West. It represents a
high order framework of conceptual markers or distinctions that unfold
and multiply from an initial pair of categories, the semantic and the
grammatical. The former is an elemental category, the latter is a relational one, and the two together epitomize the structure of codependency
that pervades and in a sense defines all textual processes at every dimension. That is to say, neither marker or category has conceptual priority
over the other, they generate meaning together in a codependent and dialectical process. However, to specify their codependence requires that one
adopt a pragmatistic or performative approach such as we see in Maturana, Spencer-Brown, and Peirce.

*The Graphical/Auditional Dimension/Dementian.*   Some kind of graphical and/or auditional state of affairs is a prerequisite for any appearance
or functional operation of a Linguistic Dimension, and that state must be
formally constrained. In Western attempts to clarify language and textuality, these forms are defined in the systematic descriptors of morphology
and phonology, which are codependent subcategories of the Linguistic
Dimension.

This Graphical/Auditional Dimension comprises the set of a text's codes
of materiality (as opposed to the specific material state of a particular
document). In print and manuscript states, the dimension includes various subsets of bibliographical codes and paratexts: typography, layout,
book design, and the vehicular components of those forms. (If we are
considering oral texts, the material assumes auditional forms, which can
have visual components as well.)

*Documentary Dimension/Dementian.*   This comprises the physical
incarnation—the "real presence," so to speak—of all the formal possi-

bilities of the textual process. We recognize it as a bibliographical or paleographical description of some specific object, or as a library or archival record of an object's historical passage (transmission history).

Note that this dimension does not simply constitute some brute chemical or physical thing—what Coleridge referred to when he spoke as the "object as object," which he called "fixed and dead." Coleridge's "object as object" is a negative abstraction—that's to say, a certain formal conception of the documentary dimension that sets it apart (a priori) from any place in a study or interpretation of textuality. A document can and—in any comprehensive approach to textuality—should be maintained as an integral function of the textual process.

. A document is a particular object that incarnates and constrains a specific textual process. In terms of print and manuscript texts, it is a specific actualized state of the Graphical/Auditional Dimension.

*Semiotic Dimension/Dementian.* This dimension defines the limit state of any text's formal possibilities. It postulates the idea of the complete integration of all the elements and dynamic relations in a field of discourse. In this dimension we thus cognize a textual process in holistic terms. It is a purely formal perspective, however, and as such stands as the mirrored antithesis of the document per se, whose integrity is realized as a phenomenal event. The document is an image of the hypothesis of total form; it appears at (or as) a closure of the dynamic process set in perpetual motion by the hypothesis at the outset.

We register the semiotic dimension as a pervasiveness of patterned relations throughout the textual system—both within each part of the system and among the parts. The relations emerge in distinct types or modes: elements begin and end; they can be accumulated, partitioned, and replicated; they can be anchored somewhere, linked to other elements, and relayed through the system.

The first of those late systems of analysis called by Herbert Simon "Sciences of the Artificial," the science of semiotics labels itself as a heuristic mechanism.[15] The pervasive order of a textual process's semiotic dimension thus emerges as a function of the formal categories, both system elements and system processes, which are consciously specified by the system's agents. Order is constructed from the systemic demand for order. As a result, the forms of order can be of any type—hierarchical or nonhierarchical, continuous or discontinuous.

*Rhetorical Dimension/Dementian.* The dominant form of this dimension is genre, which is a second order set of textual forms. Genre calls into play poems, mathematical proofs, novels, essays, speeches, dramas, and so forth. The function of this dimension is to establish forms of readerly attention—to select and arrange textual materials of every kind in order to focus the interest of the reader (audience, user, and listener) and establish a ground for response.

Readers and writers (speakers and listeners) are rhetorical functions. (Writers' first readers are themselves in their act of composition.) Mikhail Bakhtin's celebrated studies of textual polyvalence and heteroglossia exemplify the operative presence of this textual dimension.

*Social Dimension/Dementian.*   This is the dimension of a work's production and reception histories. It is the dimension of the object as subject: that is to say, of a determinate set of textual elements arrayed under names like "writer," "printer," "publisher," "reader," "audience," "user." It is the dimension that exposes the temporality function which is an inalienable feature of all the dimensions of the textual condition.

The social dimension of textuality unfolds a schedule of the uses to which its works are put beyond what New Critics liked to call "the poem itself." It is the dimension in which the dynamic and non-selfidentical character of textual works is most plainly disclosed.

In most traditional theories of textuality, the social dimension is not considered an intrinsic textual feature or function. Framed under the sign "context," it is seen as the environment in which texts and documents stand. Until the recent emergence of more holistic views of environments— notably in the work of D. F. McKenzie—this way of seeing textuality's social dimension forced severe restrictions on our ability to comprehend and study the dynamic character of textual processes. A disciplined philological study of literary and cultural works is prerequisite for dispelling the abstraction that characterizes most approaches to "context."[16]

# 6

## Digital Tools and the
## Emergence of the Social Text

I

Like another important edition of our time, Hans Gabler's *Ulysses,* J. C. C. Mays's edition on Coleridge—three volumes, each in two parts—set an inspiring example of scholarly thoroughness and integrity.[1] But the real strength of the work rests ultimately in something else—something quite rare in the scholarly editions of English-speaking authors produced in the last fifty years. Mays is deeply sympathetic to Coleridge's poetry— not unaware of or reticent to address its failings and limitations, but fronting all the work with what Desmond McCarthy, writing of Coleridge, called "the most delicate sympathy." "When he writes of it . . . his words are singularly moving in their subtlety and simplicity" (Mays, xc). That is McCarthy's description of Coleridge on the subject of "affection-love"—a shrewd judgment unearthed by Mays from a 1939 newspaper review. The words perfectly describe Mays's editorial treatment of Coleridge.

The edition also has a delicate sympathy with our own epoch and its remarkable scholarly adventures, of which Gabler's *Ulysses* has been a famous instance. Mays's edition is every bit as significant and challenging— perhaps at this point in time, more significant since its procedure throws into relief one of the great current scholarly questions: where is information technology driving literary and cultural studies and—not least of all—scholarly editing, the foundational discipline of all literary studies?

Let me briefly sketch the scholarly horizon, as I see it, of that question. We inherit two basic types of scholarly editorial method: facsimile and diplomatic editing, on one hand, and eclectic editing on the other. Both were deepened and renewed when the disciplines of modern philology emerged out of the historicism born in eighteenth-century Enlightenment.

Two systematically presented variants on these basic methods emerged in twentieth-century editorial practice: the Anglo-American critical eclecticism culminating in the Greg-Bowers school, and the European genetic methods developed by a line of German and French scholars of the mid and late century. A third variant, social-text editing, was most vigorously proposed by the late D. F. McKenzie, who unfortunately died without completing his edition of Congreve, which was to demonstrate the praxis of his theory.[2] I see my own work as a critical pursuit of views I share with McKenzie.

Mays deliberately locates his edition in relation to this general scholarly context. He is editing both the poems and plays of Coleridge, including the translations from Schiller. While he is forced to take a slightly different practical approach with the plays, a single editorial vision controls the project. In the interests of clarity, I shall concentrate my attention on Mays's treatment of the poetry.

The basic division of each "Part" of the edition into two volumes, one called the "Reading Text," the other the "Variorum Text," signals Mays's editorial purposes. Corresponding to the numbered sequence of reading texts is an equivalently numbered series of variorum texts. The symmetry between the two texts extends to the graphical editorial presentation: the Reading Text is preceded by an introductory editorial note, more or less extensive, setting the poem in its biographical and sociohistorical contexts, and (often) its later reception history. The Variorum Text begins with an editorial discussion of the textual witnesses that authorize its production. In many cases, of course, the variorum commentary discusses contextual matters that have far more than a narrowly technical (textual) import.

While Mays's editorial point of departure is, as we would expect, Anglo-American, this work is most strongly marked by the influence of the European genetic editorial methods as they were developed in various German and French editions beginning with Friedrich Beissner and Aldof Beck's edition of *Hölderlin (1943–1985)*.[3] However, certain complexities in the material, which he explains in scrupulous detail in his editorial Introduction, lead him to develop what he calls a "severely modified" (Mays, cxxi) version of a genetic edition (see especially cxxii–cxl). Mays's deviations follow from his double editorial commitment to an edition that supplies both a critical and a readerly text. "Readers approach texts for different reasons," Mays observes, so that "The distinction is not between scholarly and literary readers . . . but between different occasions for the same readers" (cxliv).

Let me briefly postpone further consideration of this presiding editorial idea. For now it is more important to complete our view of Mays's general approach to the synoptic presentation he adopts in his Variorum text. His object, he writes, is to "enable a reader to hold in mind a sense of the way the poems move . . . simultaneously in several planes: that is, the way the poems move laterally, as a series of independent versions, and vertically, as one version overlays and succeeds another" (cxxiii). Mays goes on to "promise a reader" of his edition that the "mechanics" of his graphical apparatus will not present such "an algebraic nightmare" as to obscure one's "sense of the fluid reality" of "the way [Coleridge's] poems move." These remarks are highly significant, signaling once again Mays's desire to refuse a "distinction . . . between scholarly and literary readers."

What is this "fluid reality" that Mays perceives in Coleridge's work and that he wishes us to experience? Mays uses the phrase to characterize a textual condition that is anything but continuous, uniform, or smooth. On the contrary, an unsettled restlessness and mutability is pervasive, so that Mays speaks acutely of "the bewildering, shifting detail which encumbers" the poems (cxi–cxii). Mays's general Introduction rings the changes on the changing, veering, random, and accidental characteristics of the corpus as a whole and of its individual works. "Coleridge's verse appears from the start to be unfocused and uncertain within shifting margins," Mays points out. Consequently, the reader must expect to "move between shifting centers of gravity, must constantly refocus his or her attention, is required to interpret the text on the page with reference to several other kinds of text." The original materials thus lead Mays to advise "Readers of the following pages"—readers of this edition—to "proceed like the readers of *Finnegans Wake* . . . 'fixed in a permanent state of multiple vision'" (clvi).

Coleridge's poems are not fluid Wordsworthian rivers like the Duddon or Derwent or Dove. They are fluid like that more ominous "sacred river" Alph in "Kubla Khan," moving with odd and unpredictable motions, as if hesitating and testing passages through a maze. The poetry therefore must be handled with care, always understanding that "There is no rule" (cxliv) or coherent set of rules that can guide a scholar to safe and certain editorial choices.

Mays's sure sense of the "indeterminate" character of the work helps to make him the excellent editor that he is, keeping him close to his natural, native modesty. Because Coleridge, unlike Yeats or Stevens, "had no steady idea of the literary persona he was putting before the world," very few of his poems, Mays observes, are "revised according to constant standards" (xcv). The relevant poetical materials therefore tend to be not merely unstable, but "haphazard" in their irregularities. They are fluid the way mercury is fluid. Mays's description of "Kubla Khan'"'s textual condition nicely illustrates "the pressures and considerations which a reader needs to bear in mind as he or she interprets the material in this edition":

> The lack of evidence bearing on the composition of the poem, the curious nature of its single manuscript, the context and occasions on which Coleridge is reported to have recited it, the uncertainty of its paragraphing, Coleridge's disinclination to annotate it, the obliquity and inconsistencies of the Preface, its separate half-titles and its classification as an Ode or Miscellaneous Poem in the collected editions, its dimension of political allusion. These considerations combine to suggest that Kubla Khan should be read very differently from a poem of pure enchantment. (xcv)

This editorial representation of "Kubla Khan" returns us to the "pressures and considerations" that drove Mays to the edition we have. Here is Mays's summary statement of his governing view: "Coleridge's mind operated on several levels, in several ways, and moved easily between them. An edition should display—not obscure—the variety and vitality of *his mind working*" (lxxxviii; italics added). To say this is to adopt an essentially genetic editorial position.

What brought Mays to modify it? Partly, I think, he recoiled from what he saw as the "algebraic nightmare" (cxxiii) of a genetic apparatus criticus, which in fact Mays's edition finds means to simplify. A far more salient issue is at stake for Mays, however, and it surfaces most clearly in his twice-posed Coleridgean question: "What is a Coleridge poem?" (cviii, cx). Mays clearly intends us to ride this question back to *Biographia Literaria*, where Coleridge argues that the "kind" and "essence" of "a POEM" and "of POETRY itself" are "nearly the same question with, what is a poet" (chapter 14). An edition that displays Coleridge's working brain needs to show "how the poem existed in Coleridge's mind" (cxx). A strictly synoptic procedure won't do for Mays because many of the poems have multiple ways of existing in that mazy mind: often "deliberation alternates with chance, and different intentions exist side by side" (cxx), or they shift and mutate haphazardly. "There is no clear tendency which could provide the basis of a rule" (cxxi): Mays keeps repeating versions of that formula in his introduction. Coleridge's materials are unruly. The editor must therefore be, like the poet, "fluid and opportunistic" (xv) and like the reader, "fixed in a permanent state of multiple vision."

Mays's editorial opportunism, however, always runs along genetic and intentionalist lines because the poems are always seen as Coleridge's unique—if also uniquely various—creatures. This edition is a machine for a deep critical investigation of Coleridge's "working mind." Mays assiduously sets the Reading Text and the Variorum Text in a mirroring relation in order to facilitate an intimate dialectic between the two. But the relation is uneasily maintained, as we see when he says that the Variorum Text is the "foundation" of the Reading Text, which makes the latter its completed, visible superstructure. But in fact Mays and his edition do not mean what that figure of speech implies. The figure is drawn from an editorial approach—that is to say, Greg-Bowers—which Mays himself, as he says, "do[es] not like" (cxliv) because it suggests that an "edition could be definitive." More than that, it suggests that any text of any individual poem could be definitive.

Later in the paragraph containing those remarks Mays explains himself more clearly. The Reading Text, he says, "is both clarification and simplification" of the textual condition visible in Coleridge's unruly materials. The Reading Text "is . . . necessary, given the complexity of some of the Variorum details." The Reading Text, in other words, supplies a hypothetical platform from which one can survey and study both Coleridge's materials and one's own process of investigating those materials. In this view the Reading Text is a still point—though a relative still point—in the turning world of the unruly witnesses and their fellow-travelers. It is the editorial version of what Galvano della Volpe called an interpretational quid.

It is very important to see Mays's ambivalence on this crucial point. Consider this summary sentence: "The Reading Text is literally the edition, or one edition, for which the Variorum provides the materials" (cxliv). We want then to ask: well, which is it, "the" edition" or "one" possible edition? From everything he writes in his Introduction we can see that Mays wants us to regard the Reading Text as only "one" of the possible reading texts that could have been settled upon (see especially cxliv–cxlix). As he points out, in such a complex set of conflicting "pressures and considerations" generated by the materials themselves, "choices of text are debateable" because, ultimately, "The grounds of choice are subjective and provisional" (cxlvii, cxlviii). But while the provisional character of the choices is admitted, an editor must finally make choices that will come into print: "The alternative . . . is to refrain from editing. There is no other way" (cxlix).

Because Mays is a learned and sensitive scholar we are more than happy to take his "provisional" reading texts as our points of critical departure in these volumes. Mays does not want to hide any textual complexity from our consideration, so taken is he with the mazy motions of Coleridge's mind, so committed to putting those motions on display. Nonetheless, he does not shrink from editing because, in his view, "The problem is more acute in theory than in practice. The text for each poem in all but a few cases selects itself" (cxlix). This self-selection follows from what Mays calls "The principle which has guided my choice" of Reading Text: "to give the version of the poem which reflects Coleridge's concern, up to the time he lost interest (as he so often did)" (cxlvi). The principle is simply a version of the principle of "final intentions." The reading texts select themselves because Mays's methodology has been so carefully considered and executed. The "texts" are following their marching orders, as they should. Not that other local textual choices might not have been made for particular poems, or even that wholesale differences might not emerge if one were (for instance) to take "initial intentions" rather than "final intentions" as a basic guiding principle. In any case we would look for texts that seemed to select themselves.

## II

Would computer technology be able to improve Mays's editorial project in appreciable ways? For the project as such, I think the answer is no. Online accessibility is a publishing improvement and to that extent an educational improvement as well for any work of scholarship. But now imagine Mays's six volumes transported into a browser environment. String searches would be possible, and with considerable effort one could prepare a digitally encoded version of the edition for different kinds of automated pattern analysis. All that would be clear gain. But then the downsides begin to declare themselves. We are not even close to developing browser interfaces to compare with the interfaces that have evolved in the past 500 years of print technology. A sophisticated, flexible, and stable system of graphical design and bibliographical codes stands ready to hand for a scholar wishing to build a critical machine for the complex analysis of textual works. If your object is to display "how the poems existed in Coleridge's mind"—a mind you understand to be veering, unruly, and full of contradictions—these books blow away anything one might think to develop in our current and immediately foreseeable machine technology.[4]

A good interface develops symbolic coding mechanisms that translate abstract relations into forms that a human being can optimally manipulate. In this respect, monitors—no matter how large or virtually dimensional—lack a key multitasking capacity possessed by books, which integrate visual and kinetic knowledge acquisition. When we escape the limits of the monitor that situation will change. But if Mays's edition in electronic form seems an uninviting prospect, other digital projects have distinct attractions—for instance, a scholarly edition of Campion or Burns or Tom Moore. A bibliographical presentation of their work is crippled from the start, for obvious reasons. The greatness of Burns in particular has all but escaped academic attention because our critical interfaces have been wholly bibliographical.

To the degree that a computerized environment facilitates what digerati call "interactivity," it necessarily brings a certain degree of tactile involvement. This is now far less complex and demanding than the kinetic environment summoned (and symbolically coded) in books. The difference explains itself when we recall a simple fact: that personal computers today function most powerfully as scholarly tools when we use them on our desks and in our libraries at home and elsewhere. In those places they get embraced by the more sophisticated, stable, and dispersed network of book technology. Remember how the explosion of the personal computer market took the business world by surprise? Had they a clearer grasp of their culture—the world engaged by McKenzie in *Bibliography and the Sociology of Texts* (1986)[5]—this event would not have escaped their commercially trained radar screens. Not without reason has the initial period of computerization focused on linking library resources and digitizing reference tools. These events register the depth and importance of our bibliographical inheritance.

To this point I've tried to describe as carefully as I can what the edition sets out to do and what it succeeds in doing. Now I want to ask what it doesn't do. More specifically, what does it not edit? One thing: it does not edit what McKenzie called "the social text." I give two examples, a small one and a big one. First the small one.

In preparing the variorum text for poem no. 143, "To a Young Man of Fortune who Abandoned Himself to a Causeless and Indolent Melancholy," Mays begins with a census of the documentary witnesses. These include three manuscripts (two holographs, one transcript copy in the hand of Mrs. Coleridge) plus eight printed texts (as well as a possible ninth, a variant of one of the eight). Of the transcript in Mrs. Coleridge's hand Mays has little to say except this: "An untitled transcript in the hand of Mrs. C . . . has no textual significance (II, part I, 430). For an edition aiming to expose "[Coleridge's] mind working," Mrs. Coleridge's transcript needs no further comment, especially in the case of a relatively minor poem. And of course the transcript remains separated from the critical apparatus, which is geared to analyzing the linguistic "text"—its substantives and its most substantial accidentals. The example may stand for scores of others. It follows from the kind of edition Mays has undertaken.

Although in cases like "Christabel" the discursive treatment of the witnessing documents is much more robust, the apparatus remains textual, and it scarcely begins to capture the contextual and transmissional information supplied in the commentaries and associated notes. For "Christabel" we get thirty closely printed pages that elucidate the material witnesses simply as they are bibliographical objects. This is the data that alone, for McKenzie, gives significance to the linguistic text by shaping it in terms of its social textuality. "How the poems existed in Coleridge's mind" is a dialectical not a positive function. It is in fact an idea that is in continual process of construction by Coleridge's readers and those other persons who engage to pass along Coleridge's texts. We study and reconstruct the documentary record not to know how the poems existed in Coleridge's mind but to see how they were perceived to exist.

That Mays shares this view with McKenzie is proven by these splendid editorial commentaries and notes. In critical editions, this material is arranged to introduce and subserve the apparatus criticus, and so it does in Mays's edition. But the commentary information is so replete and even excessive in relation to the needs of the apparatus that one registers a dysfunction between the two. The discrepancy is particularly urgent in Mays's interesting discussion of untraced, recited, and memorized "Christabels" and the nexus of related persons and occasions, including the secondary witnesses by which these works are known.

In the event, Mays's apparatus comes to seem no more than his edition's one publicly acknowledged analytic offspring. Other children, legitimate and bastard, wander all about. A curiously reversed dynamic thus pervades Mays's edition: the Reading Texts become, as he himself observes, devices for illuminating and negotiating a heterogeneous body of poetic materials, and the apparatus emerges as no more than one cutaway view of the complexity of that field of discourse. A traditional apparatus is organized as a body of self-identical facts testifying to the truth of the Reading Text they generate. In Mays's edition, however, as the commentaries and notes for works like "Christabel" demonstrate with special clarity, the apparatus seems but one helpful means of finding our way into a more mazy, amazing, semiotic world.

McKenzie wanted to develop more precise critical procedures for studying that kind of world. In his Panizzi lectures of 1985, *Bibliography and the Sociology of Texts*, he made his case for a "social text" editorial procedure. His critics—most notably Thomas Tanselle and T. H. Howard-Hill—remarked that while McKenzie's ideas had a certain theoretical appeal, they could not be practically implemented.[6] The ideas implicitly called for the critical editing of books and other material objects. But critical editing—as opposed to facsimile and diplomatic editing—was designed to investigate texts, which are linguistic forms, not books, which are social events.

This practical objection raised by Tanselle and Howard-Hill can no longer be sustained. It is premised in the understanding that facsimile editing and critical editing are distinct and incommensurable functions. *The Rossetti Archive* was undertaken to demonstrate that the incommensurability is paper-based and can be overcome in a properly designed digital network. The demonstration has been replicated at least twice at University of Virginia's Institute for Advanced Technology in the Humanities: in *The William Blake Archive* and, even more comprehensively, in the emerging *Walt Whitman Archive*. One can build editorial machines capable of generating on demand multiple textual formations—eclectic, facsimile, reading, genetic—that can all be subjected to multiple kinds of transformational analyses.[7]

This means that the standard dialectical mechanism of a critical edition like Mays's can be scaled up in a digital environment. One does not have to work from the pair of fixed platforms called (in Mays's volumes) the Reading Text and the Variorum Text. "Given the complexity of the materials" some sort of hypothetical position, or platform, is needed for any analysis to be undertaken at all. The underlying logic of *The Rossetti Archive* was designed so that scholars using it could make choices about their platforms of critical attention, as well about the specific kinds of analyses they would choose to undertake.

A digital organization thus makes possible a significant departure from a paper-based apparatus. Mays's edition follows the general model of lemmatized variants that all types of traditional editions use—including genetic editions, which do however develop some innovative graphical signing devices. Variant readings are culled for specific information from the apparatus' analytic options. Because this information is formally structured in the *Archive* (by inline markup), the analyses can be automated. But greater advantages follow from an automation process than analytic speed. The critical operations also acquire much greater flexibility. The scholar can define and specify the analyses, narrowing them to some particular question (e.g., which of the texts have uncorrected print material not in the chosen reference text as well as hand corrections to texts that are part of that reference text?); or expanding to questions that embrace documents outside the framework of, say, "The Blessed Damozel's" specific documentary materials (questions about genre, provenance, the physical character of documents, and so forth). For some of these analyses a database model is preferable to inline markup, and standoff markup offers other useful options. However the analyses are formally structured, a digitized approach facilitates social text editing.

A central purpose of *The Rossetti Archive* project was to prove the correctness of a social-text approach—which is to say, to push traditional scholarly models of editing and textuality beyond the Masoretic wall of the linguistic object we call "the text." The proof of concept would be the making of the *Archive*. If our breach of the wall was minimal, as it was, its practical demonstration was significant. We were able to build a machine that organizes for complex study and analysis, for collation and critical comparison, the entire corpus of Rossetti's documentary materials, textual as well as pictorial. Critical, which is to say computational, attention was kept simultaneously on the physical features and conditions of actual objects—specific documents and pictorial works—as well as on their formal and conceptual characteristics (genre, metrics, iconography).[8]

The *Archive*'s approach to Rossetti's so-called double works is in this respect exemplary. Large and diverse bodies of material that comprise works like "The Blessed Damozel" get synthetically organized: forty-four distinct printed texts, some with extensive manuscript additions; two manuscripts; thirty-one pictorial works. These physical objects orbit around the conceptual object we name for convenience "The Blessed Damozel." All the documentary objects relate to that gravity field in different ways, and their differential relations metastasize when subsets of relations among them get exposed. At the same time, these documentary objects function in an indefinite number of other kinds of relations: to other textual and pictorial works, to institutions of various kinds, to different persons, to varying occasions. With the Archive one can draw these materials into computable synthetic relations at macro as well as micro levels. In the process the *Archive* discloses the hypothetical character of its materials and their component parts as well as the relationships one discerns among these things. Though completely physical and measurable (in different ways and scales), neither the objects nor their parts are self-identical, all can be reshaped and transformed in the environment of the *Archive*.

Perhaps the most significant advance beyond copy-text editing came in 2001 when we began to design and develop *Juxta,* a computerized tool for a flexible, decentered approach to the collation of multiple witnesses. The documentary orientation of *The Rossetti Archive* had such a tool in its theoretical purview from the outset, but in 1992–1993 we lacked the resources for implementing it. When the resources became available in 2001 the tool went into development, and it is currently available as both a downloadable application and a web resource.[9]

The great advance *Juxta* brings to traditional collation procedures emerges from its ability to set any of the witnesses as the comparison base. *Juxta* can then generate multiple visualizations of the different perspectives on the textual field that emerge from the different base texts. *Juxta* demonstrates the limitations that a traditional stemmatic analysis brings to the study of textual fields, exposing as it does only a certain set of field relations; a genetic set from a hypothesized or known point of origin. That perspective obscures both the presence and the importance of other possible ways for mapping those relations. Every witness in the textual field, even a corrupt witness, supplies its own explanation of the field and the meaning of the other witnesses. Exposing those different and overlapping comparison sets is crucial for the student who wants to understand the interdependent and social character of textual fields.

The autopoietic functions of the social text can also be computationally accessed through user logs. These use records, automatically stored by the computer, supply a microscopic view of the work's reception history, which is a necessary function of all textual conditions. All textual works are works in process and they record that process at their documentary level. Even if only one textual witness were to survive—say that tomorrow a manuscript of a completely unrecorded play by Shakespeare were unearthed—that document would have recorded the process of its making and its transmission. Retransmission depends upon engaging with that evidence.

So scholars do not read, edit, or interpret self-identical texts. Each of those acts reconstructs the record of textual makings and remakings and extends that record further. No text, no book, no social event is self-identical, they evolve and mutate in their use. And because all such uses are invested in real circumstances, these multiplying forms are socially and physically coded in and by the works themselves. They bear the evidence of the meanings they have helped to make.

One advantage digitization has over paper-based instruments comes not from the computer's capacities for storage and transmission, but from its greater capacity for simulating phenomena. Monitor visualizations exhibit these simulation functions in arresting ways, but user logs are equally significant. Books are simulation machines as well, of course. Indeed, the hardware and software of book technology have evolved into a state of such micro and macro sophistication that in designing IT systems we would be reckless not to study that technology in the closest ways. The ecology of the book is an autopoietic network of social objects whose emergent functions reflect the measurements that their users and makers take for various purposes. As we now try to design digital systems that can simulate the system's realizable possibilities—the possibilities that are known and recorded as well as those that have yet to be (re)constructed— the history of book technology will take us back to the future.

This is why McKenzie's central idea, that bibliographical objects are social objects, begs to be realized in digital terms—begs to be realized in the tools and by the people who make them. Reflecting on digital technology in his lecture "What's Past Is Prologue," McKenzie saw that the computer's simulation capacities were forcing him to rethink one of his "primary article[s] of bibliographical faith": the idea of "the primacy of the physical object" as a self-identical *thing*.[10] He did not live to undertake an editorial project in digital form. Had he done so, I believe he would have seen his social-text approach strengthened by the new technical devices.

# III

# FROM METHOD TO PRACTICE

# 7

## What Do Scholars Want?

I

"Sustainability" is a dark but potent word in the field of digital humanities. It signals a broad set of concerns—both technical and institutional—about how to maintain and augment the increasingly large body of digital information that humanists are both creating and using. It is a word with far more than a contemporary pertinence, however. It could (it should) remind us that the traditional problems of philology have scarcely changed at all, and certainly have not gone away.

But the problems of the philologue and the digeratus do *look* different, so let's consider the problem of sustainability in its immediate horizon and ask: Sustaining what, precisely? How and for how long? Indeed, why do we have a sustainability problem at all?

These may seem absurdly obvious questions, and in a certain obvious sense they are. But like many obvious questions, their transparency is deceptive. This becomes clear, I think, if we pose a few more questions—the kind, in fact, that shape the ways people now tend to approach problems of sustainability. Would the problems go away if we had access to a lot more money? Or technical support? Or perhaps if all our scholarly projects had well-crafted business plans?

To think that they would is a fantasy many of us, in many different ways and perspectives, have to reckon with. Of course funding and technical support are necessary, but to fixate there is to lose sight of the more fundamental difficulties we're facing. These are primarily political and institutional difficulties. And those political and institutional pressures distort our view as we try to frame strategies and general policy. Here I will be taking some of my own experiences and myopias as instructive cases.

Our situation reminds me of the problem that organizes Kathy Acker's notorious fiction *Empire of the Senseless* (1988). At a pivotal moment in the action, Acker's heroine Abhor finds herself in a maze of difficulties. Trying to discover *what* has caused the mess of her life and how to escape, Abhor realizes she has herself been multiplying her problems. Her life takes a decisive turn for the better when she sees she has been asking the wrong question. Abhor changes the question from "what is the problem" to "who are the agents"—social and individual—shaping the field in which she has been such a dismal wanderer.[1] The shift has two important effects: it dissipates the fog of abstractions that has made such a comedy of her life; and it begins to free her from her circumstantial, and thus largely reactive, view of her experience.

So let's begin to think about the current state of humanities scholarship under that Abhorrent sign: "Not what but who."

Humanities scholarship was—and still precariously is—created and sustained through the interoperation of four institutional agents. Three of them are structurally foundational, like three persons in one secular deity: the scholars themselves (working within a network of educational and professional organizations); publishing entities, especially university presses and professionally authorized journals; and libraries and depositories, where this work is collected and made accessible for reflection and repurposing. There is also an important fourth agent, scholarship's Church Militant. This would be the various public and private funding entities that provide crucial financial support to the ongoing life of culture.

Let's do a little recollecting. Until about twenty-five years ago, that scholastic network functioned reasonably well. But a number of causes began to undermine its operations. The emergence of digital technology was not the only one but it proved to be decisive.

For obvious reasons, research libraries were the first of these agents to engage practically with the new information technologies. While the adaptation has created serious problems for libraries, the event has also restored an acute awareness of their indispensable educational position.

For the research library, digital technology has been both a problem and a boon. When digital scholarship in the humanities thrives at a university these days, the library is almost always a key player, and often the center and driving force. The digital transformation of the library has caught everyone's attention. The faculties take notice now when the library announces it's buying or subscribing to (or not buying or subscribing to) a certain database, or when it drops journals or doesn't buy certain books.

For academic publishing, on the other hand, digitization and the accompanying market changes have brought a largely unmitigated crisis that has yet to run its course.

As we all by this time know, the very existence of many university presses and specialized journals has become uncertain. As academic presses cut back their lists or even disappear, scholars—especially young scholars—have difficulty publishing their work. This serious problem has engaged the attention of our communities for some years, though our practical responses so far have not been impressive. At least as distressing is the almost total neglect of the problem of in-copyright scholarly publications—the backlists of university press monographs and the many journals with specialized subjects and audiences.[2] The digital migration of this very special library of scholarship is a clear and pressing need, but virtually no programmatic efforts have been made to address it.

In the meantime, commercial vendors have been quick off the mark to offer various kinds of digital packages to academic libraries. Until the coming of the Google Books initiative, these were specialized collections and invariably expensive, and only recently have vendors of these materials given serious thought to how users might access them for integrated online search and analysis. They were also created without effective scholarly input at the design stage, or later at the use end where these materials might be—from a scholar's point of view should be—augmented and repurposed.

In these ventures to digitize our cultural heritage, "Google Books" brought a whole new—a totalizing—approach. Because this initiative signaled toward a vast and integrated depository of our print materials, that approach was inspiring. But it has also been fraught with danger, perhaps especially in the United States, where the Library of Congress represents a national commitment to free culture and access to knowledge. The Google Books Settlement controversy exposes the disconnect between commercial-driven digital initiatives and the scholarly communities whose educational mission is to preserve, access, and augment our cultural heritage.[3]

For a scholar and educator, a most dismaying aspect of this situation is the blowback effect one sees in graduate programs. Dissertation work in literary and cultural studies, for example, is now regularly shaped to short-term market demands, which respond to a calendar that has little relation to the fundamental needs of humanities research and scholarship. Important work is not being done, is positively shunned, in graduate programs because academic presses will almost certainly not publish it any more. At the same time, as opportunities emerge for using digital resources to improve scholarly work in the humanities, programmatic responses in traditional departments have been minimal to nonexistent. Humanities students who want to pursue digital work almost always do so outside their regular institutional programs, which remain firmly oriented to print publication.

For two decades various persons and concerned institutions have been trying to address those problems. Electronic journals and journal providers; various types of digital repositories maintained by universities and their libraries; Google Books and Google Scholar; large commercial databases like ECCO and NCCO; scholar-driven and peer-reviewed research ventures like NINES;[4] and most recently print-on demand publishing: all are responses to a crisis in scholarly communication. Taken individually, each of these ventures, and even Google Books, is important, useful, sometimes inspiriting. Moreover, taken together they appear to signal a great improvement in the scholar's and educator's condition.

But further problems pervade these responses. First, their hotchpotch character is darkly eloquent, signaling a grave and now widely registered instability in humanities research education. Second, and far more troubling, the community of scholars has played only a minor role in shaping these events. We have been like marginal, third-world presences in these momentous changes—agents who have actually *chosen* an adjunct and subaltern position. We have been invisible. Because only a small minority of scholars have been active with digital work and the institutional changes it is bringing, they have been functioning on their own or in insulated venues like IATH, removed from the university's programmatic community. This is a serious institutional fracture in the world of humanities scholarship and a major source of what has come to be called "the crisis in the humanities."

Let's pause to reflect on the inaction of the scholarly community. What's going on here? Rather ask: who? The emergence of digital technology has brought a new and crucial populace into the university. So far as the university's political and social structure is concerned, they are employees hired to serve the faculties. I leave aside the fact that these people are often scholars of distinction in their own right.[5] What is chiefly pertinent here is (1) their skills are essential to digital humanities work; (2) the structure of the institution separates them from the regular faculties; and (3) they are an expensive population to support, commanding high salaries, often higher than the faculty persons they might be working with, as well as expensive resources that regular faculty don't need and wouldn't know how to use anyhow.

What to do with these immigrants? One option—it is widespread—is to set quotas on their admission. The institution hires the technicians it needs to run its basic administrative operations. Scholars who want to pursue digital work complain bitterly that the university does not give them the technical and resource support they require. But since the vast majority of the faculties do not want those persons and resources, and since they are expensive . . . etc., etc, Q.E.D.

Or if the quotas are lifted and these persons come into the university, where do they live? With some rare but notable exceptions, the answer is: outside the departments and faculties. That situation makes it extremely difficult to pursue digital research work that isn't tied directly to classroom pedagogy. It makes it virtually impossible to direct a coherent institutional policy toward the support of digital scholarship. Since the university and its faculties define themselves in relation to their scholarship and research work, the situation gets lost on both sides: it discourages the emergence of digital scholarship, and it sustains, though minimally, the traditional paper-based network. So far as digital scholarship is concerned, the result is a haphazard, inefficient, and often jerry-built arrangement of intramural instruments—free-standing centers, labs, enterprises, and institutes, or special digital groups set up outside the traditional departmental structure of the university. They are expensive to run and the vast majority of the faculty have no use for them.

The result is social dislocation both within and without the faculties. Because the dislocation registers most clearly as a struggle for scarce resources, we think we're dealing with a problem of money. But we're not. Money is the symptom of the problem of how to set university policy at a time when humanities faculties are uncertain of both their public and their intramural position.

## II

So in a time like this we are sorely pressed by the question: "What do scholars want?" I pose it thus because I'm thinking of what Freud asked Princess Marie Bonaparte about the mystery of "the feminine soul": "What does Woman want?"

The scholar's soul is a lot less mysterious or interesting than women's, or for that matter men's, souls. That's because scholars are made, not born. And there we begin to glimpse the difficulty of what scholars want. Scholarship, especially humanities scholarship, is now undergoing an historical emergency that is affecting everyone, from the most *avant* digeratus to the most retro traditionalist. Whether we work with digital or paper-based resources, or both, our basic needs are the same. We want our cultural record to be comprehensive, stable, and accessible. And we want to be able to augment that record with our own contributions. We want . . . the knowledge of what we know and have been knowing for millennia.

Those desires lead many of us—perhaps even *most* of us—to cherish the reliabilities of print-based research and traditional publication, especially monograph publication, and to resist moves toward digital venues. Alas, one might as well hope for the return of the unity of Christendom or the Holy Roman Empire. Of course book culture will not go extinct: human memory is too closely bound to it. But no one any longer thinks that scholarship—our ongoing research and professional communication—can be organized and sustained through print resources.

From that realization we might imagine that if we digitize all of our cultural heritage, if we do that with care and accuracy, we will have solved the problem. But the simplest reflection exposes how mistaken we would be. After we digitize the books, the books themselves remain. Or, as many thoughtful humanists keep insisting, *should* remain. Perhaps the greatest of the false promises of digitization is that its simulations will save our books. They will not, though they are provoking us to get seriously involved with the problems that grow, like tares among the wheat, with digitization. If our book heritage is to be saved, we will have to choose to save it intact, not simulate it electronically.

Because scholars now live—and will henceforth live—in a kind of half-world between print and digital technologies, this early period of transition has brought the confusion and uncertainty we see everywhere. We want to minimize these transitional problems. Even more, we want mechanisms that stabilize the cultural record, both print and digital, and that sustain and perhaps improve how we investigate that record and communicate what we learn. In short, we have two closely related problems on our hands: how to carry on our research in mixed depositories; and how to communicate and exchange our work?

Here's a small example—a personal experience—that may help to expose the issues.

For several years I've been spending extended periods of time in Berkeley, particularly in December and January between my fall and spring terms at the University of Virginia. I have a research appointment at UC Berkeley and thus get access to the UC libraries. I haunt the Bancroft and the Doe. But California's recent economic catastrophe forced drastic cutbacks in the Berkeley library hours.

When I arrived in Berkeley in December 2009—I had just begun my research appointment—I found the libraries were all closed. The situation threw into relief what this particular scholar sorely wanted: direct access to the printed books and journals in Berkeley's regular and special collections. Although I had privileged access to all the digital resources of two major research libraries—UC Berkeley and the University of Virginia—my research projects couldn't proceed. I had to consult certain materials in Special Collections. That was one problem, though it wasn't the most imperative. I also needed access to a large corpus of scholarly work that is only available in print. Indeed, it was this work—scholarship developed and published for the most part during the past forty years—which established my own research frame of reference. But the fact is that very little of the scholarship that is still in copyright is digitally accessible, so unless you can get the books and journals themselves, you're out of luck.

This little episode—trivial in its way—exposes two difficult issues for scholars. The first is well known but may be usefully explored a bit further. The second, less well recognized, has grown within the digital humanities community itself.

University presses control the vast majority of the copyrights of scholarly books. After a few years nearly all of these books have exhausted their salability, and in recent years that time frame—along with the sales numbers—has continued to shrink. Still older books—works, for instance, published before the drastic pricing changes that university presses began to introduce in the late 1980s—are virtually entombed. Scholars' need for these works remains as fundamental as ever. But presses resist efforts to release these works to a free culture network. In fact few are even minimally "revenue producing"—indeed, they can be serious drains on a press's finances.

The issues were highlighted in Google's negotiations with the Authors Guild and the American Association of Publishers (AAP) to establish guidelines and rights for Google's book digitization plans. These negotiations took place without any effective input from the scholarly community. Neither the Modern Language Association nor any of the large professional organizations with a fundamental interest in humanities education and cultural heritage were participants in the settlement negotiations. But whereas the chief interest of the Guild and the AAP (and Google) is in secure profits, scholars want to sustain a vigorous intramural communication, on one hand, and to maximize the public access to knowledge on the other. The interests of the educational and scholarly communities might have been defended by university presses and their association (AAUP). But this did not happen—on the contrary in fact—because academic presses have been running for years on a for-profit model that is little different from commercial publishers.[6]

Robert Darnton's series of essays in the *New York Review of Books*, begun in 2009, called attention to some of the key issues.[7] Then in the fall of 2009 a formal appeal to the court was made arguing that no settlement should be completed until the interests of the scholarly community had been assessed and addressed.[8] As it happens, the resistance to the Google Book Settlement, though mounted late, proved consequential and the settlement was rejected.[9] But of course the problem has not gone away, it has only been put back to the status quo ante the Google negotiations.

It is a problem with two programmatic faces: how to pursue scholarship into a future that will be organized in a digital horizon; and how to secure access to our inheritance of printed scholarship within that new framework. A sharp *institutional* contradiction has ensued, for whereas scholars want to preserve and integrate our print work for digital emergence, we also see the need to give up print-based forms of scholarly inquiry for born-digital forms. This means migrating the scholarly print archive—journals and publishers' backlists—and also beginning to shut down the system of print-organized scholarly research and communication and migrate to a digitally organized social machinery.

I say "begin to shut down the system" because this is not a machinery we can easily turn off. The system comes with a long history and is firmly integrated in every aspect of our scholarly institutions. Jobs, promotion, tenure, and the institutional organization of the university remain keyed to it. Understanding those relations, we talk about prying ourselves free of the system by shifting criteria for scholarly advancement from monograph to periodical work, or we plead that digital work—some of it anyhow—be put on an equal footing with print work in considering scholarly merit. But as Our Lady of the Flowers said to her judge, we're already beyond that—way beyond it in my opinion, though not—as we all know—at the level of institutional politics.

Certainly Kathleen Fitzpatrick is already beyond it, as I think many, if not most, younger scholars tend to be. Fitzpatrick's book *Planned Obsolescence* grounds its various proposals around a pair of key premises: (1) that "scholarship is about participating in an exchange of ideas with one's peers"; and (2) that the traditional "system surrounding [the] production and dissemination" of this exchange "has ceased to function" in reliable ways. She is confident that we have the technical means to reconstruct this "system" in digital forms. But the charged polemic of her book reflects her worry "whether we have the institutional will to commit to the development of the [digital] systems" that will replace the "entrenched systems that no longer serve our needs."[10] In other words, "Not what, but who."

Fitzpatrick is an energetic voice, and the practical cast of her mind is particularly refreshing. But plans for institutional changes that can actually be implemented need to rest in a comprehensive view of the scholarly scene. "To the degree that scholarship is about participating in an exchange of ideas with one's peers, new networked publishing structures can facilitate that interaction," as Fitzpatrick says, and the interaction will work "best . . . if the discussion is ongoing, always in process."

But implicit in that argument is a presentist view of scholarship that needs expanding. Our peers are both "the noble living and the noble dead." All of our ongoing discussions are rooted in the past even as they are executed in the present. That's why the crisis in the humanities is only partly— and not fundamentally—about tenure, promotion, and the obstacles to a current "exchange of ideas." It is about sustaining what Raymond Williams, a great scholar as well as a great critic, might have called "The Long Evolution"—if he had thought about the problem of culture as a socioeducational instead of a socioliterary problem, and if he had addressed it from an *Electronic* vantage point.

A Long View: this is what scholars have traditionally taken and it is still What Scholars Want, or what they ought to want, now. A Long View stretches back to the period before copyright—a territory being overrun by Google and other vendors. But it also stretches back to that middle distance where so much of our scholarship was print-published, and where copyright restrictions are such a hindrance to digital initiatives. Consider that proposals are now being drawn up to generate searchable PDF files of the in-copyright backlists of academic presses. Consider that this is precisely *not* to take a long view but a short view—one that responds to the financial difficulty of digitizing such works by avoiding the more basic needs of scholarship and education. You can look at and think about PDF files, you can even data mine them—or at any rate some of them. But you can't work with or repurpose them to any depth. For that you need structured data: TEI or XML files, databases, and ontological schemas that organize information's metadata. Traditional scholars can easily imagine that these are the requirements of digital pedants. But it isn't so. Scholars need these things because structure introduces explicitly historical dimensions into the material. Even Google takes a longer view of its digital migration of books than vendors, proprietary or open source, who resort to PDF.

Or reflect on the short view that pervades much of the thinking about (and practice with) "Web 2.0" and the enthusiasm for various kinds of "networked collaboration." Is "Web 2.0" simply "a piece of jargon," as Tim Berners-Lee has mordantly remarked?[11] I think the answer to that question hangs upon how the scholarly community actually works, as a community, with web resources. So far the signs are only minimally encouraging. Because the roots of social networking are in online practices like Flickr and other folksonomies, the considerable scholarly potential of collaborative technology remains a pursuit.

Social software technologies have a wide-spreading but shallow root system. Their most impressive result to date, Wikipedia, illustrates both its capacities and its limits. The wiki initiative delivers an encyclopedia of information that can rapidly update the range of its entries and their content. How to enlist this technology for more substantial scholarship is often speculated about but not yet realized. That is to say, while we certainly have projects that implement collaborative scholarship—NINES is as good an example as any—none of these projects is adequately integrated into the scholarly community at large. NINES, *Integrating Digital Papyrology, The Homer Multitext Project*: these and initiatives like them, while open and collaborative in various ways, are still fundamentally "stand alone" works. They are crucially limited by their weak relation to scholarship's institutional ethos—the *habitus* of our educational lives. Because internet ecology at present is volatile and promiscuous, it encourages individual initiatives and "just-in-time" collaborations rather than programmatic strategies. This happens because internet culture has yet to map itself to the complex social system that powers scholarship and education. Wikipedia and professional Listserves (our digital *Notes and Queries*) are driven by a form of that "institutional will" Fitzpatrick hopes finally to see. Higher-level online research work—there is now a good deal of it—is not.

But "institutional will" is a figure of speech that should be used with caution. It's unhelpful and untrue to imagine traditional scholars as a slacker community. The Long View of the scholar's life was well established before the emergence of the internet. Indeed, we all know that the volatile state of digital resources has made scholars hesitate to take them up. Their hesitance, like Ahab's precipitance, has its humanities.

In that respect, here's another personal anecdote that seems to me pertinent. I spent eighteen years designing *The Rossetti Archive* and filling out its content. This was a collaborative project involving some forty graduate students plus a dozen or more skilled technical experts, not to speak of the cooperation of funding agencies and scores of persons around the world in many libraries, museums, and other depositories. It comprises some 70,000 digital files and 42,000 hyperlinks organizing a critical space for the study of Rossetti's complete poetry, prose, pictures, and designs in their immediate historical context. The *Archive* has high-resolution digital images of every known manuscript, proof, and print publication of his textual works, and every known or accessible painting, drawing, or art object he designed. It also has a substantial body of contextual materials that are related in important ways to Rossetti's work. All of this is imbedded in a robust environment of editorial and critical commentary.[12]

I undertook the project partly as an experiment to explore the critical and interpretive capabilities of digital technology, and partly to create a scholarly edition of Rossetti's work. As a laboratory experiment the project was a remarkable educational experience—a clear success, I should say. I used to measure that success in theoretical and intellectual terms—as indexed in the series of books, lectures, and essays that spun off those years of the *Archive*'s development. I now measure it by its institutional position and relations: where it came from (IATH and the digital initiatives at the University of Virginia); and what it led to (SpecLab, ARP, and finally NINES).[13] I measure it even more particularly by the names of the people who worked with me in various ways and at various stages. Most important here are those young men and women, then graduate students, who are now the generation of scholars shaping the future of humanities research and education.

On the other hand, if the *Archive* is judged strictly as a scholarly edition, the jury is still out. One simple and deplorable reason explains why: no one knows how it or projects like it will be or could be sustained. And here is the supreme irony of this adventure: I am now thinking that, to preserve what I have come to see as the permanent core of its scholarly materials, I shall have to print it out. It will probably fill two dozen or more large volumes. I have also come to think that the *Archive*'s most important scholarly "content" was nothing digital at all.


## III


*The Rossetti Archive* and projects like it are most important, I now think, partly because they are already obsolete. Their own process of development has exposed the social and conceptual limits of the digital ecology that spawned them. These limits, which lie concealed by the (often) impressive appearance of such works, are institutional and not algorithmic. Currently these projects are research environments, but as the online World Library emerges, their scholarly functions will become standardized and distributed. The process is even now transforming these works into historical artifacts, less engines of scholarship than objects of scholastic interest.

They will not be sustained. They will be—we hope their most significant parts will be—preserved.

As we try to map our way to a long-term usable future, we want to reflect closely on both the recent and the more remote past. *The Rossetti Archive* is exemplary of the recent past. That is why the early history of IATH—the conceptual horizon for many such projects—is important to understand. For a dozen or so years beginning in 1992 when IATH was founded, the Institute was a focus of keen attention for humanists interested in digital technology. Part of the interest was in its groundbreaking projects—*The Valley of the Shadow, The Rossetti Archive*—and part was in the Institute's strategic commitment to high-end humanities research work.[14]

IATH's founding *modus operandi* was based in a set of four explicit working premises:

- To organize its institutional operation as a free-standing unit accessible to all UVA faculty but not answerable to the faculty member's department or dean;
- To seek out and exploit the interests and strengths of particular scholars within the university;
- To promote intra- and extra-mural research projects (rather than classroom or pedagogical projects), on the assumption that in post-secondary education important pedagogical work is a function of important research work;
- To design all projects for a global internet environment.

IATH's successes were shaped by those directives. With research agendas at the center of the Institute's work, IATH began to explore digital humanities as an autonomous disciplinary practice. Establishing the Institute as an independent unit set it outside the direct control of the university's divisional and departmental authorities. It was judged—correctly—that the faculties at large were not ready to promote the institute's work in programmatic ways. At the same time, the institute actively sought to find and support individuals in the faculty who were committed to pursuing digitally based high-end research work. Allegiance was pledged to the belief, long-held by the university community, that innovative research would drive effective and innovative pedagogy.

Finally, designing the Institute's projects for the emerging internet set all the work in a global context. That orientation had profound consequences. We were strongly biased toward Free Culture and open access, toward nonproprietary software and open source development, and toward a commitment to distributed networks and generalized standards for metadata and text encoding. So the initial premise for designing the logical structure of *The Rossetti Archive* was to assume that a distributed internet Archive of Archives already existed. Given the emergence of such a network in the future, and understanding the uncertain directions that hardware and software developments would be taking, what kind of design would most ensure that *The Rossetti Archive* would get integrated into that foreseen but unrealized situation?

When I posed that question in 1992—even in 2002—I conceived it as a question about the formal design of an information system for scholars. On one hand, we sought to construct a logical ground for the *Archive*'s content that would not be compromised by new software and hardware developments that were certain to come. On the other, we left the sociological face of the question to the global reach of the internet, which (it seemed) scholars could exploit without having to get deeply involved with infrastructural design and interface development. So we left both to forces beyond the reach or the resources of our local humanities research community.

IATH flourished in the 1990s and early 2000s because its orientation mirrored the state of play in online humanities scholarship at large. But with the turn into the twenty-first century the limitations of the IATH model began to become clear.

Of first importance was the burgeoning of various types of interactive social software in the early 2000s.[15] Mapping digital scholarship to the ontologies, but not the sociologies, of the internet not only constricts its institutional presence, it obscures the sociohistorical character of traditional philology itself. For all their "material" conditions, their hypertextualities, their internet connections, and their collaborative features, the design of IATH projects was predominantly formal and abstract. In this respect they have been a mirror and model of nearly all content-focused online scholarly projects. Like *The Rossetti Archive, The Blake Archive* is without question the most comprehensive and authoritative edition of Blake ever created, as well as the most globally accessible. Paradoxically, it is not the edition that scholars commonly work from or cite. It thus illustrates that innovative online scholarship emerged, and for the most part still remains, peripheral to the regular research and publication of the vast majority of working scholars.

The very amplitude of a project like *The Rossetti Archive* is instructive. Scholarship assumes that an investigator will have access to everything that might be relevant—everything of Rossetti's, of course, but also everything that makes up the context of his work. The *Archive* was designed to meet those requirements: on one hand it comprises those scores of thousands of files; on the other it is designed for integration into a comprehensive online scholarly environment. I thought I might build a small model of how objects in an online World Library—assuming the existence of such a library—would have to be designed.

The investigation was, I think, successful, though not at all in the way I was expecting. I was less exhilarated than sobered by the outcome. The completed Archive implicitly argued that, so far as scholarship is concerned, something as thickly empirical as *The Rossetti Archive* would have to be created for our entire mediated inheritance, which is by no means only semasiographic. Not just all the documentary (or non-documentary) remains of Rossetti or Blake or Whitman, or Washington or Jefferson, but the same for everyone they touched as well as everyone they did not touch; and not just those individuals but all the social agents, individual and otherwise, who left their mark on the record. More, it argued that the sociohistorical structures that deliver our inheritance to us must also be preserved and passed on—that would be all the metadata that organizes the complex sociohistory of our human records as well as all the imbedded forms—think XML and TEI—that define its general and local shapes.

NINES was born (2004) as a response to that Scholarly Condition. Unless they are integrated into the sociologics of an online World Library, projects like *The Rossetti Archive* are only minimally useful to scholarship. So NINES was conceived as a small model for exploring the problem of information design for scholarly work at a global scale. It developed an operational (institutional) response to the following question: assuming a distributed world network of objects like *The Rossetti Archive,* how should the network be organized and its materials integrated? This is very like the question that shaped the initial development of *The Rossetti Archive.* It differs in one crucial respect: it has a social and institutional horizon. The inquiry addresses not the formal design of a complex autopoietic system, but the institutional structures needed to promote access and repurposing by a distributed population of research scholars and educators. Most immediately, this meant that working scholars would authorize and develop the NINES content so that the traditional work of scholarship—research and publication—could be pursued in the kind of integrated environment characteristic of our inherited paper-based system. Like the latter, NINES *is designed to grow and develop through the use and input of scholars who want reliable sources and trusted materials and who expect their own work to be peer-reviewed.*

A key initial decision, therefore, was to move against the promiscuous state of information available on the web. The move operated on two fronts simultaneously. First, NINES established itself as a peer-reviewing agent that would identify and assemble a corpus of authoritative online materials. These would have to include every kind of online resource that a working scholar uses: standalone online projects like *The Walt Whitman Archive;* library and museum catalogues and accessible content; proprietary materials (like those developed by Intelex, ProQuest and the Alexander Street Press); online scholarly journals, both free culture and subscribed (for example, online journals like *Postmodern Culture, RaVon,* and *19* or aggregators like *JSTOR* and *Project Muse*); and university press publications.

Second, NINES sought a technical and disciplinary structure that would permit the range of authoritative resources to be indefinitely expandable. The particular goal here was to develop a comprehensive scholarly environment—an online corpus with, for example, the MLA's disciplinary range. So NINES from the outset was working to promote similar entities for Medieval, Renaissance, Eighteenth-century, and Modernist scholars. The first of these, 18thConnect, was formally launched in 2010 and the others are now in active development.[16] Following the initial conception of the NINES initiative, they are all imagining an eventual integration with a more comprehensive network: ARC, the Advanced Research Consortium.[17]

## IV

"Not what but who." It's a fact that most colleges and universities have not formulated comprehensive or policy-based approaches to online humanities scholarship. While resources for the use of media in the classroom, including electronic and web media, are fairly common, a resource commitment for digital scholarship is rare. Scholars who have serious digital interests regularly complain about the lack of institutional support. But it's clear that the universities are responding to facts on the ground: i.e., to the scholars themselves and their professional agents. Most scholars and virtually all scholarly organizations have stood aside to let others develop an online presence for our cultural heritage: libraries, museums, profit and nonprofit commercial vendors. Funding agents like NEH, SSHRC, and Mellon have thrown support to individual scholars and small groups of scholars, and they have encouraged new institutional agents like Ithaka, HASTAC, SCI, and Bamboo. But while these developments have increased during the past twenty years—i.e., since the public emergence of the browsable internet—the scholarly community at large remains shockingly passive.

One more anecdote and I am done. This one goes back to 1981, when I was first introduced to computer processes at the California Institute of Technology. I took a position at Caltech to help design a program of general studies in humanities and social sciences for their undergraduates—but that's another story.

Our division used VAX computers that ran UNIX. I was mesmerized by the command-line world and its powerful abstract operations. I decided I had to learn how to use these machines and the chance finally came a year later. I had just finished writing—on my typewriter—two short books, *A Critique of Modern Textual Criticism* and *The Romantic Ideology*. A young colleague in the division, an economist, was also completing a book and he had a programmer friend who was writing a computer typesetting program. His friend needed people to test out the program so we both agreed.

It was a painful experience—but that is yet another story.

In the end I actually got a handle on the program, designed the two books—one decently, the other badly—set the type, and produced camera-ready copy for the University of Chicago Press, which published the books in 1983.

I tell this story for two reasons. First there's this. Since I'd done so much of the publisher's work myself, I was pleased to think we could reduce the cost of the books dramatically. You'll recall that academic book prices at that time were beginning what would soon become their dramatic, and ultimately catastrophic, price escalation. When I asked what kind of price reduction I could expect, I was told by the press: "Very little." "What? How could that be?" "Because," I learned, "the market expects a certain price for books of this kind. If we drop the cost on your books it will skew the whole price structure of our book list."

Had I been a more imaginative person I might have seen the dark future hidden in those words. But what did I know then, what did any of us know, or foresee? The academic book market was still years away from the crisis that now engulfs it. The three persons of our one institutional god—the library, the academic press, and the institutional community of scholars—were still, to all appearances, *unam, sanctam, cetholicam*. But then came the (digital) Reformation. Now everybody wants to know how we're going to put our Humpty Dumpty together again.

But there's also something else. While I was wrestling with the bugs and deficiencies in the code and talking with the programmer, he entertained me with a little piece of black comedy. His main job was at Caltech's famous Jet Propulsion Laboratory (JPL). He said the problems we were having with his typesetting program were endemic to his work. He needed us to beta test the program so he could correct and improve it. I still remember his wicked smile when I told him I was glad to help. It amused him no end, he said, to think about the complex programming he and others were doing for JPL "You realize, don't you," he said, "that there are always fault lines and errors in the coding. Therein lies the joy of the hacker's life. And the more code we write, the more we correct and extend its functionalities, the more deeply we imbed the errors. As we improve the code, we also make it more difficult to see its weaknesses." Being a literary person I thought of Thomas Hardy's reflections on the voyage of the *Titanic:*

And as the smart ship grew
In stature, grace, and hue,
In shadowy silent distance, grew the iceberg, too.

When we pursue sustainability and try to forge policy, we want to remember: that is the horizon we're working in.

"How depressing," some might say. "Not at all," I answer. "The poet was quite right" because he knew, as still another poet remarked, that "if a way to the Better there be, / It exacts a full look at the Worst." And we're all here looking for a Better Way.

JPL is still going strong, despite its disasters, and after the *Titanic* global travel is commonplace. Another of my favorite and darkly comic poets was also right when he urged us to "Say not the struggle nought availeth." We're on "The Long Evolution." And because we are, we want to travel in the company of those a more recent poet called "The Less Deceived." Putting Humpty Dumpty back together again on a sustained basis, on the library shelves and also online, is—as they say about old age—"not for sissies." It *will* be done even though none of us knows exactly how. I also think—I hope—that all of us, even the youngest, will not live to say, as a careless and ignorant man once foolishly said, "Mission Accomplished." Much better would be to ask ourselves what Sean Connery asked Kevin Costner in *The Untouchables:* "What are you prepared to *do?*"

Which brings me back to my initial subject, Sustainability. We have to sustain our traditional cultural records. We also have to sustain our growing body of born-digital scholarship. And we have to develop and sustain digital mechanisms that give scholars functional access to both.

But there we have only the "what" of the problem. Defining it as a practical problem shifts us to ask "how." And when we make the shift we realize, like Kathy Acker's heroine, that the question ultimately comes down to "who." We know that a number of institutional agents have a serious interest in these issues. Thinking today in relation to that nexus, I've deliberately assumed the position of the scholar in order to examine sustainability (1) from the point of view of scholars as we function in our traditional institutional settings, digital and nondigital; and (2) from the point of view of scholars as we work and collaborate with nonacademic persons and institutions.

I've done this partly out of necessity, because those are the perspectives in which I experience the issues. But I've also done it to argue that the scholar's interests ought to be determining ones—perhaps, if there is such a thing, *the* determining ones. Why is that? Because it is the scholar's vocation to monitor the cultural record as the indispensable resource for public education. As librarians, publishers, funding agencies, and academic administrators engage these issues from their special vantage points, they should keep that perspective—my perspective, our perspective—clearly before their minds.

## V

Throughout the 1990s, humanists working with IT were tempted to believe they were pioneering a new disciplinary field called "Digital Humanities." In the last ten years many have begun to look back to our future. Online ecologies are leading us to imagine a new approach to traditional philology, whose center could be anywhere and whose circumference, nowhere. Indeed, as the global capacities of online networks have grown, so has the need to control and organize them for particular social and institutional needs. So while digital technology is introducing new critical methods and procedures, it does not fundamentally alter the sociologics of scholarship and education nor their institutional mechanisms. Studying the history of philology itself is especially pertinent now, as is a broad critical reflection on the current institutional state of humanities education.

In that context, we have a pressing need to integrate online humanities scholarship into the programmatic heart of the university. Twenty years ago, and for various institutional reasons, university degree programs could not support advanced work in digital humanities. So online scholarship flourished in extra-programmatic localities: typically, in the orbit of the university library, or through special agencies like IATH. The DPLA initiative is the unmistakable sign that we can no longer safely proceed in that way.

DPLA is a project to install a comprehensive online archive of authorized and reliable materials for general public education. Philology is the discipline for realizing—in a famous poet's words—"what [we] half create, and what we perceive" as the order of history and culture. The critical study and augmentation of such an archive is the foundational mission of philology, and university degree programs are sine qua non for executing that mission. To date, however, this cultural archive has been growing with little direct input or oversight by the community—humanities scholars and educators—who have a fundamental interest in its successful realization.

The Google Books Settlement was the historical event that triggered the DPLA initiative. "In what we now call the information society . . . we need a new ecology, one based on the public good instead of private gain."[18] These words show us how the DPLA ought to be an invitation and an opportunity for humanities scholars. Realizing the idea of the DPLA means developing the institutional means for reorganizing and re-editing our entire cultural inheritance, traditional as well as digital, for online access, reflection, and repurposing.

A library of this kind is so central to the educational mission of the humanities that we must insist on helping to shape its future. As it emerges, humanists will also have to begin promoting the digital transformation of post-secondary humanities programs and curricula. The institutional inertia that has been resisting these changes, while often deplored by digital enthusiasts, can and should be rethought and redirected. Traditional scholarship operates through a complex machinery of paper-based social software about which digital technicians are often deeply ignorant. The ontologies needed to organize an effective online educational system are already operating, largely transparently, within the social network of traditional scholarship and education. The Machine of the Book, perhaps the greatest social technology ever invented, should be the object of deep study by human-interface designers. But of course that kind of study, the repurposing of the work of the past, is exactly what we mean by scholarship. *The Blake Archive* is a repurposed migration not only of Blake's original works, but of all their subsequent scholarly migrations and transcriptions, and most especially the foundational editions from Ellis and Yeats to Keynes, Erdman, and Bentley.

"We will advance funeral by funeral," a learned digital scholar once ironically remarked when I was kvetching with him on these subjects. And while I'm sure he touched an important truth, it isn't a truth to help us shape reliable policy, which is what we need. Sustaining digital scholarship means sustaining our cultural resources tout court, digital and nondigital, and it also means taking a long view. It is a social problem pressing on the entire community entrusted with the care of public education. Advertising, ideology, propaganda, and entertainment are part of our public education, but scholarship is its source and end and test.

# 8

# Philological Investigations I
## The Example of Poe

AN ACUTE SENSE of what Marjorie Perloff called "the poetics of indeterminacy" has marked criticism and scholarship for at least thirty years.[1] Synthetic narratives—historicist, dialectical, psychoanalytic—have seen their truth values turn imaginary, becoming what William Blake in *The Marriage of Heaven and Hell* called "poetic tales": arbitrary constructions, "fictions of lineage," and order.[2] With the space of knowledge grown so radically volatile and complex, even "contested," the teacher's watchword became "teach the conflicts," the scholar's, "explore the contradictions." So David Reynolds dives "beneath the American Renaissance" to expose the fault lines of F. O. Matthiessen's famous normative narrative, and Timothy Powell's *Ruthless Democracy* makes a polemic on the issues: "The real subject of Ruthless Democracy is . . . not simply a revision of the canon of American literature, but rather an argument for how engaging a multiplicity of cultural perspectives (both historical and literary) can lead to a greater understanding of the richly complicated, infinitely conflicted nature of 'American' identity."[3]

Although we have long questioned the literary history—even the kind of literary history—laid out in Matthiessen's *American Renaissance,* we have found trouble devising alternatives.[4] New Historicism emerged as a corrective response to the market collapse of normative, canonical, and synthetic histories. Its work came in two forms. On one hand, New Historicists devised collage or case history approaches, building presentations—more maps than narratives—with deliberated "fissures" to provoke "reader response." On the other, they sponsored a valuable range of microhistorical investigations that could leave the rest, the synthesis, to silence.

Because of its extreme social and cultural volatility, antebellum America brings these issues of critical and scholarly method into sharp focus. Recent scholars push at the limits of New Historicist strategies when they wonder, for instance, how to develop "a[n Edgar Allan] Poe biography with multiple endings";[5] "a literary history of multiple narratives";[6] or a criticism focused on "forms of authorship" that are not "author-centered" or even authoritative.[7]

As it happens, we can actually do these things. Indeed, the tools and procedures for their implementation have been in place, have even been deployed, for quite some time. Because this work has developed in the marches of our literary and cultural centers—in bibliographical, editorial, and textual studies—it has, until recently, passed without much notice. The emergence of internet culture and, for humanist scholars, of online research and publication spaces has begun to bring such work to greater attention. Before looking more closely in that direction, however, we should return to antebellum America and consider once again the vexed cultural status of Edgar Allan Poe. For scholars and educators interested in literary history, the problem of Poe runs out far and in deep.


## I


Few literary commonplaces are more clear than the antithesis of Walt Whitman and Edgar Allan Poe. Whitman's angel, Ralph Waldo Emerson, had little interest in Poe's work, and Poe, for his part, was contemptuous of Transcendentalist optimism, its belief in social and cultural progress, and—perhaps most of all—the dominance of its social and cultural authority. In this network of antagonisms, Poe's importance in relation to the so-called American Renaissance has been greatly obscured, as we know. It has also been, until recently, misunderstood.

The nineteenth-century escape from this misunderstanding was through protomodernist aesthetic thought developed in England and France in the latter half of the period: that's to say, through Dante Gabriel Rossetti and Algernon Charles Swinburne, on one hand, Charles Baudelaire and Stéphane Mallarmé on the other.[8] Profound as this way has been, there's another way, nativist and surprising, that we have forgotten—through Whitman.

When the Poe Memorial was unveiled in Baltimore in November 1875, Whitman—remarkably—made a special point to attend. Struck by the "Conspicuous Absence of the Popular Poets" at the ceremony, he used the situation to reflect on what he would later call "Edgar Poe's Significance" for American literature and culture. His initial comments came in the *Washington Star*'s account, probably written by himself, of the memorial event, and they were elaborated several years later in a set of critical reflections that eventually found their way into *Specimen Days*.[9]

In the *Star*, Whitman records a dramatic shift from his long-standing "distaste for Poe's writings. I wanted," he wrote, "and still want for poetry, the clear sun shining, and the fresh air blowing—the strength and power of health, not of delirium." But "Poe's genius," "noncomplying with these requirements," forced Whitman "to fully admit" that it "has yet conquered a special recognition for itself."

Whitman explains this newly realized appreciation of Poe and his work by recounting "a dream I once had" of "a vessel on the sea, at midnight, in a storm." This was "no great full-rigg'd ship, nor majestic steamer, steering firmly through the gale," but a "superb little schooner yacht" like those Whitman often observed in the waters around New York. But now it was not "lying achor'd, rocking . . . jauntily," but was

> flying uncontroll'd with torn sails and broken spars through the wild sleet and winds and waves of the night. On the deck was a slender, slight, beautiful figure, a dim man, apparently enjoying all the terror, the murk, and the dislocation of which he was the center and victim.[10]

"That figure of my lurid dream," Whitman adds, "might stand for Edgar Poe, his spirit, his fortunes, and his poems—themselves all lurid dreams."

Five years later, in a journal entry of January 1, 1880, Whitman elaborated his thought and dream and then published the entry in *Specimen Days*. The significance of Edgar Poe, Whitman says, is "in diagnosing this disease called humanity."[11] Accustomed to reading Whitman out of his reiterated polemic for the ideal *literatus* of an ideal America—the bard of "a grand, secure, free sunny race"[12]—we often forget the extreme darknesses that emerged as he peered through his *Democratic Vistas*:[13]

> I say we had best look our times and lands searchingly in the face, like a physician diagnosing some deep disease. Never was there, perhaps, more hollowness at heart than at present, and here in the United States. . . . [F]or all this hectic glow, and these melo-dramatic screamings . . . [t]he spectacle is appalling. We live in an atmosphere of hypocrisy throughout. . . . A scornful superciliousness rules in literature. . . . The great cities reek with respectable as much as non-respectable robbery and scoundrelism. . . . In business,

(this all-devouring modern word, business,) the one sole object is, by any means, pecuniary gain. . . . The best class we show, is but a mob of fashionably dress'd speculators and vulgarians. True, indeed, behind this fantastic farce, enacted on the visible stage of society, solid things and stupendous labors are to be discover'd, existing crudely and going on in the background, to advance and tell themselves in time. Yet the truths are none the less terrible. I say that our New World democracy . . . is, so far, an almost complete failure in its social aspects, and in really grand religious, moral, literary, and esthetic results.[14]

As the vocabulary of disease indicates, here is where "Edgar Poe's Significance" begins to emerge, in this dark night of the American soul. Because, as Whitman says, "I wanted, and still want for poetry, the clear sun shining, and fresh air blowing," Whitman's most direct access to the nightmares of America is a prose access.

Let's briefly explicate Whitman's text. What he sees in Poe is an imaginative exposure of "the age's matter and malady." In the intransigence of Poe's revelation lies its great "significance." Whitman's own imaginative vision, committed to "a perfect and noble life, morally without flaw," is a daytime vision, as Whitman knows and declares. Whitman's power is thus exemplary rather than diagnostic. He then proceeds to reflect on "another shape of . . . the artist sense . . . where the perfect character, the good, the heroic, although never attain'd, is never lost sight of, but through failure, sorrows, temporary downfalls is return'd to again and again." This is another exemplary way—a romantic way, "dearer far to the artist-sense" of the nineteenth century, Whitman says, than his own healthy and sunny way. This romantic way, emblemized in the great popular poets of the time, "we see more or less in Burns, Byron, Schiller, and George Sand."

"But," Whitman then avers, "we do not see it in Edgar Poe." Poe's is instead a third way, different from both of these. It is to make himself and his work the unappalled "center and the victim" of the dislocated world, "apparently enjoying all the terror" of the maelstrom. In choosing this way, Poe becomes that arresting dream figure, what Whitman calls the "entire contrast and contradiction" both to Whitman's ideal of an American literatus and to those romantic poets who make a drama of their perpetual struggles toward "something evermore about to be."[15]

The heart of Poe's greatness lies, paradoxically, in his imaginatively deliberated heartlessness, what Whitman calls "a strange spurning of, and reaction from" all customary forms of human commerce and sympathy. To gain access to the truth of America's nightmares demands giving up, in Jesus's words, "all that a man hath," everything connecting him to daylight illusions: "the author's birth and antecedents, his childhood and youth, his physique, his so-call'd education, his studies and associates, the literary and social Baltimore, Richmond, Philadelphia and New York." Poe moves through these realms only to spurn them, and in that gesture he enters the land of transcendent darkness.

> Almost without the first sign of moral principle, or of the concrete or its heroisms, or the simpler affections of the heart, Poe's verses illustrate an intense faculty for technical and abstract beauty, with the rhyming art to excess, an incorrigible propensity toward nocturnal themes, a demoniac undertone behind every page—and, by final judgment, probably belong among the electric lights of imaginative literature, brilliant and dazzling, but with no heat.

Every reading of that great passage known to me sees it as a dismissal of Poe. It is not. It is rather Whitman's effort to describe a poetic "genius" that is at once apparent and incomprehensible to him. The passage recalls (or forecasts) the famous moment in *The Education of Henry Adams* when Adams, introduced to Swinburne, acknowledges that he has encountered an imagination that has passed beyond his ken.

## II

What is the significance of "Edgar Poe's Significance"—a text of barely two pages published in a book that runs to many hundreds? It is significant because it shows Whitman trying to remedy a previous blindness with a new insight. Remarkably, his key descriptors set Whitman's Poe close to Baudelaire's and Mallarmé's: Poe as happy terrorist and technician of the imagination, amoral, demoniac, heatless and heartless, abstract. And we know that Whitman read both Baudelaire and Mallarmé.

But there is a significant difference. To Baudelaire and Mallarmé, Poe's heartless, abstract, and demoniac texts define their heroic character and their modernity. To them Poe is an imaginative hero because he is master of the modern imagination. So in his "Notes to the Poems of Poe," Mallarmé accepts the account of Mrs. Suzan Achard Wirds that Poe wrote "The Philosophy of Composition" "under the heading of ingenious experiment. It had amused and surprised him to see it so promptly accepted as a *bona fide* declaration."[16] Mallarmé takes the prose commentary as "a pure intellectual game" and thus entirely in keeping with Poe's project toward "pure poetry." For Mallarmé, Poe is a crucial intellectual force because he makes "the beauty of the word" a theatrical event. "And from this special point of view is there mystification? No. What is thought, *is:* and a prodigious idea escapes the pages which, written afterwards (and without foundation in fact—there it is) did not therefore become . . . less sincere. The idea is that all chance ought to be banished from the modern work, and if it is there, it must be feigned. The eternal wing-thrust does not exclude a lucid gaze studying the space consumed by its flight."[17]

That prodigious Poe is rarely proposed by Americans, enthusiasts or detractors. Indeed, in most American perspectives until recently Poe is a subaltern character—diminutive, even infantilized, he and his readers alike. Not a "majestic" vessel—that would be Byron or Herman Melville—but a "little schooner yacht." Whitman has in view a world different from tormented modernity—what he called, after Richard Wagner, "the Future." Because Whitman daydreams of a morally healthful world and the heroism of the democratic Individual, he is puzzled, perhaps even appalled, certainly disturbed, at precisely those features of Poe's work that Baudelaire and Mallarmé celebrate.

But suppose the nightmare America is as true as Whitman's daydream America? That possibility haunts Whitman's text. His little commentary on Poe ends, after all, in a pair of unanswered questions: "The lush and the weird . . . what mean they? . . . abnormal beauty—the sickliness of all technical thought or refinement . . . what bearings have they on current pathological study?"[18] Unlike Baudelaire and Mallarmé, who are confident in the Poe of their dreams, Whitman cannot answer those questions, which conclude his little essay. But that our American Lohengrin should have posed those questions is crucial.

History, like love, is its own avenger. Now that Baudelaire's and Mallarmé's dreams of modernity have been played out, the deep truth of Whitman's dream and bafflement has emerged. It is written all over our recent academic commentaries on Poe and antebellum America: most notably in the work of Jonathan Elmer, Betsy Erkkilä, J. Gerald Kennedy, Meredith McGill, Scott Peeples, Timothy Powell, Louis Renza, David Reynolds, Eliza Richards, John Carlos Rowe, and Terence Whalen.[19] Each has been searching "beneath the American Renaissance" for a response to Whitman's questions and to the larger issues implied in those questions.

Whitman's arresting image of Poe as the "centre and victim" of a storm-tossed world appears recurrently in the work of these scholars. Perry Miller's 1956 study of Poe and Melville and their cultural context was prescient of much that would follow. Consider Miller's description of Melville:

An artist can, once he has caught the ear of his people, abruptly discover himself cut off not because he thunders some clear sanity against their insanity, but because he participates completely in their befuddlement. He accepts as the terms of his problem precisely the terms they propound to him . . . ; then he finds himself, despite the power of genius, no more capable of resolving the antinomies, or of making good the pretensions, than they are. If at the end of his exertions, no matter how titanic, he confronts the blank emptiness of defeat . . . , the tragedy is not so much his overreaching as an inescapable collapse of the structures his society provided him—indeed, imposed upon him, with no allowance for alternatives.[20]

There precisely is the artist as center and victim of a maelstrom—what modernism taught us to see as "the tragedy" of "the power of genius." But suppose the scene were constructed closer to Whitman's dream, as a dark comedy with the "slight figure" of a confidence man as the genius loci? That would be the scene mapped by Jonathan Elmer's "Cultural Logic of the Hoax."

Matthiessen famously excluded Poe from his study of the American Renaissance not so much because Poe was "hostile to democracy"—Nathaniel Hawthorne and Melville took dim views as well, and Whitman was often mortally troubled, as we know. Poe is expelled because his skepticism lacked "the moral depth" of his contemporaries.[21] But since Matthiessen, many have learned to see how Poe's mordant comic skepticisms reach a depth of insight unachieved elsewhere at the time. This comes because his works reflect so completely the contradictions—the "befuddlement"—of his age. Thus Terence Whalen's study of *Edgar Allan Poe and the Masses* usefully examines how "many of Poe's overt political pronouncements—progressive and reactionary—were largely derived from the words of others, which indicates a negative political capability rather than a rigid ideological agenda."[22] This is acute, though the Keatsian reference can easily distort Poe's work with irrelevant Romantic categories. Poe does not so much sympathize with the contradictions of his age as exploit and theatricalize them. They emerge less through an affective engagement—in that respect, his work *is* cold and abstract—as through his willing suspension of belief in them.

In this Poe assumes an aesthetic posture toward the contradictions of his antebellum world. From its every form of worship—the idols of cave and market, whether sublime (as in *Eureka*) or ridiculous (as in "The Case of M. Valdemar" or "Von Kempelen and His Discovery")—he makes poetic tales. Or, as T. S. Eliot famously lamented, Poe merely "entertains" his ideas, he does not believe them.[23] His negative capability is of the mind, not of the heart, as is quite clear from the poetic argument he develops in *Eureka*, where he distinguishes two kinds of "belief": the one operating when we say "We *believe* in a God," the other being what he calls "belief proper," i.e., the "mental conception" constitutive of "intellectual belief."[24]

Poe's work reflects the ideological conflicts of his time by participating in their expression, by conscious acts of identification, including conscious acts of false consciousness—what Miller called "befuddlement." "Far from being removed from their world, Poe's poems and tales may be the most powerful artistic representation we have of the traumatic psychic and cultural effects of the social crisis and political breakdown that marked the post-Enlightenment . . . in the United States." Poe's moral elusiveness—what James Russell Lowell famously saw as his fudge-factor, "There comes Poe, with his raven, like Barnaby Rudge, / Three-fifths of him genius and two-fifths sheer fudge."—sets him apart and supplies his moral depth.[25] Reading Poe we realize how it is intellectually dangerous to take what one writes or reads too seriously. Or, as Betsy Erkillä succinctly observes: "There is no such thing as a pure poem."[26] Thence comes the negative space, the dark matter of Edgar Poe, a Kosmos to disturb and befuddle the kosmos of the heroic artist by folding it back into its true source and end and test: the man of the crowd, aspiring, befuddled, self-deceived, ultimately tragicomic.

A modernist orientation on Poe's work, still common and useful, recognizes how it casts a cold and mocking eye on the hypocrite *lecteur*. Irony, satire, hoax, an amoral posture ("the heresy of the didactic"), cold ratiocination, theatricality, and "de la musique avant toute chose": these are all the marks of that *Poetic* world. Another modernist orientation, the obverse of Baudelaire's—Henry James, Laura (Riding) Jackson, Eliot, and later Matthiessen and Bloom are its exemplary characters—reads those same signs as shallow, immature, and ultimately unserious.[27]

Inserting "mass culture" as a neglected category in these modernist designs on Poe, Jonathan Elmer's 1995 study decisively shifted the critical territory. "If [Poe] offers us a rich imagination of the mass culture of the day—a view of the democratic "mob," a sampler of most of the popular and mass literary forms of antebellum magazine culture—he is also, and equally, imagined by mass culture: he is, in fact, its symptom."[28] Elmer's work exposes the symmetry marking the two modernist lines of critical reception, both of which assess Poe's work as a function of his individual talent (or lack of it). While different criteria for measuring this unique Poetic talent will yield diverse judgments, ultimately "the achievement of Edgar Allan Poe" is the issue.

But what if the personal achievement of Edgar Allan Poe can only be measured as a social function? More, what if the social context of an individual talent is mapped along volatile, discontinuous, and severely relativistic lines? Those two questions have shaped the orientation of the antebellum scholarship I have been referencing. Perhaps even more significantly, they indicate the need we have for what Eliza Richards calls "a model of literary and cultural production that . . . is intersubjective and interactive."[29]

Poe's case is crucial because his work reveals the extreme dispersal of textual and literary authority.

> Poe's investments in genre, his adoption of the literary values of the miscellany, and his attempts to establish authorship by disrupting the process of reprinting are authorial strategies made possible by the heterogeneous and uncontrolled distribution of antebellum periodical literature.[30]

Poe shamelessly echoes, mimics, plagiarizes, and refashions the work of others, as we have known for a long time. But in operating this way he becomes subject to other agents and social forces. "Poe's career passes through nearly all of the important antebellum publishing centers," Meredith McGill observes, "and his shifts between them chart a progress toward the embattled center of the struggle over a national literature."[31] This is the decentered "centre" that Poe explores in Eureka, the field of relations in "which the centre is everywhere, the circumference nowhere."[32] As a consequence, Edgar Poe becomes what he beholds, a textual being to be echoed, mimicked, plagiarized, and refashioned in his turn:

> The crisis for Poe is not that he is forced to embrace literary nationalist ideals in order to advance his career. Rather, his autonomy is jeopardized when the literary nationalists embrace *his* principles, invoking him as an idealized figure of independent judgment within [the] discourse [of Lowell and Duyckinck]. Poe does not abandon his critical ideals so much as lose control over them as they are translated into the literary nationalist idiom.[33]

Here is Richards's intersubjectivity and interactivity with a vengeance. Poe's case ultimately shows that the autonomous author might be "victim" of other agents, confidence man, "symptom" of seriously unstable social conditions, or even, perhaps, all three at once.

Scott Peeples drives straight to a heart of the matter when he reflects on *The Afterlife of Edgar Allan Poe:* "One could perhaps write a Poe biography with multiple endings or in some other way foreground the unreliability of the evidence surrounding his death, highlighting the fact that we don't know Poe so much as we know the documentary evidence related to his life."[34] The ambiguous death of Edgar Poe is a dramatic emblem of our difficulties with this period: we know the documents—at least the ones that survive—but we have come to know them only in their differences and unreliabilities. So scholars now dream toward a literary history of multiple narratives, a literary history in which "the poetics of creation are inseparable from the poetics of reception."[35] And McGill gives the issue an explicit general form: "An author-centered criticism necessarily collapses the range of obscured, withheld, projected, and disavowed forms of authorship" that "necessarily" characterize social and cultural life.[36]

## III

The first issue of *New Literary History (NLH)* (1969) opened with "A Note on New Literary History" by the editor, Ralph Cohen. His journal, he argued, would provide a forum for discussing the historical foundations and social function of literary studies. The forum was needed for two reasons. First, literary studies in society at large seemed to have turned marginal and inconsequent. Second, the discipline had grown uncertain of itself and its cultural mission. Cohen pivots his "Note" on "the feeling of uneasiness prevalent in our profession" and the related "feeling of inadequacy involved in the teaching of English studies."[37] For Cohen, both are a consequence "of the current rejection of history either as guide to or knowledge of the present."[38] Cohen does not mention the antihistoricism of the New Criticism as his critical point of departure. He does not have to.

Now, more than forty years on, Cohen's message seems more pertinent than ever. The emergence of internet culture—what Siva Vaidhyanathan calls "the Googlization of everything"[39]—has exacerbated the crisis of the literary and historical imagination that Cohen addressed in 1969. But if literary culture seems still in peril, the antebellum American scholarship I've been examining tells us something important about the legacy of *NLH*. History-oriented investigations of literature and culture are now impressively widespread, diverse, and learned, in no small part because of the example of *NLH*. Moreover, these sociohistorical approaches are peculiarly relevant to the problems humanist educators face because of the rise of internet culture.

A new literary history will direct—the process has already begun—the great obligation facing literary studies now: the reediting, for online environments, the entirety of our cultural inheritance. The example of current antebellum American scholarship, and the problem of Poe in particular, has been important for exposing some of the basic philological issues that will have to be addressed if the task is to be successful.

Before the advent of hypermedia, virtual texts, and semantic webs, textual studies had begun to worry the limits of author-centered and text-delimited editions and editorial method. For Anglo-American scholarship, this began in the 1980s with the publication of two books, *A Critique of Modern Textual Criticism* (1983) and *Bibliography and the Sociology of Texts* (1986).[40] Both argued the need to rethink the crucial distinction scholars traditionally make between a text and its context.

When Eliza Richards speaks about a "model of literary production that . . . is inter-subjective and interactive,"[41] we want to ask: what would such a model look like? "Intersubjective and interactive" is internet idiom summoning a world of wikis, blogs, and social software. But those media forms are nothing like the essays and monographs where Richards's model, like an obscure object of desire, is called after.

The question can be sharply defined if we pose it with respect to the basic form that a "model of literary production" must be able to take. That form is the scholarly edition. The complete genetic information about any cultural work is coded in the double helix of its DNA, i.e., in the codependent relation of its production history and its reception history. The idea of the scholarly edition, Variorum and fully critical, is to represent the textual DNA of the work(s) to be edited. While much more could and should be said about the structure of that codependent relation, the essential point to realize is that each strand of this double helix is produced by the collaboration of multiple agents. The terms "the poet" and "the reader" are high-level generalized descriptors of a dialectical process of various persons and institutions.

In its fullest theoretical articulation, the scholarly edition realizes that codependent relation: not just putting the relation on display as an historical record, but putting it in operation as a machine to be used for accessing, analyzing, and evaluating the record once again, a process that necessarily includes evaluating the edition's own particular scholarly presentation of the record. All books are knowledge machines, but the scholarly edition is a specially sophisticated type. One doesn't *read* a scholarly edition as one reads a narrative, fictive or historical, nor even as one reads markedly reflexive texts like *The Waste Land* or *Philosophical*

*Investigations.* One uses a scholarly edition as one uses a cookbook or an encyclopedia.

As the work of Richards and McGill explicitly indicates, the documents from the discursive field of antebellum America present a daunting critical/historical, and therefore editorial, challenge. This is at the same time a fundamental challenge to literary interpretation, although it is rarely so recognized. We have learned about the poetics of indeterminacy. We need to know what constitutes the scholarship of indeterminacy.

## IV

"A Poe biography with multiple endings"; "a literary history of multiple narratives"; a criticism focused on "forms of authorship" that are not "author-centered." These stirring calls are made, however, in the teeth of a scholarly condition that makes their realization very difficult. The problem is simple yet fundamental. Consider that the primary act of scholarship and criticism is editorial—establishing reliable documents and explaining the grounds of their reliability (or lack of it). The model of that foundational act is the critical or scholarly edition and its normative form is the edition of a specific author. That editorial model underpins our investigations, framing the way we perceive and approach the "objects" we will study. Like Laocoön and his children, the scholars I've been discussing all struggle in the coils of that tradition.

As have their distinguished precursors. The great Poe scholar Burton R. Pollin once again exposed the issues when he undertook a complete edition of Poe's works, *The Collected Writings of Edgar Allan Poe.* The basic problem is present in each of the volumes so far published, but it appears with greatest clarity in Pollin's heroic effort to produce a "Poe edition," as it were, of the *Broadway Journal.*[42] This edition comes in two parts—an editorial volume with scholarly introductions and notes, and a volume of the text—in this case, a photofacsimile of the annotated copy of the journal that Poe gave to Sarah Helen Whitman.

Or I should say a *selected* photofacsimile—a necessary caveat that begins to explain the difficulty. The journal ran from January 4, 1845, through January 3, 1846. Although Poe was contributing from the first issue, he did not become associate editor until March 1845, assuming complete editorial control in July. The journal was published by John Bisco and its initial chief editor was Charles F. Briggs.

From the outset Poe is a major contributor to *The Broadway Journal,* and from July he is the chief contributor. The facsimile presentation of the texts supplies a useful bibliographical context for Poe's work. But in going this far to present Poe in his journalistic context, Pollin exposes the deficiencies of his author-centered approach. Two things are especially crucial. First, by giving only those texts that Pollin judges to be Poe's writings, we are left with an expurgated view of Poe's important work as editor. Second, while Poe has annotated his contributions in the Whitman copy of *The Broadway Journal,* the reliability of those identifications is controversial in many ways. Pollin of course discusses the attribution issues—nearly all of them—in excellent detail.

The most notorious of the controversial attributions comes in "The Little Longfellow War" controversy. This event is worth rehearsing in some detail since it illustrates in a relatively brief space the general problem that's at stake. The dispute began with Poe's severe critique of Longfellow in the January 14 issue of the *Evening Mirror,* edited by Nathaniel Willis, at that point a friend and supporter of Poe. The subsequent controversy included a long "attack" on Poe signed "Outis" ("No Man"). Poe quotes this essay in full when he replies to it in *The Broadway Journal* on March 8, the pseudonymous essay by Outis having been originally published on March 1 in Willis's *Evening Mirror.* Pollin is certain that Poe wrote the "Outis" essay and he argues his position very well. But others see it differently and the editorial controversy is not settled. Even more problematic, however, is the critical issue, which Perry Miller long ago outlined with brilliant economy:

> There is reason to suppose that Poe blew [the controversy] up by writing at least one attack on himself (signed "Outis") in order to get the maximum of publicity; he was entirely capable of such a ruse. There is equal likelihood that Briggs entered the game deliberately, writing against Poe with Poe's contrivance [or perhaps without it?] so as to excite further retorts [and thereby promote the circulation of the journal].[43]

Miller writes "at least one attack on himself" because Briggs published another anonymous attack on Poe in *The Broadway Journal* (on February 15). Pollin does not provide us with this text because it was not, in his view, written by Poe (but even so, could it have been written by Briggs?). Then various other parties entered the fray, some named, some not, in different periodicals.[44] The whole affair is so interesting in itself that one wants an editorial environment more equal to its complexities—an environment that does not make Poe the pivot point of everything, the "center" determining what we see and how we see it, but only one possible center and "perspective."

The publishing world that enveloped Poe and his contemporaries is re-plete with these kinds of situations. Poe is so important because he had an acute understanding of the dynamics of his publishing scene, exploiting it—or being exploited by it—repeatedly. McGill's discussion of a publica-tion problem with "Lenore" is arresting and important. The long-line ver-sion of the poem was first published in Willis's *Evening Mirror* on Novem-ber 28, 1844, the Pindaric version having appeared the previous year in Lowell's periodical *Pioneer*. Although Poe was working in Willis's offices at the time, Willis published the poem as if by an unknown author, stating that it came to him through his correspondence with the Kentucky poet Amelia Welby, who—according to this account—saw it in a badly printed text in the Jackson, Tennessee, *Advocate*. Not only has the latter text never appeared—did it ever exist *in fact?*—Mabbott and others assume its reality in order to infer the existence of another printing of the poem in some New York periodical sometime before October 1844—also a text that has never appeared. Reflecting on the situation McGill rightly wonders:

> Is Poe's presence in [Willis's] office and his penchant for literary deception enough evidence to suggest that the entire correspondence might have been a . . . ruse to generate publicity about a poem to which Poe would soon lay claim in an extended analysis of . . . Welby's poems in the *Democratic Re-view?* Does the unauthorized circulation of "Lenore" point to reprinting as a problem for Poe, or to Poe's successful manipulation of these conditions of publication? How would we be able to decide without access to Poe's signature?[45]

As I've already suggested, many more questions could justifiably be raised in this context. But McGill's questions expose the key issue: that these textual conditions are marked by radical uncertainties. The surest way to handle the situation, from an editorial point of view, is to provide all of the documents, not just those that an editor, however learned, may judge pertinent. In Pollin's case, "pertinence" is determined in "author-centered" terms: did Poe write the text or didn't he? If Pollin thinks he did, it goes into the edition. If not, not. So the "Outis" review goes in but the anonymous attack on Poe printed by Briggs in the February 15 issue of the *Broadway Journal* is left out.

After Poe took control of the journal in July the problem grows more pressing because he is responsible for, even if he does not write, the en-tirety of the journal. Pollin's edition not only removes crucial contextual materials from our attention, it directs us to read in perspectives that are far from certain.

A notable example comes with a series of entries in the December 13, 20, and 27 issues of the *Journal,* all dealing with the veracity of the tale we now know as "The Facts in the Case of M. Valdemar," which Poe had just published in the December issue of the *American Review* under the title "The Facts in Valdemar's Case." In the December 13 issue of *The Broadway Journal* Poe prints a notice of a review of the *American Review* "article" that had just been published in the New York *Tribune* (December 10). Possibly written by Margaret Fuller, the review condemns Poe's work both for its subject matter and for the misleading "style of giving an air of reality to fictions." In his *Broadway Review* rejoinder to this review Poe asks: "*Why* cannot a man talk after he is dead?," observing with pertinent if wicked irony that "we find it difficult to understand how any dispassionate transcendentalist can doubt the facts as we state them."

Then in the next issue, December 20, Poe prints the *American Review* text under a slightly altered title. He heads "The Facts in the Case of M. Valdemar" with a note stating that the reprint comes at a reader's request and in order to let "the article . . . speak for itself." Pollin's edition does not include the *Broadway Journal* reprinted text—an unfortunate omission since Poe mischievously refers to the work as an article, not a story or a tale.[46] The sequence of entries is then completed in the December 27 issue when Poe prints the following: "Mr. Collier, the eminent Mesmerist, has written to us in reference to the extraordinary case of M. Valdemar. We quote a portion of his letter." The quoted letter attests to the veracity of such mesmeric resuscitation, remarking that "I did actually restore to active animation a person who died from excessive drinking of ardent spirits. He was placed in his coffin ready for interment."

If Collyer actually wrote those words Poe must have found them perversely, comically, gruesome.[47] But the authenticity of this letter has never been corroborated—indeed, its need for corroboration has never been pointed out. Pollin—like Mabbott before him—accepts its veracity. Referring to its author as "Collier" in his headnote, Poe then gives a text dated December 16, 1845, and signed by "Robert H. Collyer." Under the circumstances, we might lift some words from the letter to say of the letter itself: "I have not the least doubt of the *possibility* of such a phenomenon" as the veracity—or the hoax—of this letter. Poe had created false documentation for real and living authors before—in "Autography," for example, and "The Balloon Hoax." Whatever the case in *this* case, the management of the entire event is, if not pure poetry, pure Poe.[48]

This example illustrates a salient deficiency in both author-centered and text-centered approaches to literary works and literary history. The

*American Review* text of "The Facts in Valdemar's Case" gives only a certain view of that work. *The Broadway Journal* then gives, along with its different title and intercalary texts, an altogether different view. With the publication of those materials we move into a close encounter of a third kind with this work: a view where all the printings—authorized or not, skeptical or otherwise—configure a textual network of remarkable wit and complexity. In publishing his tale, or "article," Poe makes *un coup de dès* that summons the great god chance, who summons in turn various unpremeditated characters. The Valdemar matter gets taken up in the periodical press on both sides of the Atlantic by many readers and reviewers, publishers and editors. All bring their own ideas and dispositions to the event, all contribute to the field of discourse by seeing it in a certain way and letting others know what they see.

## V

The antebellum publishing scene in America and Poe's grasp of its expressive possibilities can be misleading. We must not think of this as a special case. It is not, it simply gives us a graphic picture of the complex nature of every textual condition. Restoration England supplies us with another dramatic case, as we know from the notorious problems of "attribution" that dog the work of Rochester, Dryden, and their respective circles of friends and enemies. Nor is it without reason that D. F. McKenzie focused on Congreve's work in his pursuit of the idea of a "sociology of texts."

But if the case of Poe and his world is not singular in an ontological sense, it is historically notable for two reasons. First, it clearly, and perhaps even more significantly, capaciously defines a publishing scene dominated by a volatile mix of periodicals pursuing a variety of different purposes and goals—political, commercial, regional, cultural, and religious. Authors and textual works mesh or collide in many different ways under the pressure of conflicted, overlapping, or shared interests. It is a scene ripe for gaming and hoaxing. Second, given the relatively ephemeral character of the principal means of public expression—newspapers and periodicals—the documentary materials that survive from the period are comparatively rich.

For a scholar, these two historical conditions hold out a promise—or is it a temptation?—that new and more comprehensive methods might be developed for studying the complexity of cultural materials and social texts to depths and at ranges not previously possible. Poe's work is crucial in that context because, while it is intensely personal in its perspective, it is not at all subjective, as the work of his celebrated contemporaries—Emerson, Thoreau, and Whitman, for instance—so clearly is. To edit Poe adequately requires that the work be clearly located in the full range of its social relations. Poe is a man of that crowd of relations, nor must we imagine that his heart could be laid bare for us. What can be exposed more fully, however, is the network of intersecting interests and relations that comprise antebellum American print culture.

An "author-centered" edition will not do. We require an editorial environment where multiple relations can be exposed from a wide range of different perspectives. Some would be individual authors, but others would be centered in a certain time or place, and still others in a particular social agent—for instance, a periodical or a certain social or religious institution. Scholars should be able to shift their focus on the total field at will.

Of course, the whole point of the traditional scholarly edition is to supply readers with the means to gain multiple perspectives on the work being edited. Pollin's edition of *The Narrative of Arthur Gordon Pym*—the first volume of his projected edition of the *Collected Writings*—shows this purpose very clearly. The edition deploys the basic format that has evolved through centuries of development—a format that is, moreover, within the limits of the print medium, flexible and powerful.[49] There is first of all a central reading text—a document that has emerged from the editor's evaluation of the multiple witness texts that make a claim to this central position. All of those witness texts are identified, though only the central text—the so-called critical text—is presented in toto. Readers are informed in editorial notes where the other witnesses vary from or agree with the critical text, and in many of these cases commentaries are supplied that try to explain the significance of the variations or agreements. The edition also supplies a series of scholarly essays that elucidate—in this particular case—Poe's "Aims and Methods" (Pollin 4–16), the work's "Sources" (17–28), "The Growth of the Text" (29–36, an essay in this case contributed to Pollin's edition by Joseph V. Ridgely), and Pollin's essay on "The Text" (37–52). Finally, it presents facsimiles of the title pages of the first American book publication (1838) as well as the title pages of the first two English printings (1838, 1841).

The problem in the case of *Pym* is slightly different from what we saw in the case of the material in *The Broadway Journal*—a fact borne out by the presence of Ridgely's important essay, with its discussion—at once learned and speculative—of the work's stages of development over a period of some twenty-two months ("from the late fall of 1836 to July 1838"; Ridgely, 29), and perhaps as long as twenty-eight.[50]

*Pym* has always been studied in relation to its two initial textual states: the first printing in the *Southern Literary Messenger (SLM)* (in two installments in January and February 1837) and the much longer book publication by Harper and Brothers in July 1838. These two texts represent completely different—what shall we call them?—works (?). Because they bear similar titles, and because Poe used the *SLM* materials as the basis for what would become the first four chapters of the Harper book, scholars have commonly approached these works as a problem in bibliography: what is the relation between the *SLM* and the Harper texts—most importantly, what changes were made and what do they mean? And while these bibliographical issues can scarcely be avoided in any serious study of *Pym,* they serve primarily to bring into focus the complexity of the interpretive questions that populate the *Pym* gravity field.

Here are some of those questions.

1. What is the status of the *SLM* text (which is to ask: Why did T. H. White, the editor of *SLM,* publish only two installments? Or, why did he publish any installments at all, since he had just fired Poe in early January 1837? Or, had Poe written any more of the tale to that point in time? Or, did he have specific plans for further installments? Or, whatever be that case, did Poe make new plans after being cut off from his serial publication? Or, what relation, if any, does the *SLM* text have to the book that Harper and Brothers contracted to publish in the spring of 1837?)

2. What is the status of the Harper text? Which is to ask: what are the specific textual differences between Harper and *SLM?* And, can we date the changes in any reliable way? And, what are we to make of the gross inconsistencies between the *SLM* and the Harper text, or the hoaxing and bizarre "Preface" and closing editorial Note? And, what are we to make of the "wholesale borrowing" (Pollin, *The Imaginary Voyages,* 9) that characterizes so much of the new material in the Harper text? And, what is the relation of the Harper text published in July 1838 and the work contracted in the spring of 1837—for instance, is the "long delay in the publication of *Pym* [due] to Poe's failure to supply copy [or perhaps] to business conditions"[51] and the Panic of 1837? And, since Poe was talking with Harper early in 1836 about publishing a long connected narrative, what if any relation does that fact have to the *Pym* materials?

3. What is the status of the nonauthoritative printings, i.e., the subsequent dissemination of *Pym* through the culture of reprinting? And, what relation do these texts have to the *SLM* and Harper's texts—other than

exhibiting a record of nonauthorial readings? And, what is the status of the first two English editions (1838, 1841) and the changes they introduced to the title and the Preface in particular? And, what special status, if any, does the so-called Griswold text (1856) have, considering that it was the most widely disseminated well into the twentieth century?

As Ridgely and Iola Haverstick first showed us in 1966, there are "Many Narratives of Arthur Gordon Pym."[52] Like any good scholarly edition, Pollin's tries to call the salient issues to attention. But the editorial procedure is such that everything pivots around the reading text: justifying it as reliable and authoritative and annotating specific passages so that we can track Poe's intentions, conscious as well as nonconscious. But the fact is that *Pym* has multiple narratives; and while Poe's intentions, conscious or otherwise, are invested in many of them, all are social texts brought into being—i.e., into their events of meaning—by multiple agents involved in the work's production and reception histories. A critical edition like Pollin's acknowledges the presence of those many agents and narratives but it also works to organize them in a stable hierarchy of relations. In doing that, it seriously distorts our access to a comprehensive view of the discourse field—a distortion, ironically enough, that actually moves against the inertia toward social textuality that Poe worked so hard, and so successfully, to gain. When McGill charts some of those moves, by Poe and others, she says they "chart a progress toward the embattled center of the struggle over a national literature."[53] In fact, it is precisely the kind of "center" that Poe explicates in *Eureka*. It is a field of relations *"of which the centre is everywhere, the circumference nowhere."*[54]

## Concluding Unscientific Prescript (An American Dream)

That kind of field is much less a psychological space of personal expression than a social space of dialogue and dispute. Poe's individual work is exemplary because, more than anyone else in the period, his writings regularly make a spectacle of their social relations. The "Longfellow War," the witty theatrics of the "Valdemar Case," the entire record of Poe's multiple publications and subsequent republications and reprintings: through these events we observe Poe's demonstrative explanation and interpretation of the social dynamics of his world and the people who live in it. The work holds a mirror up to that life. The spectacle is framed, at least initially, by something Poe writes and then circulates. Once put in circulation, however, the writing get seized and reframed by others—eventualities with which Poe may or may not engage again, to give further definition to the complexity of the scene. More than most, Poe's writings demonstrate why a throw of the dice can never abolish chance. Indeed, each throw of the dice only proves the authority of chance.

As Whitman's dream of Poe would reveal, Poe's is a stormy, turbulent, and "dislocated" world. Few historians have ever seen the period otherwise. Antebellum America is a virtual byword for a society torn by many illusions, conflicts, and extreme violence of many kinds.[55] Poe's first book, *Tamerlane and other poems* (1827), was published in the year of Andrew Jackson's first presidential term; and the period of his "three" administrations fairly defines the extreme dislocations that made such a fearful turmoil of antebellum America.[56] Coming after Poe, Whitman would respond to that dark historic page by trying to see the American world otherwise, by imagining it—representing it—as healthful and harmonious, or at least as a world dreaming toward health and harmony. But as is clear from the pivotal role Whitman gives to Poe in "Out of the Cradle Endlessly Rocking,"[57] Whitman's dream of America had first to pass through the strait gate of his dream of Poe.

A great reward awaits the scholar who will also pass through that gate. Digital environments offer the means for constructing editorial machines that can usefully simulate the complex hyperworld that Poe's work exposes. Fear and Illusion are the watchwords of antebellum America, as Poe more than anyone realized, because its high and conflicted energies were only barely held in control, and often went altogether out of control. The Panic of 1837 is a virtual index of the chaotic energies that were ripping through antebellum America. Poe's comic parodies of Enlightenment, like his quest for a *poesie pure,* are inverted expressions of the signs of the time, the reign of Fear and Illusion.

Scholars have been pursuing machines for editing discourse fields of that kind for some time, the earliest being efforts to design and build different kinds of hypermedia environments. Some recent digital works that explore integrating timelines with geospatial information have been provocative. And there is Timothy Powell's adventurous project, *Gibaga-dinamaagoom: An Ojibwe Digital Archive,*[58] an attempt to construct an online design for a set of cultural materials that do not map to Western Enlightenment design models. Because Ojibwe "history" is conceived and organized along a "sacred landscape," *Ojibwe* identities—objects, agents, actions, and locations—are radically discontinuous from the cultural formations that shape the logic of our Western databases and metadata ontologies. The structural and interpretive demands, and consequences, of this situation are significant. In Powell's words,

> The metadata schema and the database structure we have created thus inscribes a sacred landscape which allows animikii and other oshkaabewisag ("messengers") to move freely between the realm of the ancestors and this world. In doing so, we offer a spatio-temporal paradigm that, if acknowledged by Americanists, would perhaps allow us to free ourselves of the deeply problematic concept of periodization and our seemingly endless obsession with nationalism, postnationalism, transnationalism. . . . It is sacred landscape that is distinctly Ojibwe, yet still part of American literary history.[59]

Powell's *Ojibwe Digital Archive* indexes the general need we have for editorial spaces that can integrate the decentered scholarly present, with its variable critical and cultural interests, with equivalently dynamic fields like antebellum America, where multiple agents and relationships have been in play well before scholars in the present thought to investigate them. But critical editions have always been far more than collections of authoritative texts, as these new kinds of editorial ventures show.[60] They set the ground and the terms by which we try to remember and then explain who we are.

# 9

## Philological Investigations II
### A Page from Cooper

I

When Armitage, the Wanderer in Wordsworth's *Excursion*, tells "The Story of Margaret," he takes the scene of a ruined rural cottage for his text.

> I see around me here
> Things which you cannot see: we die, my Friend,
> Nor we alone, but that which each man loved
> And prized in his peculiar nook of earth
> Dies with him, or is changed; and very soon
> Even of the good is no memorial left.
> (*The Excursion*, Book I, 469–474)

The tale recalls a dark passage from the inscrutable Book of God. Because Armitage has read the passage before, he is well acquainted with its night. He is proposing to make its darkness a visible darkness by his retransmission. Writing in a special dialect of Romantic language, Wordsworth then reflects that retransmission so that it becomes for us a codicological homily on the nature of the Textual Condition. This is always a condition of loss. For if it is true, as Don McKenzie averred, that documents bear within themselves the history of their own making, it is equally true that those histories are defeatured from the start. The Book of God himself reminds us that documents are replete with obscured memory. How replete? To discover that, you must enter the document's world, like Armitage, with an alert attention. And even so, much will remain inaccessible—perhaps even lost forever.

Armitage is a scholar of a particular field of British popular culture. He does here what all scholars do: he rereads a text that he knows intimately and—most important—that he assumes we know as well, but much less intimately.

Was there ever a time when we didn't know how to read a book? No, there never was, though our subsequent life in books can sometimes lead us to imagine what such a moment was like. For the scholar and educator in any event, elucidating texts and documents is always rereading. Many will not have read James Fenimore Cooper's *The Pioneers,* but I write about it confident that you will find my commentary as familiar as Armitage assumed his tale would be for his interlocutor. Part of the history of their own making that books always carry is the meta-history of books and textualities as such.

Look at the title page of *The Pioneers* (Figure 1). You all know what it is even though you may not know all that it is or might be. For that you have to become familiar with it. And while I'm about to discuss what I see around me here on this title page—things I believe you cannot see—I'll begin by recalling things that I think you all *can* see.

Like any title page, this one sets down coded instructions for reading what follows, where further instructions come into play. When we read, we decipher the instructions embedded in what digital scholars call Marked Text. All texts are marked texts, i.e., algorithms—coded sets of reading instructions. This important fact about textuality comes to dramatic focus when we pay attention to a document's graphical and bibliographical features. Unlike a text's linguistic elements, bibliographical codes lay bare their devices: they announce that they are executing a "non-natural" language system. Consequently, their instructional or "performative" character is apparent for those who have a will to see: tables of contents or indices; type font, trim size, and book design; chapters and all the many protocols for divisioning (pagination, paragraphing, and punctuation).

Different books code for different kinds of reading. A dictionary is not coded like an instruction manual, which resembles a novel in significant ways, whereas a dictionary is much closer to a cookbook. In the case of a fictional narrative like *The Pioneers,* deciphering the code will not be finished until the reading is finished. I do not say "until the reading is completed" because no reading can execute all of a work's reading instructions. Another reader always awaits the document. Indeed, that Other Reader will appear as Yourself when you have finished your reading—that is to say, when you're positioned to reflect on how and

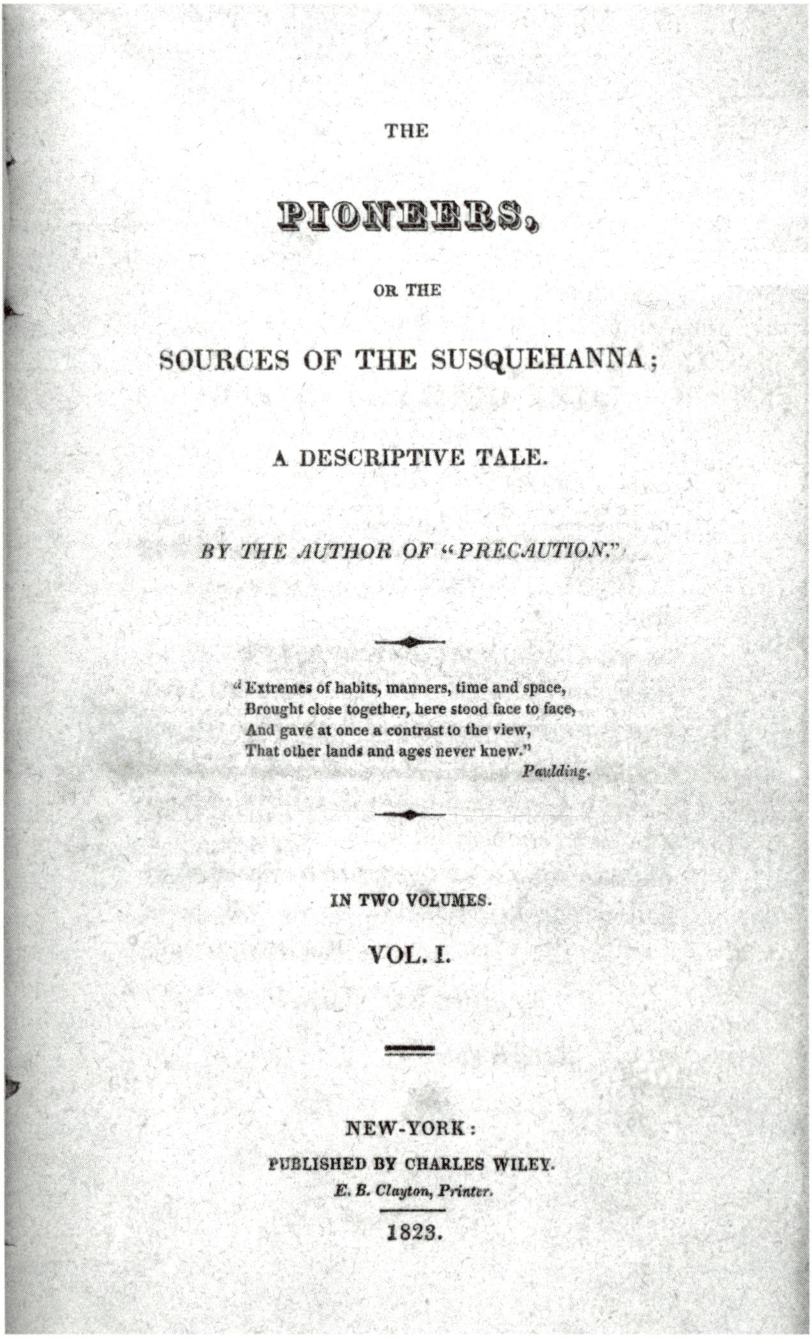

THE

# PIONEERS,

OR THE

## SOURCES OF THE SUSQUEHANNA;

A DESCRIPTIVE TALE.

*BY THE AUTHOR OF "PRECAUTION."*

—◆—

"Extremes of habits, manners, time and space,
Brought close together, here stood face to face,
And gave at once a contrast to the view,
That other lands and ages never knew."
                                        *Paulding.*

—◆—

IN TWO VOLUMES.

## VOL. I.

═══

NEW-YORK:

PUBLISHED BY CHARLES WILEY.
*E. B. Clayton, Printer.*

1823.

*Figure 1.* Title page of Cooper's *The Pioneers,* first edition, first issue (courtesy of *Albert and Shirley Small Special Collections Library, University of Virginia*).

what you've read, including every context of relations with which your reading chose to get engaged. For in reading, as Milman Parry observed, we make for ourselves a picture of great detail. And none of us ever finishes the pictures we make.

The very first Other Reader is the person called The Author, who has not only written the first iteration of the codes, s/he has written them reflexively, with purposes and an end in view, some conscious, many not. Like every reader, the author makes choices, which also means that other possible choices are not made or are deferred or only partially realized: choices about events, characters, locales, temporalities, all kinds of language investments, choices about publication venues. Those choices bring into play materials or even agents—a publisher for example—that impose an authority of their own, and therefore introduce additional horizons of meaning. Furthermore, in a work like *The Pioneers* Cooper necessarily submits his tale to precedent and even dead authorities: historical persons, places, and events. To see that is to realize how different interpretive moves will privilege some limited set of codependent agents, each of whom is as well the subjective center of an interpretation, empirically located or not. "The Ruined Cottage" is a special reading of a larger world, and so is *The Pioneers*.

So it happens that when we read in the same spirit that the author writ, as we should, we will—and the author will as well—be reading in a codependent counter-spirit. That counter-spirit is the offspring of the complex lifeworld of the original work. Here in 2013, we can know Cooper's work only through the ways it has come to be known through its past, emergent, and shape-shifting shape.

Elusive as it is, the shape does have an identity, however much it may keep getting redescribed. Everyone knows, for instance, that Cooper's work was written to explore and explain America and its history. We also know that, paradoxically, he leveraged his study from an improbably insignificant place and time: a small town in southwest-central New York state named after Cooper's father, who began its settlement in a by-moment of the early republic: the anti-climatic years 1785–1794, *not* the epochal revolutionary years 1776–1783.

Yet, as Thomas Philbrick has acutely remarked,

> The true country of Cooper's fiction is the world, stretching from Venice to Antarctica, from the deserts of northwestern Africa to the islands of the Pacific. It is a mistake, I think, to insist upon Cooper as a novelist of one region. . . . [And] at the center of the scheme . . . is a lake, the axis mundi of the little world of Otsego County.[1]

That is to see the world in a grain of sand, as Armitage could see a world through fragments scattered in a desolated rural place. It also helps to explain why I see, and want you to see, the title page of *The Pioneers* as a bibliographical axis mundi.

These are all commonplaces about *The Pioneers,* which is a fictional narrative that maps itself to an actual history, so that various dates, persons, events, people, and places continually impinge on and overlap the fiction. Crucially, because the mapping occurs as a documentary event, a student might take any documentary moment as a point of departure. My focus is the first edition title page, which represents a severely abbreviated summary of Cooper's book. In contemporary terms, it lays out the initial codescripts in the file's Header element. These scripts enable the coded subroutines that follow and depend upon it. The title page is the primary reading protocol in what we traditionally call the book's front matter.[2]

Before proceeding I must qualify my remark that "The title page is the primary reading protocol." That statement is largely true for the first edition of *The Pioneers,* but if applied to, say, Whitman's *Leaves of Grass* or almost any twentieth-century American book, the statement would be false. In those cases the primary reading protocols are laid down in the bindings and, if present, the dust jackets. *The Pioneers* was first published in dull boards. Not that those nondescript boards themselves lack significance. Are they present in the copy of *The Pioneers* I'm looking at? If they are, that's important, and if they're not that's important too. How important? Only a close investigation will tell.[3] For the codes that organize the documentary front matter of an early nineteenth-century book differ as much from a sixteenth- or seventeenth-century book as they do from a late nineteenth-century or twentieth-century book. And while different historical conventions can and should be recognized, ultimately every copy of every book—even every copy of every mass produced book—is, in a philological perspective, unique.

### *The Pioneers,* First Edition Title Page

This first printed page of Cooper's novel (Figure 1) delivers more significant information about the work than is apparent to a cursory view, which is what most title pages are given, except by specialist scholars.[4] We won't see what it's saying—how it prepares us to read on—until we know more of the whole story. A title page, *this* title page, establishes the general contours of the work's contextual relations. But it anticipates all those soon-to-be-unfolded relations in contoured and schematic form. That form is precisely what makes this document so valuable to scholarship and criticism. Unlike the ensuing fictional narrative, which affects completeness and completion, the title page declares itself a compressed and encrypted data file. For the reader, its bibliographic image aims to establish a horizon of reading interest. For the scholar, it fairly defines the character of the tale to come, which is itself, for all its elaborations, a contoured and schematic treatment of the historical world it recalls. As such, it needs explication. So if the body of the book of *The Pioneers* has unzipped the title page, its relation to the title page indexes its own relation to its referred historical field. An edition of *The Pioneers*—any edition—is itself a compressed and encrypted file. The set of all these files—the entire production and reception history of the book—is a fractal archive.

Thus the very form of the title page announces the need of a correspondent form of explication for the work as a whole. The pertinent form would not be interpretive exposition but a collage of annotation and glossing. As such, it would not only preserve the distinctive character of the field elements, subordinating coherent exposition to localized particulars. It would also license deep (expository) investigations of each of the distinctive field elements.[5]

So to develop a comprehensive critical account of *The Pioneers,* we want to watch carefully how its title page works as a bibliographical field.[6] We can begin with the printing layout of the page, which is in three sections arranged top to bottom in descending order of importance: title and author; epigraph; and finally publication and printing information. For rhetorical purposes I shall read the page from bottom to top—that is to say, from the text that the page's own conventions declare the least pertinent to the work's meanings, thence to the epigraph, and finally to the title/author texts, which properly dominate the page and the book. I take this reverse route through the page as an initial move to deform slightly our sense of its familiar features. Even a modest estrangement like this helps to open our doors of perception, since phenomena come to us wrapped in what Shelley called veils of familiarity.

I shall leave the subject of the type fonts unremarked except to point out a few matters of generally recognized pertinence: that different point sizes signal degrees of importance within the three page areas; that while the epigraph is in a small ten-point upper and lower case font, it gains special significance partly because of its central page position, and partly because all the other texts are either caps or small caps; and that this title is especially arresting because it is presented in an open face font. That

font does more than draw attention to the title, which is already the focus of the page. Because they mirror themselves, the characters turn
slightly iconic, artfully self-reflective.[7]

A word about the implicit significance of the general page design,
which is thoroughly conventional. Each element of the page identifies an
interpretive horizon for readers, whom the page itself declares the book's
immediate agents of meaning. Addressing those readers, the page identifies the readers' other participating agents and their authority-fields. The
printer names the work's medium of expression, the publisher its initial
(social) reading horizon. The epigraph signals the presence of the intertextuality that characterizes all expressive forms, here being more precisely signaled. The author specifies the conscious intentionality that first
organizes the work, and the title specifies an initial conceptual frame for
reading. Following the title and here unnamed author and title, the epigraph and the printing/publishing data thus further define the work's
field of intentionality in terms of agents other than the author. All of this
metadata is place and date-stamped, setting history in general, and a certain historical horizon in particular, as a special context of agency. By
specifying those agents the page declares that they all function in codependent relations to each other.

The physical form of that declaration—the title-page display—is crucial. The extensive white spaces move readers to see each page element
as distinctive, while the general page layout holds those separate parts in
a loose if also very clear relation, as in a collage. But unlike the layout of
the unfolding narrative in the body of the book,, the title page does not
work to weave everything into a seamless garment. Rather, it invites us to
register and initially grasp certain key general features of the discourse
field to come. The complexity of the book will be only weakly experienced if we are not ready to encounter its representations as a richly
partitioned matrix.

All of the front matter of a book like *The Pioneers* has this quality of
extranarrative distinctiveness. Front matter is replete with white page
space and the conceptual distinctions that such space fosters. Cooper's
dedication to his old friend Jacob Sutherland, his preface to his publisher,
and the changes to the front matter that come in later editions, from
Cooper or other parties, are important early glosses that get added to the
title page.[8]

With that as my own interpretive metadata, let's turn to the document
and try reading its code.

New York: / Published by Charles Wiley. / E. B. Clayton, Printer. / 1823.

Although rarely folded into interpretive readings, this conventional text is always full of significance, and never more so than in the present case. First, then, some explication of the characters.

The publisher is Charles Wiley (1782–1827), founder (1807) of the New York firm that is still operating, the oldest family-owned American publisher. He published five of Cooper's books: *The Spy* (1821), *The Pioneers* (1823), *The Pilot* (1823), *Tales of Fifteen* (1824), and *Lionel Lincoln* (1825). He was a close friend of Cooper's as well as the only publisher in Cooper's famous Bread and Cheese club. Cooper's 1823 preface underscores the personal relation between the two men and thereby their common interest in promoting the institution of American letters at this important moment of its history. Indeed, that project might be judged the principal object of all Cooper's work, an object he successfully gained, as we know from Cooper's reception history, not least of all in England and Europe. The back room of Wiley's New York offices, known as "The Den," was a regular gathering place for New York City intellectuals until Wiley died in 1827. The event induced Cooper to switch to Carey and Lea for his next novel, *The Prairie* (1828). The house of Wiley was responsible for some of the most important works of nineteenth-century American literature: two more books by Cooper, plus works by Poe, Irving, Melville, and others.

The place of publication is equally notable since New York was beginning to emerge at this time as a center of American letters to vie with Boston and Philadelphia, where religion and politics strongly shaped the publications. The ethos of New York publishing was notably marked by more practical and social interests, an inflection very clear in Cooper's case. Religion and politics certainly figure prominently in his work, not least in *The Pioneers*, but they are always brought forward and operate under a distinctively sociohistorical horizon. Cooper is "a New York Author."

E. B. Clayton, Printer. A complex history is signaled in that simple name, as James Franklin Beard's scholarly edition of 1980 makes abundantly clear.[9] The printer named on the first edition (first and second volumes) is the then prominent New York printer Edward B. Clayton. While his life dates are uncertain, he was printing books as early as 1819 and his offices were then located at 64 Pine Street. E. B. Clayton and Sons was operating out of 157 Pearl Street until late in the century. What needs to be stressed here, however, are three other related matters: first, that while the initial New York edition was printed by Clayton, it was issued at the beginning of February 1823 more or less simultaneously with a second edition; second, that the title page of volume one of the second edition reads "J. Seymour, Printer" (even as its second volume still reads "E. B. Clayton, Printer"); and third, that these texts all signal a prolonged and fraught initial printing process in which Wiley and Cooper were deeply engaged, not only with text changes and corrections, but with negotiations for an English edition. These were concluded with the famous John Murray firm, which issued the first English edition a few days after the American edition(s).[10]

J. Seymour is Jonathan Seymour (1778–1841), the most distinguished printer in New York at the time. He is perhaps most closely associated with the famous publishers Harper Brothers (James and John). John was a journeyman printer with Seymour until he and his brother founded their firm in 1817. Briefly, then, Seymour's name comes to the title page of the first volume of the second edition because Wiley and Cooper were trying to get control of the printing process. The first edition turned out to be full of Clayton's printing errors (for details see Beard 467–495, especially 469–473). In addition, however, the prolonged printing of the first two editions—from the spring of 1822 to late January 1823—led Cooper to a process of extensive revision. The printing delays had the fortuitous effect of bringing the book to public attention over a considerable period before its eventual publication. The book was announced to appear in early October 1822, but when circumstances blocked that event, Wiley made sure that newspapers during the next few months kept noticing the book and its anticipated appearance. Because Cooper's previous book, *The Spy*, had been a great success, much was expected of this new work. *The Pioneers* would achieve an even greater success when it was finally published.

Two other matters to observe. In a bibliographical sense, the information "IN TWO VOLUMES. VOL. I." comes at the top of the third section of the page. But its information has reference to both the publishing and printing information and the author/title information given in the first title page section. To observe this is also to realize the general rationale of the page's typographical design. Because they connect to each other through this shared information, sections one and three of the title page also rhyme with each other typographically, a fact underscored by their marked difference from the second section carrying the epigraph.

That typographical relation connects the last line of the title page, the 1823 publication date, with the first line, "The Pioneers," a tale descriptive of a pioneer settlement that other information in the book informs us was set in 1793–1794. Drawing this connection is important since the very different historical perspectives of 1793 and 1823, as well as their relation, shape the way we receive the fictional representations.

Extremes of habits, manners, time and space,
Brought close together, here stood face to face,
And gave at once a contrast to the view,
That other lands and ages never knew.
                                    —*Paulding.*


James Kirke Paulding (1778–1860), a prominent early New York literary figure, the close friend of Irving, and a member of the group of "Knick-
erbocker" writers. He was not a member of the Bread and Cheese Club.
It is probably coincidental, but nonetheless significant, that Cooper's first
effort to write a fiction in the mode of Walter Scott was published the
year that Paulding did the same with his novel *Koningsmarke.* The more
pertinent aspect of the epigraph is its source, Paulding's *The Backwoods-
man* (1818), a long, heavily moralized poem in heroic couplets of six
books and 176 pages. Cooper quotes book II, lines 571–574.

The suggestiveness of the epigraph is strongest if one is familiar with
Paulding's entire poem, as Cooper was and as he must have hoped his
readers would be. Though we often forget it, the resonance of retrieved
quotations is often as much a function of what they leave out as of what
they recover. This is certainly the case here. Cooper is opening a dialogue
with other representations of frontier America, using Paulding as a point
of contrast to set off his own very different representation. Simply, Paulding's poem is the story of a journey rather than, like *The Pioneers,* the
story of a place; and a journey past the "dear haunts of social men,"
which are Cooper's focus, to "rougher scenes" beyond the western frontier of the Ohio River. The hero of the poem is Basil, who leaves his home
near the Hudson to travel west and eventually settle on the frontier. The
villain of the poem is a renegade Briton who musters the western tribes
to a battle against a settlement, where the poem sets its bloody climax.
When Cooper in his preface to the first edition urges readers to "throw
[his book] aside at once" if they are looking for "strong excitement" as
from gods, spooks, witches, battles, or murders, he sets his work far apart
from Paulding's, and of course from other sensational fictions as well.

Paulding's verse is constructed around a set of very simple contrasts.
First, fierce Indians stand opposed to intrepid white settlers. Second,
while the settlers come from various parts of Europe, they divide neatly
into heroes and villains—or in this case, heroes and villain, for white
wickedness is poured into a single man called the "renegade," all other
settlers being adventurous and brave lovers of liberty. For Cooper, such
impoverished distinctions pervade the Euro-American view of the society
of the New World. Cooper assembles a host of very different characters

in his tale in order to expose the complexities of what might to a superficial view appear as a "bland society" of white America.

Two further points raised by the epigraph deserve comment. First of all, Cooper's "Extremes of habits, manners, time and space" are largely tracked through white society and his understanding of that society. The coming *Leatherstocking Tales* and their associated books—most importantly *The Wept of Wish-ton-Wish, Wyandotté,* the *Home* volumes, and "The Littlepage Trilogy"—radically expand and deepen one's view of those extremes, and not only for the Euro-American world. If Euro-America always remains Cooper's chief focus and interest, his works show that engaging its complexities requires a sympathetic investment in at least some of the sociohistory of native America. The books that follow *The Pioneers* thus involve extended commentaries on these other, native "Extremes of habits, manners, time and space."

Second, Cooper measures these extremes along multiple axes. We register this perhaps most clearly in *The Pioneers* through secondary characters like the palatine descendant Major Hartmann and the Frenchman Le Quoi. Le Quoi, who is unimportant for the book's central plot action, is particularly interesting. When we reflect on how he is presented—a refugee from his Martinique plantations who will return to his native France at the end of Cooper's book—a perspective enters *The Pioneers* that is both surprising and important. Cooper wants us to see that the history directly viewed in *The Pioneers* is indirectly calling up other, related world histories. As we shall we, the French Revolution and the history of Caribbean slave revolts are oblique but significant presences in *The Pioneers.*

But the most extreme of the "Extremes of habits, manners, time and space" are those that set "face to face" the native and the colonist. While Cooper's representations stand far apart from Paulding's cartoon, his book has only one native American, Chingachgook. Paradoxically, while he is clearly represented in a white and western perspective, Chingachgook emerges nonetheless as a complex character whom neither we nor any of the white characters in the book understand, not even his old friends and companions, Natty Bumppo and Edward Effingham. He is mysterious because even the most sympathetic white perspectives (which include Cooper's) leave him alienated. Critics of Cooper often discount his work because of its undernourished representation of native Americans. But a slight shift of perspective shows that this dimension of his work is one of its greatest strengths. Chingachgook in *The Pioneers* functions quite like the doubloon in *Moby-Dick*. Seen differently by the various characters, he becomes a distorted mirror of each. The mirror is distorted because Cooper fashioned it from the critical sympathy he brought to his characters, including Chingachgook. Cooper's racism, integral to his sympathetic metabolism, is integral to the representational strength of his work.[11]

THE

## PIONEERS,

OR THE

SOURCES OF THE SUSQUEHANNA;

A DESCRIPTIVE TALE.

*BY THE AUTHOR OF "PRECAUTION."*

Cooper's story supplies his particular and extended gloss on this title page, and especially on these words. But the story is in fact only one account of "the history" represented in the book. In his preface to the 1832 (English) edition Cooper tells that audience that "the history of this district of country [i.e., "The interior of the province of New York"], so far as it is connected with civilized man, is soon told." But Cooper's ensuing account—eight brief paragraphs—drastically truncates the conflicted and often exceedingly violent years that make up the context of his story. Indeed, the very length of his fictional representations will only further clarify how much that is pertinent to this history—not least its understanding of "civilized man"—has been left mis- or un-represented.

Let's begin with a striking absent presence. Why is Cooper's name not spelled out? The situation is nothing like, for instance, the title pages of Scott's Waverley novels. Here no mystery is involved about "The Author of 'Precaution'" (1820), whereas mystification was a key purpose in those famous words "By the Author of Waverley." If the words here mean to inform the reader that Cooper is a known and successful author—a conventional bibliographical formula—why not name *The Spy* (1821), which Wiley published, as he did not publish *Precaution?* Besides, while *Precaution* was well received, *The Spy* had a celebrated debut.

Whatever other explanations might serve, the bibliographical move clearly subordinates the author to the work. In that respect it underscores Cooper's view of his purpose as a writer: "All fine writing"—he is talking about imaginative writing or "polite literature"—"must have its roots in the ideas" that drive the writing.[12] Aesthetic and formal concerns were for him secondary, a means "to elucidate the history, manners, usages, and scenery, of his native land."[13] For a book that draws so much of its material from very personal sources, everything on the title page marks the author not primarily as an individual but as an American.

Even more consequent are the title and elaborate subtitle and their three key words: Pioneers, Sources, and Susquehanna. As we shall see, Cooper is notably alive to the social and political importance of words and names. The title invokes three languages, though two are subordinated to the dominant language, English. In that respect the title marks the ethnopolitical focus of Cooper's "Descriptive Tale," where important matters will often be made invisible or left to inference. Two words in the title have a French source, though here they are "Englished." The other is native American—in fact, it is a word from the Delaware or Lenni Lenape language.

English so dominates these title words that we become aware of the other languages only by conscious effort. French is least important because it has but an etymological presence, and only twice does Cooper ask us to reflect on the French connections in his book, one of which I will discuss below.[14] But the Delaware language is literally present and quite significant. While the word references a river in both Delaware and English, the meaning of the word (and the river) in each language is different. Cooper himself suggests this when he gives the name Chingachgook to the old Delaware chief, who to English speakers is known by the condescending English nickname "Indian John" or "John Mohegan." Because Cooper represents his book's two key Delaware words, Susquehanna and Chingachgook, as ethnographic rhymes—an important matter I will shortly examine—he has also coded the word "Sources" linguistically and geopolitically.[15] That coding is further exposed by the two syntaxes the title has put into play: one marks an equation between "Pioneers" and "the Sources of the Susquehanna," the other marks a difference (people *vs.* places). The words "Sources" and "Susquehanna" both have multiple and overlapping reference points within the discourse fields of American "history, manners, usages, and scenery." Of what, then, is this book a "Descriptive Tale"?[16]

That is a far more complicated question than might at first appear, as Cooper's revealing introduction to the 1832 English edition of *The Pioneers* shows. "New York having but one county of Otsego," he writes, "and the Susquehanna but one proper source, there can be no mistake as to the site of the tale." But if the river has only one true source, why does the title refer to its "Sources"?

In one respect we understand what he has in mind. When Cooper insists on the "one proper source" he is assenting to the then emerging scientific view that the North Branch—which rises at the foot of Otsego

Lake—is the Susquehanna's single "proper source," rather than the West Branch, which rises in western Pennsylvania and never leaves that state, flowing east to join the North Branch at present-day Sunbury.[17] So Cooper is using the controversy—very much alive in the eighteenth century—about the "proper source" of the Susquehanna in order to emphasize the importance of the Upper Susquehanna region of New York. This was a fraught and violent scene of the "Border Wars" during the years of the Revolution. *The Pioneers* describes the aftermath of those wars, the period when Cooper's father William established a pioneer settlement with cultivated social ideals. The book is a "Descriptive Tale" of the sociohistory of the late colonial and early republican periods "of this [New York] district of country, so far as it is connected with civilized man." That final remarks glances at the violent histories, native and nonnative, that the book, like Cooper's father, meant to leave behind.

But the words "one proper source" itself recognizes the presence of other Sources, and the widely meandering Susquehanna is an index of those multiple sources. If in a geophysical sense there is only one proper source of the Susquehanna, it has multiple tributary sources, as any riverine map of the Susquehanna watershed shows—not least the region of the upper watershed defined by the river's North Branch (Figure 2).

That topographical condition invests the word "Sources" with a much wider range of significance. If Otsego Lake is the point of reference and the people of the Templeton settlement area specify the book's subject, then we track the region's sources to the people involved with the settlement. The histories of those people then become important sources for understanding the settlement. Although Cooper will focus our attention on a frontier region of New York, a more expansive view of America pervades the book and is signaled on the title page.

The 1832 preface summarizes, in eight succinct paragraphs, what Cooper regards as the salient information about the geography and history of his story's focused area. Strikingly, half of that account treats the famous (or infamous) Sullivan Expedition of 1779, which mounted a three-pronged extermination campaign to lay waste the native American villages in central and western New York, Pennsylvania, and Ohio, the remaining stronghold of the Six Nations of the Iroquois federation (Figure 3).[18] This is the region of both the upper and the middle Susquehanna watersheds, and as we shall see, Cooper's tale is deeply connected to the whole region. With the exception of certain of the Oneidas and Tuscaroras, the federated tribes sided with the British in the Revolutionary War. Cooper's preface indicates that Sullivan's expedition effectively opened the region to non-native settlement on a broad scale, which in this case

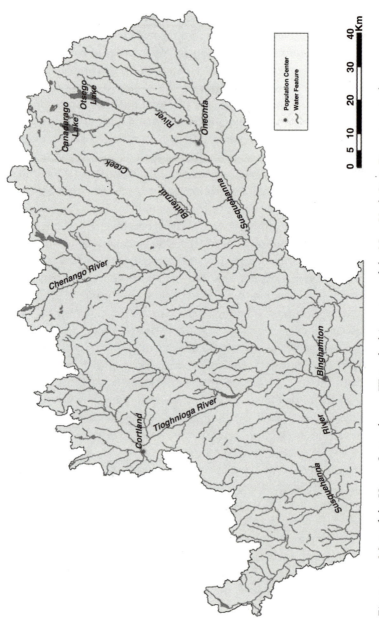

*Figure 2.* Map of the Upper Susquehanna Watershed (courtesy of the New York State Department of Environmental Conservation, http://www.dec.ny.gov/lands/53674.html).

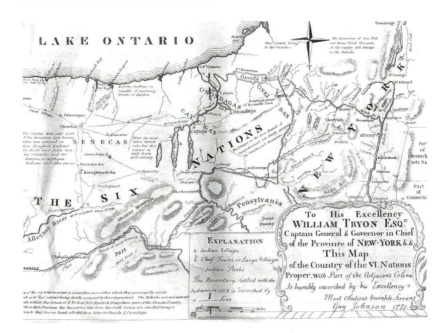

*Figure 3.*   Guy Johnson's 1771 *Map of the Country of the VI. Nations* showing the Fort Stanwix Treaty Line (1768) (from reproduction in Edmund B. O'Callaghan, *Documentary History of the State of New York* [Albany: C. Van Benthuysen, 1851]: IV. 1090; courtesy of *Albert and Shirley Small Special Collections Library, University of Virginia*).

Cooper dates to 1785, eight years before the year of his story's action. As early maps of the region show, the land west of colonial New York's Tryon County—including the region of Cooper's tale—was designated "Indian Country" before the Sullivan Expedition, after which the Iroquois were driven away and settled further west and north. At that point the descriptors "Indian Country" or "Country of the Six Nations" disappears from the maps.

Cooper tells an important truth about the border region when he recalls the Sullivan Expedition for his English readers. But he does not tell anything like the whole truth. The Sullivan Expedition was the climactic event in the "Border Wars" that ravaged the country of central and southwestern New York and northeastern Pennsylvania between 1774 and the end of the Revolution in 1783.[19] Cooper's account of the expedition is as important for what it says as for what it leaves unsaid. The account means to explain how the expedition made possible the "civilized" settlement of a place like Cooperstown/Templeton. It thus glosses the title word "Pioneers," but strictly limits the word's focus to the years following the expedition, and in particular to the years 1785–1794. Thrown out of focus, however, are the previous years of frontier settlement, and especially—so far as *The Pioneers* is concerned—the previous ten years.

A more unequivocally "patriotic" book than *The Pioneers* would have marked those as the triumphant years of the Revolutionary War. But for Cooper's book—and his other related books reinforce this[20]—those are primarily remembered as the tormented years of an American internecine war that pitted neighbor against neighbor, Crown Loyalist against Colonial Rebel.[21] Nowhere were those Border Wars more fierce and bloody than in the region of what we now call the Upper Susquehanna watershed. One has only to name a few of the famous battles and massacres that took place during the period: Oriskany, Springfield, Cherry Valley, Wyoming, and of course Sullivan's culminant scorched earth campaign designed to break British power in the region by utterly destroying the world of Britain's Indian allies.

A full recovery of that history is important for understanding key elements in Cooper's book, each of which gets focused in those three key words: Pioneers, Sources, and Susquehanna. Consider the principal word in the title, "Pioneers," which we initially identify with the people of Cooperstown/Templeton. But there were earlier settlers, and it is a striking fact that the word only appears in the book three times. Two of these are particularly strategic, framing as they do the whole book: first on the title page, and then again in the final sentence, when it specifically refers not to the "civilized" settlers of Templeton, but to Natty Bumppo.[22] Natty is a sixty-eight year old *coureur des bois*, very much an anachronistic figure in the time frame of *The Pioneers*, a man whose frontier life in the region dates back to the mid-1740s. If Judge Temple/William Cooper brought "civilization" to the region, as Cooper argues, earlier pioneers brought exploration, settlement, and violence. Cooper represents the region before the emergence of Cooperstown/Templeton as a wilderness. It was not, as the Sullivan Campaign itself testifies. But the region was not just inhabited by native Americans. Years before the Revolution, Augustin Prevost and George Croghan, for example, had set up residences at the northern and southern ends of Otsego Lake itself, and the early history of New York records the residences and activities of many others.[23] The lives of these settlers became as precarious as the lives of the Indians during the Border Wars, when thousands were either killed or forced to flee.

The pioneers marked by the title are thus a distinct second generation who occupy the land after it has been cleared of those who preceded them, both native and immigrant. These earlier people are all but cleared from *The Pioneers* as well. But not altogether. Cooper preserves their trace memory in Major Effingham, Natty Bumppo, and Chingachgook. All three haunt the book and its sources, but one—the early pioneer Major Effingham—dominates the plot.

None of that Border War history is explicitly present in *The Pioneers,* however—an anomalous fact in light of Cooper's 1832 preface. Yet it is but a portion of other and larger histories that pervade the action. One of these—the book's most extensive historical context—I shall leave unexamined. But I briefly note its presence here since it shows how the local histories in all of Cooper's tales are invested with large historical import. The New York Border Wars located merely the northernmost extent of conflicts that began to rage all along the Allegheny frontier in the aftermath of the French and Indian War (1763). After that bloody conflict England tried to bring peace to the region by establishing a definitive border between colonial settlement and Indian Territory. But the effort not only failed, it hastened another war, the American Revolution. The royal Proclamation of 1763 set the border vaguely at the Alleghenies, the Treaty of Fort Stanwix (1768) tried to reset it more firmly and further to the west (see Figure 3). But in the southern regions of the border a different line was drawn at the Treaty of Hard Labour (1768), and the contradiction with the Fort Stanwix Treaty was only resolved with the Treaty of Lochaber (1770). In truth, as those volatile treaties indicate, the border was continually being violated by American settlers, and the Indians continually retaliated with corresponding violence. Lord Dunmore's War (1774) is a Virginian equivalent of the New York Border Wars. The sources of the American Revolution on the western frontier had little to do with taxation without representation. They had everything to do with American land and the problems of its settlement, legal and nonlegal. For Cooper, the Susquehanna watershed supplied a perfect example of the historical complexity of those problems.

In *The Pioneers* that larger context emerges into view only occasionally and in oblique ways. Yet it is the history that organizes the plot of the book, which is fundamentally gothic, being driven by the mystery of a man whose very name is uncertain: Oliver Edwards, Young Eagle, or Edward Oliver Effingham.[24] The mystery of this person is bound up with the secret histories of the other principal characters, all of whom define features of the social domain announced in the book's elaborate title. Cooper works to reveal the secrets of this domain only in a very special point of view. His book's primary purpose is to reconcile the interests of two groups of American pioneers who fell out with each other over the Revolution: Crown sympathizers, on one hand, and colonial revolutionaries on the other.

That is not the history *The Pioneers* was written to *tell*, it is the history it was written to conceal and then, in a final *eclaircissement,* expose. That is precisely the argument of its gothic machinery. Both the concealment and the exposure touch other hidden histories that therefore come to us only in the somewhat distorted mirror of Cooper's perspective. Because he does not treat all of his book's secrets candidly, when plot resolution comes, as it does, not all the conflicts are resolved. So in reading the book we inevitably face certain questions about what and how Cooper wants us to see, as well as what and how he makes it hard for us to see.

A useful place to begin deciphering that perspective is at Natty Bumppo's pioneer hut, which is situated up the eastern shore of Otsego Lake (Templeton is located at the extreme southwestern tip). Little about this hut is explicitly told in the book, but once we finish the story its concealed truths become available. The hut, for example, was built on the lake well before Templeton was founded. It represents a period of pioneer settlement before what Cooper calls the "civilized" period of Templeton. (Many years later Cooper will write two books about that earlier period, *Deerslayer* and *Wyandotté.*) Moreover, Natty Bumppo and Chingachgook have not been the only inhabitants of the hut. Oliver Edwards is a recent and known arrival, though we don't understand why until the book's conclusion. Also living with them—a crucial secret unrevealed until the plot has been completely unwound—is the now senile major Effingham, whose pre–Revolutionary War land rights, as we eventually learn, rested in his Delaware identity.

Much of the significance of major Effingham is left to inference. He has a native-American name, Fire Eater, because he became an adopted chief of the Delaware nation. Like many other early frontier settlers, he gained his Crown patents because of his connection to the Delaware people. According to Chingachgook, the connection established a blood right in his grandson, Young Eagle. At the end of the book, as he tells his personal history to Judge Temple, his future father-in-law, he denies that he has any Delaware blood (chapter 40). Perhaps the truth was kept from Oliver, or perhaps he is lying to the judge, who would not be pleased to learn that Oliver is "a man with a cross." *The Pioneers* maintains a majestic silence about Oliver's native, matrilineal heritage. Early settlers like Sir William Johnson and George Croghan—the historical models for major Effingham—regularly married or had children with native women, as Cooper was well aware.[25] Cooper deplored racial mixing, however, and as Barbara Mann has clearly shown, he worked hard to convince his readers that, whatever Chingachgook tells us about Oliver, Natty was "a man without a cross."[26]

Only traces of that history remain visible in *The Pioneers,* where the action has shifted from lower down in the Susquehanna watershed—the land of the Delaware nation in eastern Pennsylvania—to the western frontier of central New York. The geographical shift is important because it suggests not only how major Effingham came to be secretly housed in Natty Bumppo's hut, but what his presence there signifies. Once again Cooper supplies only sketchy details about matters of significance, and once again the dominant issue is land title.

Oliver's father, Edward, whose death is discovered (but not revealed) in the midst of the unfolding tale, had been Judge Temple's business partner in Pennsylvania. The two men fell out during the Revolution, Edward Effingham siding with the Crown, the judge with the insurgents. Like many Crown loyalists, Oliver's father left Pennsylvania in 1783 or soon thereafter, fleeing east and north to Nova Scotia, where he left Oliver with major Effingham to seek redress in England for the property confiscated from his father after the war. Major Effingham's title claim is primarily a native claim, however, not British, as Chingachgook explains (chapters 12 and 36).

In fact, the dispute about the land claim has much less to do with British cession or American confiscation than with a much earlier dispute between the Iroquois and the Delaware people. That too figures among the Sources of this tale. The dispute is the foundation for Cooper's mythic presentation of the hatred between the Mingoes (Iroquois) and the Delaware, famously elaborated in *The Last of the Mohicans,* the next book in Cooper's Leatherstocking series. When the British sought to establish land claim to large areas of Delaware territory, principally in eastern Pennsylvania, the Iroquois wanted to cement good relations with the Crown by granting its request. At the Grand Council of 1742 when the Iroquois ordered the Delaware to give way to the British, they refused. That falling out between Delaware and Iroquois—which Cooper knew from John Heckewelder, if not from various other possible sources—sets up the famous antagonism in Cooper's Leatherstocking fictions, spectacularly presented in *The Last of the Mohicans.*[27] It is equally the ground for the plot action of *The Pioneers,* where Cooper works to reconcile all conflict about the future of the land. This reconciliation is figured at the novel's end in the marriage of Judge Temple's daughter Elizabeth to Oliver Edwards/Young Eagle, now also identified as Edward Oliver Effingham, the son of the judge's deceased business partner and grandson of Fire Eater/Major Oliver Effingham.

Given what Oliver tells us about his history after 1783, we must infer that the major moved with his son and grandson to British Nova Scotia, whence the father went to England while the grandfather and Oliver moved to Connecticut. Oliver eventually joined his father in England, returning to America shortly before the action of Cooper's tale. While Oliver was in England, Natty and Chingachgook brought the old man from Connecticut to live on the land that had belonged to him, according to both British Colonial and native American law, before the Revolution. Since Oliver was able to track his grandfather to Natty's hut on Otsego Lake when he returned to America in early 1793, we realize that he, Natty, and Chingachgook had somehow maintained contact during these years. In fact, their connection is more intimate still, dating back to the period before the Border Wars when they all resided in the Pennsylvania region of the Middle Susquehanna watershed. This is where Natty and Chingachgook, a Delaware chief, met and grew up together, as Cooper later told his daughter Susan.[28] We finally learn (chapter 40) that Natty was the major's devoted attendant even before the Border Wars.

Judge Temple gained title to the land around Otsego—which is but a small portion of Fire Eater's domain—by buying up the original Crown patents which, as he finally reveals, he has held in trust for his former business partner, Oliver's father. In that move the judge signals his conviction that the United States now has complete land sovereignty and that if he is to secure rights to the land, and protect the original rights of the Effinghams, he has to buy the land in the American speculative market. But in the view of Natty, Chingachgook, Oliver, and (were he *compos mentis*) major Effingham, Oliver retains his right to the land through his Delaware bloodline. To Chingachgook, Oliver's name is Young Eagle. Indeed, Cooper's books repeatedly remind us, as *The Pioneers* and *Wyandotté* make especially clear, that the Treaty of Paris would not, even in American law, have extinguished certain Indian land rights. The forfeit of British claims would not necessarily entail the forfeit of native claims, a fact that the new American government itself acknowledged when it set about trying to renegotiate various Indian treaties after the Revolution.[29]

That Cooper takes seriously Oliver's claim to the land is evident in the book's plot. As his names imply, Oliver is a kind of double agent in *The Pioneers,* the descendant of both a British loyalist and a Delaware chief. That he has a Delaware rather than an Iroquois identity is crucial since, in Cooper's reading of native history, the Delaware never relinquished their land rights to the British.[30] Indeed, in the Treaty of Fort Pitt (1778)— the first treaty ever made between an Indian nation and the emerging American government—the lands as far west as Detroit were explicitly declared to be sovereign Delaware territory. This is the claim that Chingachgook speaks of in chapter 12. As Edward Oliver Effingham—the direct descendant of Edward and Major Oliver Effingham—his marriage to Elizabeth heals the cultural breach between loyalist and rebel American that emerged in the Border Wars. As Young Eagle, the descendant of Eagle (his father's Delaware name) and Fire Eater, his marriage effectively resolves the question of Delaware and American land rights.

What this does not resolve, however, is the position of Leatherstocking and Chingachgook in the "civilized" world projected at the end of the book. One dies and the other moves on. As a mythic imagination of the future of America, *The Pioneers* does not imagine where or how they will fit in that promised land. That irresolution is especially notable because, as Cooper's reception history shows, these two men represent a moral center far more mysterious and powerful than the moral outcome—the marriage—produced by Cooper's gothic tale. Rather than plot a definition of what they represent, Cooper locates and then tracks them in a vast and transhuman Otherworld with a magically realist name— Susquehanna—whose meaning ramifies from its initial double significance. Susquehanna is both a vast watershed extending from Virginia to central New York; and also a once powerful native American tribal federation. Taking a large perspective one might think of *Moby-Dick*. As Melville sails the world under the sign of an extinct down east nation, the Pequots, Cooper's global journeys begin under the sign of the extinct Susquehannocks. And I remark in passing that Melville, a great admirer of Cooper, would have known Heckewelder's (correct) view that these two tribes came from a common native American stock. In this respect, *Moby-Dick* is a dark interpreter of Cooper's Leatherstocking Tales.[31]

The native word Susquehanna is as mysterious in its meaning to this day as Cooper's Chingachgook. "Hanna" means river but no agreement has yet been reached about the meaning of "Susque." Cooper, however, decides to tell his readers that it means "Crooked River" (in a note to chapter 12). He does this to associate the Delaware chief Chingachgook, "the Great Serpent," with the river.[32] He and Natty both trace their early history to the middle portion of the Susquehanna watershed near the mouths of the Delaware and Susquehanna rivers—the territory of the Susquehannock tribes who occupied the land when it was first explored by Captain John Smith in the early seventeenth century. The upper right quadrant of Smith's famous (1612) map of Virginia (Figure 4) is dominated by the majestic figure of an Indian and carries the legend: "The Sasquesahanougs are a Giant like people and thus atyred." At the mouth of the Susquehanna Cooper locates a key set of sources for events that his book tracks to the middle and upper regions of the great river.

*Figure 4.* John Smith's (1608) *Map of Virginia,* first published in 1612. The map is oriented to the west (facsimile reproduction courtesy of *Albert and Shirley Small Special Collections Library, University of Virginia*).

The Susquehannocks were the controlling power in the region from the upper Chesapeake Bay to central New York throughout the seventeenth century. They were a federation of tribes who waged wars with adjacent tribes and made tributaries of those they mastered (including the Lenape or Delaware—i.e., Chingachgook's—tribe). The authority of the Susquehannocks was itself finally broken in the late seventeenth century and they were made tributary to the Five Nations (Iroquois), their principal enemy. But in Cooper's myth, Chingachgook and his father rejected assimilation, as his friendship and travels with Natty Bumppo and the Effinghams signifies.

In the context of the Susquehanna watershed and its 200 years of complex and fraught American histories, those personal relations imagined by Cooper become a symbolic constellation that he will expand and explore in all of his works. Chingachgook in particular reveals the historical significance of his allegiance to Oliver Edwards/Edward Oliver Effingham/Young Eagle when he remarks in chapter 12: "Go to the highest hill, and look around you. All that you see, from the rising to the setting sun, from the head-waters of the great spring, to where the 'crooked river' is hid by the hills, is his. He has Delaware blood, and his right is strong." Cooper is plainly looking to the four quarters of the horizon from Mount Vision, which rises 500 feet above Otsego Lake just to the east of Cooperstown/Templeton. The view from that point would encompass the patents bought up by William Cooper/Judge Temple.

Chingachgook's words have a double meaning, and while Cooper intimates both, he makes only one of them clear. The speech is plainly relevant to the question of land rights, supplying terms that help Cooper arrange the final resolution of claims. In that resolution Oliver denies his Delaware blood right but claims his Western patrimony. But Chingachgook does not assert Indian ownership of the land, though Young Eagle's "[Delaware blood] right is strong." What he describes is a sacral rather than a legal right, part of a native American ethos that Cooper—like Heckewelder and many Euro-Americans—quite understood. Indeed, understanding it allowed many colonists, especially British colonists, to assert land claims by right of purchase from nations that were dealing in rights of use—famously, "hunting grounds"—rather than ownership. After the Revolution, that native American conception of right was simply "extinguished" by American law.

All that is relevant to *The Pioneers* (and its related books) because of Cooper's interest in the complex political and ethno-history of the American continent. The conflicts between the colonial powers, and for Cooper especially the conflicts between the loyalist and revolutionary English populations, mirror the conflicts that marked and divided various tribal federations and nations.[33] But that representation of native American wars and violence comes in a Western mythic mirror. It is a Euro-American translation of native history and culture into a Western ontology.

The ecological history of the Susquehanna watershed dates from about 20,000 years ago as the glaciers began receding from northeast America. For Cooper, the human knowledge of that ecological history was most deeply understood by the native peoples, who alone, in the purview of his work, had an extensive historical investment in it. The great original settlement of North America occurred in several migrations sometime before 12,000 BCE, and developed forms of native culture were clearly in place throughout the continent as early as 5000 BCE.[34]

Cooper begins to describe in earnest the special native American relation to the land in *The Last of the Mohicans*, and he continues to explore it as late as *Satanstoe* (1845).[35] However deracinated they may have become in his view, his Indians appear learned in the secret lore of the natural world, and their histories are coded in the environment. Because the biosphere is for Cooper the book of God himself, native American culture is for him a primitive (and so a failed) effort to translate the word of God. But then because that culture is so alien to his Western mind, he translates it to the language of Leatherstocking, in whom it can regain at least a measure of its original alien genius. That is why Cooper's most intensely spiritual natural scenes and events—the view of Glens Falls in *The Last of the Mohicans*, for instance, or his remarkable essay on the eclipse he witnessed in June 1806, or the conclusion of *The Crater*—all seem his white and western translations of a native American ecological consciousness.[36]

That Cooper's knowledge of these matters was not merely bookish—he was raised in Cooperstown from his fourth year—is clear from various small details in his stories—for instance this passage in *The Pioneers*, chapter 12:

> After following the course of one of the streets of the village, for a short distance, Mr. Grant, who led the way, turned into a field, through a pair of open bars, and entered a foot-path, of but sufficient width to admit of only one person to walk in it, at a time.

This path is an Indian trail, though Cooper has not explicitly marked it for his readers. He then adds a further, even more telling detail for those who are able to understand: "The path was beaten so hard, that [a person] moved with ease along its windings." Such trails have been there a

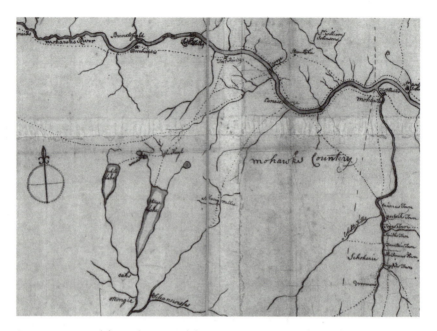

*Figure 5.*    Detail from the map of the *Country Between the Mohawk River and [the] Wood Creek from an Actual Survey in November of 1758,* known as the *Map of the Country of the Five Nations* (courtesy of the Library of Congress: LOC Map no. 156). [The dotted lines show some of the Indian trails.]

very long time, and colonial maps of "Indian Country" mark their presence (Figure 5).

As several of Cooper's books show in much greater detail—*The Last of the Mohicans, The Pathfinder,* and *The Chainbearer,* for example—those trails were crucial features of the social space of the colonial world of the great Susquehanna watershed.

## II

To this point my commentary has been excavating historical contexts that stand behind the book as its events are imagined during the year of December 1793–December 1794. That corresponds to the ninth year of the settlement of Cooperstown by Cooper's father. But as the title page shows, the book's other historical pivot point is 1823. That year primarily turns the reader's attention forward from 1793, rather than backward. In that respect and from *our* vantage, *The Pioneers* turns up Cooper's effort to develop a conception of the social and political significance of the United States in the world historical context of his own time. Cooper's entire *oeuvre* unfolds as the execution of that purpose. The subsequent works in the Leatherstocking series and the books closely related to the series—*Wyandotté* and *Home as Found* are perhaps the most prominent—show Cooper adding new documents to his imaginary historical archive. These are the founding documents of Cooper's America, and in the chronology of their publication we observe the evolution of his interpretation of his own, heavily documented, ideas.[37]

An extensive commentary, related to the present one, would thus work its way forward from 1823. An ecocritical view would note that Cooper's book foretells the extinction of two significant American fauna: the eastern cougar and the carrier pigeon, whose migrating flocks were so vast they could darken the sun for days. Or another exercise in critical bibliography might take its focus from the first English or the first French edition (both also published in 1823), where the global significance of Cooper's work begins to become apparent. Important as that study line is, I want to end my commentary by reflecting on the thirty years after 1793, rather than the thirty years before. Digging into the date on the title page offers, as Whitman might say, a backward glance o'er roads that Cooper's mind traveled between 1793 and 1823. I'll focus on just two matters.

The first involves the one French connection that is pertinent to *The Pioneers* in both its 1793–1794 and its 1823 historical relation. It comes through the minor character Le Quoi, the only person in the book whose fictional name corresponds to his historical identity.[38] Le Quoi is a political refugee from Martinique, and at the end of Cooper's tale he is about to leave for Paris. Like all the pioneers in the book, including the minor ones, Le Quoi is a representative type who calls attention to historical issues that Cooper wants to bring forward. Having recently fled his plantation on Martinique, he is presented as one of the many royalists who fled the island when civil war broke out between royalists and revolutionaries in 1790–1791. Cooper is also calling attention to the British invasion and occupation of the island in 1794. The British reinstated the Old Regime authorities on the island and rescinded the abolition of slavery that had been promulgated in Paris earlier in 1794. Le Quoi's planned return to Paris at the end of 1794 is clearly meant to recall the death in July of Robespierre and the emergence of the reactionary White Terror in France. Equally important is the recollection of those events in the context of 1823, the year after the French authorities put down a slave revolt on the island. Forty eight slaves were severely punished: twenty-one were

executed, ten were sent to forced labor for life, and seventeen were ordered to severe whippings.[39]

Cooper was far from an abolitionist nor even friendly to the idea of
emancipation. He himself owned slaves, and all his African American
characters are cloaked with derision. Le Quoi and Martinique do not
come into *The Pioneers* to urge readers to think critically on the question
of slavery. That, however, is an inevitable consequence of their presence.
Cooper uses Le Quoi primarily to draw a contrast between the American
and the French revolutions, as we see when Le Quoi's marriage proposal
to Elizabeth is refused. The American Revolution distinguished itself by
founding a stable republican government as well as a relatively stable
social order. For Cooper, the French failed in both respects. In seeing
Cooper's purpose here, however, later readers—certainly ourselves—
recognize how Le Quoi might have functioned in the political arguments
mounted by *The Pioneers*. Precisely because Cooper does not exploit the
slavery questions that Le Quoi's history brings forward, later readers
get licensed to think critically about Cooper's racism and its American
foundations.

We get an even more important critical view of *The Pioneers* from another post-1793 historical perspective. Cooper wrote and published the
work in the final years of the debacle that was wiping out virtually the
entire land wealth that his father had so spectacularly, and so precariously, built. The story has been well told by Alan Taylor, who sums up the
events this way: "The estate that [William] Cooper had built upon the
controversial auction at Mabie's Tavern in 1786 vanished in the forced
auctions of the 1820s. Ultimately Cooper's vision of entrenching an
enduring lineage of wealth and power proved as evanescent as George
Croghan's."[40] The lands passed to his family by the great speculator
William Cooper[41] would be bought up by a new generation of equally
enterprising and unscrupulous speculators. Of this darkly ironic symmetry Walter Scott might well have said that "coming events cast their
shadow before"—a poetic text that was, or would become, a favorite of
Cooper's.

The final words of Cooper's elaborate title, "A Descriptive Tale," could
well have been—and in certain respects would better have been—"A
Gothic Romance." The book has a clear gothic plot and is in that respect
a book of many secrets. One of those secrets—"the forced auctions of the
1820s"—is an important source for the book's romantic view of an
American frontier settlement founded in much blood and ruthless capitalist enterprise. But that is not how Cooper wanted his book to remember
the "civilized" settlement founded by his father. Cooperstown/Templeton

was made to illustrate the American republic as a "compassionate country," as he called it in his first edition's preface. The world evoked in the book, he says in that preface, was "dear to me," and his "feeling" for it—again, his word—was perhaps more dear than ever as he kept a dismal watch over its loss after his father's death.

My commentary on this title page might have gone out much further and in much deeper. I'm sure that Randall McLeod, in one or another of his incarnations, would have quickly observed that I've actually been commenting much less on a document than on a generalized documentary event: the first edition title page of the book rather than the particular copy of the first edition that I was working with and that I've reproduced here. And he would be right, for that copy has its own buried memory that is most clearly signaled in the manuscript markings on the title page, about which I have said nothing at all. This copy is meta-coded (and hence explicated) in the library catalogues of the University of Virginia, where the copy resides along with three other, quite different copies of the first edition. The early printing history of Cooper's famous book can be glimpsed in those four copies, as can the book's subsequent reception history, which encompasses the provenance of those copies.[42] Nor is my personal part in that history irrelevant, for University of Virginia's Special Collections is where I do much of my work. Not without reason have I taken this document for my text. Indeed, it's important that we should see what a special case I've been laying out here.

A properly critical understanding—a philological understanding—would regard every document as a special case, even when the documents are machine printed. The reason is simple, though in our interpretive pursuits we often forget it: on one hand, a document is a specific material object that has passed through a particular, if also vastly complex, transmission history; on the other hand, the interpreter of the document is equally, *codependently* shaped to a specific moment, location, and set of interests. Reception history is merely (exactly) transmission history unfolding through a different phase space, and both are functions of particular acts of reading.

Medieval manuscripts foreground the general interpretive issue I'm talking about because their provenance is an imperative topic for the interpreter. But the multiplied and duplicated copies of print technology do not alter the basic interpretive issue: who produced, who distributed, and who read the document, and how was it retransmitted? Our immediate readings are shaped by those histories, whether we are aware of them or not. A scholar wants to be so aware, but such awareness is difficult, and not simply because of the complexity of the historiated past. For as we turn our critical attention to the objects we study, we inevitably struggle to engage the subjective status of our own work and, most important of all, the pertinence of that subjectivity.

When interpretation, or theory of interpretation, addresses **the** *Constitution of the United States* or **a** poem by Keats, it makes an abstract of the documentary situation actually in play. Those kinds of interpretive moves have served the humanities long and well because some level of abstraction is a requirement of interpretation. But the question for the interpreter remains: how much am I willing to abstract from attention? Or—to recall Milman Parry—when and why do I stop making "for myself" my detailed interpretive picture? Empirical, even positivist, as he was, Parry understood the subjective character of his pictures.

Interpreters regularly throw a host of variables into a black box so that the complexity of the interpretive conditions can be limited and controlled. Like Ahab, this move has its humanities for, like Ahab, it defines a particular quest that has been shaped to work its will. But how willful do we mean to be? Even more pertinently, how aware do we mean to be about our willfulness? In such circumstances—they are widespread in the humanities—a philological conscience becomes the critical monitor of our interpretive moves to remember and understand. Such a monitor is important because the interpretation of history and culture is always threatened by Faustian temptations—the Dialectic of Enlightenment, the Poverty of Theory. Framing our studies as the particular act of a reader among other readers can help to remind us of that threat, if we choose to remember. For as the old song has it, "how little we know, how little we understand."

# Conclusion

## *Pseudodoxia Academica;* or, Literary Studies in a Global Age

I

Since all the cultural materials discussed in this book are resolutely Occidental, I should perhaps say something about how I've tried to engage with the global issues facing anyone interested in these things. For my argument holds that digital technology has realized the idea of a new Library of Alexandria. That institution's dark reciprocal, however, is the global character of the threat to memory, epitomized in the crisis of our languages. Linguists expect that by the end of this century some half of the 7,000 currently recognized languages will be extinct. In a narrow Western view, those losses occur at the periphery of the familiar world, in tiny isolated communities. But as Wittgenstein once famously reminded us, every language entails an understanding of the World *tout court*. We lose an entire imagination of the World when we lose the language, the culture, which was able to use it to see it. We lose a history of the World and a memory of the World.

The work of the skeptical anthropologist Marshall Sahlins is useful to consider here. For Sahlins, history and culture are always mapped along multiple timelines and memories.

> Tropes of every kind can be used to make sense of the resources of a given historical scheme. This is the endemic possibility of 'heteroglossia'—not an undifferentiated, shared culture but, as Bakhtin said, a complex relationship of shared differences—that explains how history can be culturally ordered without being culturally prescribed.[1]

Sahlins steps away from a Greenwich Meridian view of history and culture. Chronological time, seasonal time, corporate time, and family time: their names and types are legion even in a cultural field we might otherwise see as unified. Sahlins's study of Captain Cook's voyages to the Sandwich Islands, *Islands of History*, brings the consequences of such differentials into dramatic focus.[2] In that wonderful book, he tracks how two histories, one Polynesian, the other European, collide in a single event. Captain Cook's death occurs in both the cyclical/seasonal time of a god's eternal return and the chronological time of the Western imperial calendar.

Reading Sahlins's narrative, one may well recall another close student of the unexpected and the unforeseen, Thomas Hardy. Remember how he characterizes the "crass casualty" that took the "smart ship" *Titanic?*[3] Hardy's *Titanic* sinks, Sahlins's Cook dies, "According to [a] Mighty Working" that we inevitably fail to see, no matter how capacious or enlightened we imagine ourselves. The spinner's wheel flees on forever "outside perception's range."[4]

Hardy's world—what he called Wessex—is a lot more circumscribed than Sahlins's, and I shall return to that difference, and its relevance for us, in a moment. Hardy "thinks locally," as we say these days. Not so Sahlins. But thinking as globally as he does, beyond his native Chicago, he has gained an acute insight into his Enlightenment inheritance. His ear has not lost its ability to recognize the eloquence of vulgarity:

> More and more, I am convinced, these [indigenous] people are 'marginal' to history and modernity in nobody's eyes but our own. Indeed, at the point of social action, the field on which indigenous peoples struggle to encompass what is happening to them in the terms of their own world system, theirs is the encompassing move on a peripheral culture of modernity.[5]

These comments represent far more than a gloss on Trotsky's theory of "the privilege of historical backwardness."[6] Trotsky's thought is firmly located in a Western, high-Hegelian ethos. Sahlins is arguing something different. He is arguing that one of the great modernist instruments of Western imperialism and enlightenment—ethnography, the discipline in which Sahlins became a recognized master—has inverted the categories of cultural dominance and cultural marginality.

## II

Sahlins's cultural relativism helps to clarify what Pascale Casanova argued in her much-discussed *The World Republic of Letters*—an explicit effort to imagine a place in that republic for "all deprived and dominated writers on the [Occidental] periphery" (354).[7] This can happen, she argues, if the republic is founded outside any imaginable political or economic order. "The final definition of universality" (152)—a universality "that escapes the centers" of Western economic power—is an aesthetic definition (355). The subaltern world discovers its global identity by joining the "eccentric writers" (355) of "the [European] avant-garde" (152).

To an anthropologist, cultural distinctions are important but they are not drawn in the field of aesthetics. So when she considers a decentered Herderian model for literary history—in simplest form, "the existence of two synchronic and equally literary worlds"—she simply observes: "Plainly, this will not do" (103). The point is plain for her because the issue is aesthetic value: "The unification of literary space through competition presumes the existence of a common standard . . . an absolute point of reference recognized by all contestants" (87). This is what she means by "Parisianization, a universalization through denial of difference" (154)—or, "the structural ethnocentrism of the literary world" (155). Casanova wants to imagine a world republic of letters because she is troubled by what she names "the present-day structure of world literary space" (169). This space and its traditions of "autonomy" are being invaded.

> What is being played out today in every part of world literary space is not a rivalry between France and the United States or Great Britain but rather a struggle between the commercial pole, which in each country seeks to impose itself as a new source of literary legitimacy through the diffusion of writing that mimics the style of the modern novel, and the autonomous pole, which finds itself under siege not only in the United States and France but throughout Europe, owing to the power of international publishing giants. The American avant-garde is no less threatened than the European avant-garde. (169)

In the face of those profane forces, Casanova writes to "show how literature . . . managed, through a gradual acquisition of autonomy, to escape the ordinary laws of history. . . . What I have called literary space is this very process by which literary freedom is invented" (350).

As we know, anxieties of this kind emerged in the late eighteenth century when the very concept of aesthetic autonomy began to be explored.

The category of "the aesthetic"—the secular sacred—is a commercial function and, for the past 200 years, of capitalist economics in particular. Casanova's book replicates various texts from Kant and Wordsworth to Yeats and Adorno. The life's work of one of our first global writers, Byron, is a running commentary on literature's involvement with market forces. But Casanova argues that "the power of international commerce" has today become so great as to "have called into question the very idea of literature independent of commercial forces" (171–172). She writes to establish the authority of Western literary culture—the "idea" of the aesthetic—in a metastasizing global network of cultural agents.

Bracketing for the moment the pertinence of the theory of aesthetic autonomy—in Marx's formulation: "art is not among the ideologies"—we can still see that Casanova's sweeping historical representations have problems. If we look at the nineteenth century alone, France and Paris are clearly peripheral to the cultural authorities set loose in England and Germany, not even to speak of Russia. Simply in terms of poetry and fiction, Goethe, Byron, Pushkin, Sir Walter Scott: these men bestride the cultural world like colossi. David Harvey's Parisian capital—Harvey is not mentioned in Casanova's book—only begins to arise with Baudelaire and only then as a meditation on Byronism.[8]

This factive inadequacy of Casanova's account does not measure a failure of scholarship, it marks her ideological purpose. Like the artwork that interests her, Casanova's discussion "escape[s] the ordinary laws of history." It isn't a history at all, it is a theory, and "Paris" for her is a myth—"a modern myth created by literature." "It is for this reason," she then adds, "that historical chronology is of little importance" (27).

But if Paris is a myth escaping the ordinary laws of history, the myth is itself a historical formation and is important as such. It is clearly important if people put faith in the myth—or if they don't. Casanova's belief allows her to distinguish commercialized literary simulacra that "mimic" the real thing—at any rate, allows her to believe that the myth of autonomy has this distinguishing power. But faith in the myth of autonomy has waned dramatically since 1930, even in the sphere of literature, as the names of Laura Riding, Flann O'Brien, and Nathaniel West (among many others) testify. And it could easily be shown that a host of unbelievers throve very nicely throughout the Age of Aesthetic Faith. Contemporary art long since went so completely pagan that aesthetic autonomy shifted from a desired end to a stylistic resource—a set of procedures to be used as needed. This is the great insight and argument of Johanna Drucker's recent study *Sweet Dreams: Contemporary Art and Complicity.*[9] The book's cover design—Gregory Crewdson's stunning C-print "Untitled

(Ophelia)"—tells the whole story. And of course there are the movies—
the twentieth century's dominant scene of artistic practice: utterly commercial and profane in Casanova's frame of reference.

We want to remember that Casanova's myth of aesthetic autonomy is
a European invention. In a single couplet of great wit, wisdom, and wickedness, Byron called this myth "western sentimentalism" and then showed
how easily it might be translated—sold—as "samples of the finest Orien-
talism" (*Beppo* 407–408).[10] There in 1818 is a clear warning to all subaltern writers to beware these belated Greeks bearing gifts—and right from
the horse's mouth, the first and in many ways the greatest of self-marketing
poets! But Casanova's message to marginal cultures is the opposite.
"There is a kind of universality that escapes the centers," she argues: the
myth of Paris, the myth of aesthetic autonomy (355).

But what if, like Sahlins, we call into question this way of mapping the
world's cultural territories? What if we decide that the center/periphery
map has been drawn Under Western Eyes only and that it gives poor service in a truly globalized world? What if—going further still—we were to
propose, to theorize, that in such a world, such a myth resembles less a
map than a kind of equilibrium device, a cultural gyroscope for maintaining cultural status quo? It seems to me, looking from my marginal American position, that such thoughts are now common among non-Euro-
Americans. If that is indeed the case, I think, with Sahlins, it's a good
thing. But there's an even more pertinent question for all of us: what if
we decide the map is wrong, and that the map's aesthetic derivative—the
idea of literary autonomy—might be usefully disbelieved?

First, then, let's think about the center/periphery map, and let's frame
the problem in the sobering terms of day-to-day education programs.
What kinds of curricula would we devise that could adequately encompass the boundaries of the present and fast-expanding global network of
cultural agents? The question boggles the mind when we begin to consider the range of possibilities. It's already painful trying to devise a
thirteen-week course that gives some samples of the finest Occidentalism,
even for, say, a particular literary (not to speak of a cultural) period. Although the scale of the problem for a literary curriculum of "Global
Studies" is more severe, it's the same kind of problem. You need a canon
for a curriculum. Casanova's canon would presumably pivot around a
certain subset of "eccentric" and avant-garde writers and their "global"
inheritors. But Casanova's array of twentieth-century eccentricities appears to my view quite conventional—as they should be, I suppose, given
her commitment to the myth of Paris. The problem is that once you embrace an eccentric model you're entering—what shall we call it?—a *mise*

*en abyme?* That great eccentric Byron once again comes to mind. In face of the coming orthodoxy of the romantic revolution, he offered this revelation:

> If ever I should condescend to prose,
>     I'll write poetical commandments, which
> Shall supersede beyond all doubt all those
>     That went before; in these I shall enrich
> My text with many things that no one knows,
>     And carry precept to the highest pitch:
> I'll call the work "Longinus o'er a Bottle,
> Or, Every Poet his own Aristotle."
>                              (*Don Juan* 5.205)

Byron did not annotate the meaning of his comic proposal. Is it mere anarchy loosed upon the literary world? Or perhaps it's saying "Let a thousand flowers bloom" (or, in the dialect of a very orthodox medium—the book of Numbers: "Would to God that all the Lord's people were prophets," *Numbers* 11:29).

Leaving aside the difficulty of drawing a reliable map from Casanova's vantage, what about its ideological basis, the commitment to the autonomy of the literary work? As she makes clear in the "Preface to the English Language Edition" of her book, Casanova's idea of autonomy derives from an interpretive tradition framed at one end by Kant and Schiller and at the other by Marcuse and Adorno.[11] "The central hypothesis of this book . . . is that there exists . . . a literary universe relatively independent of the everyday world and its political divisions" (xii).

I've already suggested that this interpretation may be less disinterested than it appears—might indeed be seen as a move in the everyday world to preserve a Parisian myth about the literary universe. Seen as such, it might not claim our allegiance—even the allegiance of we who sit in our Western rooms. Indeed, Casanova's own commitment to eccentric models might warn us from this way of thinking about the Enlightenment myth of aesthetic autonomy.

It's of course true that from Kant forward the myth has been scaled up to a general theory of art. But therein lies the problem. Alexander Baumgarten's original 1735 study, *Meditationes philosophicae de nonnullis ad poema pertinentibus* (Philosophical Meditations on Some Requirements of the Poem), is not a philosophy of art or even a poetics.[12] It's much more modest: an inquiry into issues of poetic style and method. Its historical importance lies in a view of poetry not as a mimetic undertaking but as a discourse of sensibility. As Kai Hammermeister succinctly observes in his important study *The German Aesthetic Tradition:* "Philosophical aesthetics originated as an advocacy of sensibility, not as a theory of art."[13] It's true that Baumgarten himself later became a professor of philosophy and initiated the passage that led to Kant's third critique. As a theory of art, however, aesthetics may now best be seen as a secular form of worship drawn from a poetical tale about sensibility.

## III

Let me stop arguing with Casanova for a moment. I agree with much that she writes, and I especially agree that we in *das Abendland* have an obligation to help lay bare the devices of the Western myth of Paris. One of those devices is the general theory of the autonomy of art that was erected upon Baumgarten's early treatise on poetic style. Briefly, the explicit purpose of Baumgarten's treatise was to establish the autonomy of aesthetic or sensate knowledge apart from the knowledge we gain through cognition. Because Baumgarten was as much a rationalist as Plato and Gottfried Leibniz, aesthetic knowing was to him inferior to the powers of reason. Aesthetic awareness is strictly phenomenal. But Baumgarten showed that standards for determining aesthetic value could be established without invoking rational concepts. The aesthetic order was autonomous exactly because its principles, so to say, were entirely sensate—in his new word, aesthetic. The aesthetic order was an order of what Blake would shortly call "minute particulars." Philology would soon claim dominion in that order.

Baumgarten did not go on to put the aesthetic order back under the authority of the new and "higher reason"—the "pure reason"—developed in Kant's renovated form of foundational philosophy. This is crucial to recall because it exposes how a General Theory of Aesthetic Autonomy was extruded from Baumgarten's Special Theory. Kant's is a General Theory and so is Marcuse's, and Adorno's, and—to come back home— Casanova's: "there exists a literary universe relatively independent of the everyday world and its political divisions." Thus does the myth of Paris enter Casanova's world republic by the back door.

If, like Casanova, we want to put a "critical weapon in the service of all deprived and dominated writers," we might look not to philosophy but to philology—the republic of grammarians, rhetoricians, and the poets they study. Textual scholars stay close to a ground that is not "the transcendental ground," close to words that call to each other rather than to The Word.

Besides, Parisian myths obscure just how complex and ramifying are the possibilities of centrality and marginality. Scholarship is a vulgar office where dialects and dead or disappearing languages are as pertinent as imperial tongues. Nor can the scholar honorably think that to study Felicia Hemans or Ogden Nash is less an obligation than Milton or Dante.

Thinking about aesthetics in these lower cases, I close with a brief comment on the verse of that fastidious aesthete Marianne Moore. Her ways of thinking (poetically) illustrate what Baumgarten was trying to express in his Latin treatise. Moore is particularly relevant because, like Alexander Pope, she combines a high degree of surface artifice and verbal gaming with an insistence on clarity of plain prose statement.

Artifice in Moore—in all poetry—keeps attention on the surface of the text, the ordering of the signifiers. Her resort to syllabic versification, Moore's signature device, gains special aesthetic force by being combined with prosaic dictions.

> I remember a swan under the willows in Oxford
>     with flamingo-colored, maple—
>         leaflike feet. It reconnoitered like a battle
> ship. Disbelief and conscious fastidiousness were the staple
>         ingredients in its
>             disinclination to move.[14]

A text like this illustrates why "Inspection" is one of her keywords. Her verse makes a drama of a mind looking carefully at phenomena, including the phenomena of her language as she is in the act of using it, the particular act of the writing we are particularly reading.

>                                                 the bat
>     holding on upside down or in quest of something to
>
>     eat, elephants pushing, a wild horse taking a roll,

And so the catalogue of particulars continues, observing this and that and then often stopping to think again, as the thinking drives a shift of attention:

>                             nor is it valid
>     to discriminate against "business documents and
>
>     school-books"; all these phenomena are important.[15]

Why? Well, "not because a / high sounding interpretation can be put upon them but because they are / useful."

The Kantian tradition of philosophical aesthetics moved Baumgarten's argument about poetic autonomy to a separate, transcendental sphere of "purposeless purpose." But as Moore's verse reminds us, fundamental thinking—moves to discriminate experience—governs the sensate order. Poetic expression is "useful" because it exposes and illustrates that kind of fundamental thinking: the acts of attention where even abstract terms ("discriminations," "inspections") once again breathe their human air.

Modest, lucid, catholic, and secular: those are the recognizable virtues of Moore's verse. I bring them forward here to define how we children of the Faustian West might better imagine our position in the world republic of letters Casanova so much desires. She has set a face of flint "against the presumptions, the arrogance, and the fiats of critics in the center." That is well done within the patrolled region of the Western imperium. But in the world elsewhere? As Sahlins reminds us, we here should be wary of imagining "deprived and dominated writers on the periphery of the literary world." In a Western mind the idea is at best insular, at worst something mildly shameful.

# Notes

## Introduction

1. Although the primary focus of this book is the need to rethink and reorganize humanities research and education, I am well aware of the enveloping economic and social context and problems. In this connection I mention Richard Grusin's *Premediation: Affect and Mediality after 9/11* (London: Palgrave, 2010) because his book examines some of the most important aspects of those problems. His concerns and judgments are very close to my own. I believe, however, that practical headway can be made through concrete changes in institutional policies and programs in humanities research and education. That conviction has shaped the arguments of this book. See also the important work of Alan Liu, in particular his two recent books *The Laws of Cool: Knowledge Work and the Culture of Information* (Chicago: University of Chicago Press, 2004) and *Local Trasncendence: Essays on Postmodern Historicism and the Database* (Chicago: University of Chicago Press, 2008).

2. IATH (The Institute for Advanced Technology in the Humanities: www.iath .virginia.edu); NINES (Networked Infrastructure for Nineteenth-Century Electronic Scholarship: www.nines.org); *The Rossetti Archive* (www.rossettiarchive .org); *IVANHOE* (www.ivanhoegame.org); *Juxta* (Juxta Collation Software for Scholars: www.juxtasoftware.org). For related discussions see Jerome McGann, *Radiant Textuality: Literature after the World Wide Web* (New York: Palgrave, 2002) and the special issue of *Text Technology* 12, no. 2 (2003).

3. The relations of this book to the now lively field of memory studies will appear in due course. I mention here three very recent works that came to my attention too late for me to take them up in a detailed way, though their general approach, as will be apparent throughout, is one with which I am very much in sympathy: Friederike Eigler, *Heimat: At the Intersection of Memory and Space* (Berlin: De Gruyter, 2012); Sebastian Conrad, *Memory in a Global Age: Discourses, Practices and Trajectories* (Basingstoke: Palgrave Macmillan, 2010); Aleida Assman, *Cultural Memory and Western Civilization: Arts of Memory* (Cambridge: Cambridge University Press, 2011).

4. "The Return to Philology," in *Humanism and Democratic Criticism* (New York: Columbia University Press, 2004), 57–84. See also the essays in Jan Ziolkowsky, ed., *What Is Philology?* (University Park: Penn State University Press, 1990).

5. Hans Gumbrecht, *The Powers of Philology* (Urbana: University of Illinois Press, 2003), 37.

6. The term "implicate order" was made famous through David Bohm's *Wholeness and the Implicate Order* (London: Routledge and Kegan Paul, 1980).

7. The two men most associated with an object-oriented philology are August Boeckh (1785–1867) and Hermann Sauppe (1809–1893). For a good presentation of how the distinction between *Wortphilologie* and *Sachphilologie* played out in the Wilamowitz-Nietzsche controversy, which I take up in Chapter 1, see Anthony K. Jensen, "Geschichte or Historie? Nietzsche's Second Untimely Meditation in the Context of Nineteenth-Century Philological Studies," in Manuel Dries, ed., *Nietzsche on Time and History* (Berlin: Walter de Gruyter, 2008), 211–226.

8. See my essay "On Creating a Usable Future," *Profession* (2011): 182–195.

9. August Boeckh, *Enzyklopädie und Methodologie der gesamten philologischen Wissenschaften,* ed. Ernst Bratuschek (Leipzig: B.G. Teubner, 1877), 11. Boeckh made this famous formulation very early in his career, when he was twenty-five years old.

10. D. F. McKenzie, *Making Meaning: "Printers of the Mind" and Other Essays,* ed. Peter D. McDonald and Michael Suarez, SJ (Amherst: University of Massachusetts Press, 2002).

11. Derrida, *Archive Fever: A Fruedian Impression*, trans. Eric Prenowitz (Chicago: University of Chicago Press, 1998).

12. I borrow this term from Randall McLoud, the most distinguished documentary scholar of the past fifty years. See his "Obliterature: Reading a Censored Text of Donne's 'To his mistres going to bed,'" *English Manuscript Studies* 12 (2005): 83–138.

13. One of the most persuasive contemporary calls for a recovery of philology came from Edward Said, "The Return to Philology," in *Humanism and Democratic Criticism* (New York: Columbia University Press, 2004), 57–84. See also the essays in Jan Ziolkowsky, ed., *What Is Philology?* (University Park: Penn State University Press, 1990).

14. Danièlle Hervieu-Legér's *Religion as a Chain of Memory* (Cambridge: Polity Press, 1993, 2000), 127.

15. Maurice Halbwachs, *The Collective Memory,* with an introduction by Mary Douglas (New York: Harper Colophon Books, 1980), 48.

16. Paul Connerton, *How Modernity Forgets* (Cambridge: Cambridge University Press, 2009), 147.

17. It is collected in *The Prose of Osip Mandelstam,* trans. with a critical essay by Clarence Brown (Princeton, NJ: Princeton University Press, 1965).

18. Mandelstam in 1921 was still an adherent to the revolution, though he took a perverse line on its (for him, spiritual) importance. The revolution marked

the "classical" inheritance with the great prophetic sign of sociohistorical revolution: alienation, or what Trotsky would call "the privilege of historical backwardness."

19. Mandelstam is implicitly recalling Ovid's famous remark about his exile to remote Thrace: that the people there could not understand Latin.

20. *Memory and Literature: Intertextuality in Russian Modernism* (Minneapolis: University of Minnesota Press, 1997), 238–240.

21. That is to say, globalized internetworks that aspire to make massive amounts of linked data and information accessible to the broad public for regular use. Europeana: http://www.europeana.eu/portal/; DPLA: http://dp.la/.

22. McGann, *Radiant Textuality.*

23. Some friends and collaborators at the time were severely critical of the assumption. It proved to be "correct" in the sense that it proved to be fruitful.

24. See *Radiant Textuality,* 1–27, but especially 7–10 where the extraprogrammatic character of work at IATH is discussed. What was a virtuous necessity in the 1990s has turned to something much less virtuous two decades on.

25. In titling his second novel *The Longest Journey* (1907) Forster was quoting Shelley's *Epipsychidion* (1821). The conclusion to *A Passage to India* (1924) is taken from the first edition.


## 1. Why Textual Scholarship Matters

1. See my "Textonics. Literary and Cultural Studies in a Quantum World," in *The Culture of Collected Editions,* ed. Andrew Nash (Basingstoke: Palgrave Macmillan, 2003), 245–260.

2. Discussed at length in *The History of the Russian Revolution,* vol. 1, chap. 1.

3. Jerome J. McGann, *A Critique of Modern Textual Criticism* (Chicago: University of Chicago Press, 1983) and D. F. McKenzie, *Bibliography and the Sociology of Texts* (London: The British Library, 1986).

4. See Eliza Richards, *Gender and the Poetics of Reception in Poe's Circle* (Cambridge: Cambridge University Press, 2004), 1.

5. *The Scholar's Art: Literary Studies in a Managed World* (Chicago: University of Chicago Press, 2006), 160–171.

6. This work by Talan Memmott is now available from the Electronic Literature Collection under the slightly revised title *Lexia to Perplexia* (http://collection .eliterature.org/1/works/memmott_lexia_to_perplexia.html). It was originally published in 2000 by the Iowa Review Web (link now inoperable).

7. Bethany Nowviskie on the Collex design: www.nines.org/about/software /collex.html.


## 2. "The Inorganic Organization of Memory"

1. See also Sheldon Pollock's moving essay "Future Philology: The Fate of a Soft Science in a Hard World," *Critical Inquiry* 35, no. 4 (Summer 2009): 931–961. Pollock's title is lifted from Wilamowitz's pamphlet attack on Nietzsche.

Perhaps because I am not an intercessor for Sanskrit studies, as Pollock is; and/or perhaps because I am encouraged by the scholarly opportunities emerging through internet technology, my view of a "future philology" is guardedly hopeful. It is also far more in sympathy with Nietzsche than Wilamowitz. See Chapter 3, pages 71–73, where I discuss Milman Parry's trenchant commentary on the respective limits of the Wilamowitzian and the Nietzschean lines of thought. My approach in this book is a conscious effort to reconcile these two approaches to humane studies.

2. For Lyotard's objection to Habermas's pursuit of legitimation as consensus see the appendix to *The Postmodern Condition* (hereafter cited as PC). Originally published in 1979 as *La condition postmoderne: Rapport sur le savoir,* it was published in English in 1984 in a translation by Geoff Bennington and Brian Massumi (Minneapolis: University of Minnesota Press).

3. PC was delivered initially as a set of lectures for the Council in the spring of 1979. The typescript is available online at: http://www.cse.gouv.qc.ca/FR/Publications_CUniv/.

4. Stanley Fish, "The Old Order Changeth," *New York Times,* December 26, 2011: http://opinionator.blogs.nytimes.com/2011/12/26/the-old-order-changeth/.

5. I cite the English translation, *Technics and Time,* vol. 1: *The Fault of Epimetheus,* trans. Richard Beardsworth and George Collins (Stanford, CA: Stanford University Press, 1998) (hereafter cited as TT).

6. D. F. McKenzie, in *Making Meaning: "Printers of the Mind" and Other Essays,* ed. Peter D. McDonald and Michael Suarez, SJ (Amherst: University of Massachusetts Press, 2002), 267–268; Dino Buzzetti and Jerome McGann, "Critical Editing in a Digital Horizon," in *Electronic Textual Editing,* ed. Lou Burnard et al. (New York: Modern Language Association, 2006): online at http://www.tei-c.org/About/Archive_new/ETE/Preview/mcgann.xml.

7. Seth Lerer's recent lively study of how European philology fared in the mid-twentieth-century United States moves from one of the key ground-points of philology: that it is an inquiry into the history of error. See *Error and the Academic Self: The Scholarly Imagination, Medieval to Modern* (New York: Columbia University Press, 2003).

8. "The Historical Method in Literary Criticism," in *The Making of Homeric Verse: The Collected Papers of Milman Parry,* ed. Adam Parry (Oxford: Clarendon Press, 1971), 411.

9. *Too Big to Know: Rethinking Kowledge Now That the Facts Are the Facts, Experts Are Everywhere, and the Smartest Person in the Room Is the Room* (New York: Basic Books, 2011).

10. See http://about.galileo.usg.edu/.

11. Aleida Assmann, "Canon and Archive," in *Cultural Memory Studies: An International Interdisciplinary Handbook,* ed. Astrid Erll et al. (Berlin: Walter De Gruyter, 2008), 99. Assmann elaborated her views in *Cultural Memory and Western Civilization: Functions, Media, Archives* (Cambridge: Cambridge University Press, 2011), a translation of a work published in German in 2006 (*Erinner-*

*ungsräume: Formen und Wandlungen des kulturellen Gedächtnisses* [München: Beck, 2006]).

## 3. Memory

1. For a more detailed exposition of the scholarly conditions and tensions at the time see James I. Porters's *Nietzsche and the Philology of the Future* (Stanford, CA: Stanford University Press, 2000).

2. My translations from *Wir Philologen* (hereafter cited as WP) are taken from *We Philologists*, trans. J.M. Kennedy, in volume 8 of the first comprehensive English edition of Nietzsche's works, *The Complete Works of Friedrich Nietzsche*, ed. Oscar Levy (Edinburgh: T.N. Foulis, 1911). The citations are to WP and aphorism number. The text is available online from Project Gutenberg: http://www .gutenberg.org/files/18267/18267-h/18267-h.htm.

3. "For life" refers to the important related document of the period, the famous second part of the *Untimely Meditations, Vom Nutzen und Nachteil der Historie für das Leben* (commonly Englished as "On the Use and Abuse of History for Life"). I use Ian C. Johnston's translation, available online, and cite it as UM 2: http://onlinebooks.library.upenn.edu/webbin/book/lookupid?key=olbp25214.

4. For a good treatment of various issues relating to "The Woman Question" and Nietzsche see Peter J. Burgard, ed., *Nietzsche and the Feminine* (Charlottesville: University Press of Virginia, 1994). Closely related to this problem is "the racism and nationalism" (Porter, *Nietzsche and the Philology of the Future*, 24ff.) that pervades both Nietzsche's work and the work of all his scholarly contemporaries.

5. From *The Birth of Tragedy*, sec. 20, in *"The Birth of Tragedy" and "The Geanealogy of Morals,"* trans. Francis Golffing (Garden City, NY: Doubleday, 1956), 122.

6. From the *Nachlass*, in *Werke: Kritische Gesamtausgabe*, ed. Volker Gerhardt et al. (Berlin: Walter de Gruyter, 1967–), IV/1, 3, [69].

7. See *The Case of Wagner, Nietzsche Contra Wagner, and Selected Aphorisms*, trans. Anthony M. Ludovici (Edinburgh: T.N. Foulis, 1911). Nietzsche's critique, a late work, was first published in 1895.

8. See Arnold's "Preface" to his *Poems* (1853).

9. The translation is from J.M. Kennedy's, from volume 9 of the Levy edition cited from the online text: http://archive.org/stream/dawnofday02967 5mbp/dawn ofday02967 5mbp_djvu.txt.

10. Christian Emden, *Friedrich Nietzsche and the Politics of History* (Cambridge: Cambridge University Press, 2008), 322–323.

11. See David S. Thatcher, "Nietzsche and Byron," *Nietzsche-Studien* 3 (1974): 130–151.

12. Quoted from William M. Calder III, "How Did Ulrich Von Wilamowitz–Moellendorff Read a Text?," *The Classical Journal* 86, no. 4 (April–May 1991): 350–351.

13. It is important to remember, however, that the epochal German philologists were themselves by no means in complete agreement of various key matters. For one of the best *critical* discussions of such differences see Ingo Gildenhard, "*Philologia perennis?* Classical Scholarship and Functional Differentiation," in *Out of Arcadia: Classics and Politics in Germany in the Age of Burchhardt, Nietzsche, and Wilamowitz,* ed. Ingo Gildenhard and Martin Ruehl (London: Institute of Classical Studies, University of London, 2003), 161–203.

14. See the famous remark in he second *Untimely Meditation:* "it is possible to live almost without remembering, indeed, to live happily, as the beast demonstrates; however, it is completely and utterly impossible to live at all without forgetting."

15. Babette Babich, "Future Philology! by Ulrich von Wilamowitz-Moellendorff," trans. G. Postl, B. Babich, and H. Schmid" (2000). *Articles, Book-Chapters, etc. by Babette Babich.* Paper 3. http://fordham.bepress.com/phil_babich/3:11.

16. See Chapter 8.

17. *The Philosophy of Literary Form,* 3rd ed., rev. (Berkeley: University of California Press, 1974), 89.

18. The correct logical form would be "The 'The Rime of the Ancient Mariner,'" which I suppose helps to explain why Lewis Carroll's logical games are so amusing (and instructive).

19. "Er entnimmt daraus, da das Groe, das einmal da war, jedenfalls einmal *möglich* war und deshalb auch wohl wieder einmal möglich sein wird."

20. Raymond Geuss, "Genealogy as Critique," *European Journal of Philosophy* 10 (2002): 212–213; Bernard Williams, *Truth and Truthfulness: An Essay on Genealogy* (Princeton, NJ: Princeton University Press, 2002), 37.

21. See Emden, *Friedrich Nietzsche and the Politics of History,* 262–263.

22. Byron, *Childe Harold's Pilgrimage,* IV. 125.

23. See Peter Burke, "Strengths and Weaknesses in the History of Mentalities," in *Varieties of Cultural History* (Cambridge: Polity Press, 1997), 162–182.

24. Pierre Nora, "Between Memory and History: *Les Lieux de Mémoire*" (trans. Mark Roudebush), *Representations* 26 (1989): 10. Nora's sentence is not easily rendered: "Interroger une tradition, si venerable soit-elle, c'est ne plus s'en reconnaitre uniment le porteur," "Entre Mémoire et Histoire," *Les Lieux de Mémoire* 1: *La République* (Paris: Gallimard, 1984), I. xxi).

25. Raphael Samuel, *Theatres of Memory: Past and Present in Contemporary British Culture* (London: Verso, 1995), 11. See also Peter Carrier's excellent critical account of Nora's project, "Places, Politics, and the Archiving of Contemporary Memory in Pierre Nora's *Les Lieux de Mémoire,*" in *Memory and Methodology,* ed. Susannah Radstone (New York: Oxford University Press, 2000), 37–57.

26. "*Monuments aux morts?* Reading Nora's *Realms of Memory* and Samuel's *Theatres of Memory,*" *History of the Human Sciences* 12, no. 2 (1999): 139. Taithe distinguishes Samuel's work as a project of "fragments," whereas Nora's "was 'hailed as the publishing event of the decade [1980s]' as the wrapper in-

forms us. Raphael Samuel's was entirely a labor of subversion, a critique of the authority of classically trained historians and a work which invited readers and critics to reconsider their own intellectual legitimacy and respect the dignity of un-academic visions of the past. Nora's is a publishing masterpiece, a collection reflecting the achievements of a handful of eminent French scholars" (126).

27. Andreas Huyssen, *Present Pasts: Urban Palimpsests and the Politics of Memory* (Stanford, CA: Stanford University Press, 2003: 46. Huyssen's move to resist the seductions of monumentality is essentially deconstructive: "Only if we historicize the category of monumentality itself can we step out of the double shadow of a kitsch monumentalism of the nineteenth century and the bellicose anti-monumentalism of modernism and postmodernism" (ibid., 40).

28. Nora specifically resists this view of *Les Lieux:* "Although these objects must be grasped in empirical detail, the issues at stake are ill suited to expression in the categories of traditional historiography. Reflecting on *lieux de mémoire* transforms historical criticism into critical history" (Nora, "Between Memory and History," 24). And for Nora, the organization of *Les Lieux* institutes that reflection.

29. The ground of Ricoeur's arguments come in volume 1 of *Time and Narrative,* trans. Kathleen McLaughlin and David Pelauer (Chicago: University of Chicago Press, 1984), where he lays out his tripartite analysis of mimetic action (52–87).

30. Paul Ricoeur, *Memory, History, Forgetting* (Chicago: University of Chicago Press, 2004), 458–506.

31. See Keats's letter to his brother George, December 17, 1817.

32. The phrase is Alfred Jarry's summary definition of 'pataphysics: see his *Selected Works,* ed. Roger Shattuck and Simon Watson Taylor (New York: Grove Press, 1965), 191.

33. *A Companion to Cultural Memory Studies,* ed. Astrid Erll and Ansgar Nunning, in collaboration with Sara B. Young (Berlin: Walter de Gruyter, 2008), 2.

34. Alon Confino, "Memory and the History of Mentalities," in ibid., 81, 79.

35. This is Jan Assmann's position—see his essay "Communicative and Cultural Memory," in Erll and Nunning, *A Companion to Cultural Memory Studies,* 109–118, and Martin Zierold, "Memory and Media Cultures," in ibid., 400.

36. Danièle Hervieu-Legér, *Religion as a Chain of Memory,* trans. Simon Lee (New Brunswick, NJ: Rutgers University Press, 2000).

37. The cultural-historical "break," as it commonly called, has been variously dated to the twelfth through thirteenth centuries; to the period of the Reformation; and most frequently to "about 1800": Paul Connerton, *How Modernity Forgets* (Cambridge: Cambridge University Press, 2009), 132. The rise of Memory Studies, however, has pushed speculation about the date forward because, as Connerton remarks, "the process of cultural forgetting characteristic of modernity is accelerating" because of "the emergence of megacities, the increasing importance of electronic media and the development of information technology" (ibid.).

38. *Mark Twain's Notebook,* ed. Albert Bigelow Paine (New York: Harper and Brothers, 1935), 240.

39. "God's Education" was published in *Time's Laughingstocks and Other Verses* (London: Macmillan and Co., 1909), "God-Forgotten" in 1901 in *Poems of the Past and the Present* (London: Macmillan and Co.,1901).

40. The fascicles for letters A to E appeared between 1884 and 1895. The fascicles for the letter F were published in 1896.

41. Milman Parry, *The Making of Homeric Verse: The Collected Papers of Milman Parry,* ed. Adam Parry (Oxford: Clarendon Press, 1971), 411.

42. It was then first printed in the *Harvard Alumni Bulletin* 38 (1936): 778–782.

## 4. The Documented World

1. *The Need for Roots: Prelude to a Declaration of Duties toward Mankind,* trans. Arthur Wills with a preface by T.S. Eliot (New York: Putnam, 1952), 283–284.

2. D. F. McKenzie, *Making Meaning: "Printers of the Mind" and Other Essays,* ed. Peter D. McDonald and Michael Suarez, SJ (Amherst: University of Massachusetts Press, 2002), 271.

3. For a discussion of this important Rossettian idea see my "DG Rossetti and the Art of the Inner Standing-Point," in *Outsiders Looking In: The Rossettis Then and Now,* ed. David Clifford and Laurence Roussillon (London: Anthem Press, 2004), 171–187.

4. *The Letters of Emily Dickinson,* ed. Thomas H. Johnson and Theodora Ward (Cambridge, MA: Belknap Press of Harvard University Press, 1958), III. 916.

5. Johanna Drucker, "Graphical Readings and the Visual Aesthetics of Textuality," *TEXT* 16 (2006): 267–276.

6. *Dante Gabriel Rossetti: Collected Poetry and Prose,* ed. Jerome McGann (New Haven, CT: Yale University Press, 2003), 239.

7. Reprinted in Alan D. Sokal, "What the Social Text Affair Does and Does Not Prove," in *A House Built on Sand: Exposing Postmodernist Myths about Science,* ed. Noretta Koertge (Oxford: Oxford University Press, 1998).

8. The following schema is slightly but significantly revised from its first published version in *The Beauty of Inflections: Literary Investigations in Historical Method and Theory* (Oxford: Oxford University Press, 1985).

9. Reprinted in *My Way: Speeches and Poems* (Chicago: University of Chicago Press, 1999). The essay first appeared in the *Michigan Quarterly Review* 35, no. 4 (1996): 644–652.

10. *Critique of Taste,* trans. Michael Caesar (London: New Left Books, 1978) (originally published in 1960).

11. René Wellek and Austin Warren, *Theory of Literature* (New York: Harcourt Brace, 1949; rev. 1956, 1970).

12. *The Complete Poetry and Prose,* rev. ed., ed. David V. Erdman, with a commentary by Harold Bloom (Berkeley: University of California Press, 1988), 634.

13. See *"The Poetic Principle": Edgar Allan Poe. Essays and Reviews,* ed. G. R. Thompson (New York: Library of America, 1984), 75.

14. See *The Marriage of Heaven and Hell,* plate 10.

15. Lyn Hejinian, "The Rejection of Closure," in Bob Perelman, ed., *Writing/ Talks* (Carbondale: Southern Illinois University Press, 1985), 290.

## 5. Marking Texts in Many Dimensions

1. See Henry Thompson and David McKelvie, "Hyperlink Semantics for Stand-off Markup of Read-Only Documents," in SGML Europe 97, Barcelona, 1997: http://www.infoloom.com/gcaconfs/WEB/TOC/barcelona97toc.HTM.

2. *Electronic Texts in the Humanities: Principles and Practice* (Oxford: Oxford University Press, 2000), 20.

3. See Humberto Maturana and Francisco Varela, *The Tree of Knowledge: The Biological Roots of Human Understanding* (New York: Random House, 1992).

4. Humberto Maturana and Francisco Varela, *Autopoiesis and Cognition: The Realization of Living* (Boston: D. Reidel, 1980), 78.

5. "What Matters?," http://www.w3.org/People/cmsmcq/2002/whatmatters .html.

6. This is the "OHCO Thesis": see Allen Renear, Elli Mylonas, and David Durand, "Refining Our Notion of What Text Really Is: The Problem of Overlapping Hierarchies," final version, 1993: http://www.stg.brown.edu/resources/stg/mono graphs/ohco.html.

7. See Mark Caton, "Markup's Current Imbalance," *Markup Languages: Theory and Practice* 3, no. 1 (2001): 1–13.

8. See René Thom in his classic study *Structural Stability and Morphogenesis: An Outline of a General Theory of Models,* trans. D. H. Fowler, with a foreword by C. H. Waddington (Reading, MA: W. A. Benjamin, 1975).

9. Pierce's seminal statement on existential graphs was given in the so-called MS 514, published online with commentary by John F. Sowa: http://www.jfsowa .com/peirce/ms514.htm.

10. See Johanna Drucker, *Speclab: Digital Aesthetics and Speculative Computing* (Chicago: University of Chicago Press, 2009).

11. See the special issue of *Text Technology* 12, no. 2 (2003) devoted to *IVANHOE.*

12. The project came out of McGann and Drucker's SpecLab: see Bethany Nowviskie's 2003 online report on the project: http://www2.iath.virginia.edu /time/time.html. That frankly experimental project is now being practically pursued by Nowviskie and her collaborators at the University of Virginia's Scholar's Lab as the Neatline Project: http://neatline.org/.

13. See G. Spencer Brown, *Laws of Form* (London: George Allen and Unwin, 1969).

14. A classic statement of field poetics is Charles Olson's "Human Universe" in his *Selected Writings,* ed. Robert Creeley (New York: New Directions, 1971). See also Donald Wellman, "Field Poetics (a Compleat History of De-individualizing Practices)," *EOAGH* 5 (2009): http://chax.org/eoagh/issuefive/wellman.html.

15. *The Sciences of the Artificial,* 3rd ed. (Cambridge, MA: MIT Press, 1996). The book was originally published in 1969.

16. For a set of provocative investigations of the idea of context see the special issue of *New Literary History* 42, no. 4 (Autumn 2011).

## 6. Digital Tools and the Emergence of the Social Text

1. *Ulysses: A Critical and Synoptic Edition,* ed. Hans Gabler et al., 3 vols. (New York: Garland, 1984); *The Collected Works of Samuel Taylor Coleridge: Poetical Works,* ed. J.C.C. Mays, vols. 1–3, parts 1, 2 (Princeton, NJ: Princeton University Press, 2001). For my discussion of Gabler's edition see "*Ulysses* as a Postmodern Text: The Gabler Edition," *Criticism* 27 (Summer 1985): 283–305.

2. This Congreve edition has just appeared, though I have not yet been able to evaluate its achievement: *The Works of William Congreve,* 3 vols. (Oxford: Clarendon Press, 2011).

3. Friedrich Beissner and Adolf Beck, eds., *Hölderlin Sämtliche Werke,* 8 vols. (Stuttgart: Cotta, 1943–1985).

4. A glimpse of a possible future for a digital environment that might overgo the traditional book interface may be had in the Juxta collation software: see http://www.juxtasoftware.org/about/. But of course this powerful collation tool is only one function—albeit perhaps the essential function—of a critical edition.

5. McKenzie, *Bibliography and the Sociology of Texts* (London: The British Library, 1986).

6. See T.H. Howard-Hill, "Theory and Praxis in the Social Approach to Editing," *TEXT* 5 (1991): 31–46; and Thomas Tanselle, "Textual Criticism and Literary Sociology," *Studies in Bibliography* 44 (1991): 83–143.

7. See the various projects sponsored by the Institute for Advanced Technology in the Humanities: http://www.iath.virginia.edu/projects.html.

8. Since its initial conception, *The Rossetti Archive* has been subjected to further digital transformations—most notably a translation into XML format—that extend the Archive's trans-linguistic critical functions. The digital logic of the Archive's structure leaves it open to more comprehensive scales of interoperability such as those being developed through the Semantic Web and the Open Knowledge Initiative (OKI). For an introduction to the latter see: http://web.mit.edu/oki/.

9. See *Juxta. Compare. Collate. Discover:* http://www.juxtasoftware.org/about/.

10. See McKenzie, "'What's Past Is Prologue': The Bibliographical Society and the History of the Book," in *Making Meaning: "Printers of the Mind" and Other Essays,* ed. Peter D. McDonald and Michael Suarez, SJ (Amherst: University of Massachusetts Press, 2002).

## 7. What Do Scholars Want?

1. Kathy Acker, *Empire of the Senseless* (New York: Grove Press, 1988), 112.

2. The ACLS-sponsored Humanities E-Book project is one response but its approach is decidedly random. Google Books has already digitized a vast number of these works but few are accessible to the scholarly community, and when the Google Book Settlement is finally achieved, no one knows how these works will be accessible.

3. The literature on this controversial event is very large. For a good summary that is kept up to date see: http://en.wikipedia.org/wiki/Google_Book_Search _Settlement_Agreement#Further_reading.

4. ECCO: http://gdc.gale.com/products/eighteenth-century-collections-online/; NCCO: http://news.cengage.com/library-research/gale%E2%80%99s-nineteenth -century-collections-online-arrives-at-academic-institutions-worldwide/; NINES: http://www.nines.org/.

5. Much of the most important work in humanities scholarship today is done completely outside the university's programmatic structure and by persons who have little or no faculty status. The case of *The Scholar's Lab* at University of Virginia is a notable instance of a widespread situation (http://www2.lib.vir ginia.edu/scholarslab/). A notable counterexample would be the *Center for Digital History and New Media* at George Mason University (http://chnm.gmu .edu/).

6. Libraries, universities, and private enterprises continue to explore new procedures for making educational materials accessible online, either freely or at reasonable costs. See for example the Hathi Trust (hathitrust.org), the Internet Archive (archive.org), and, in general, the entities associated with the Internet International Preservation Consortium (netpreserve.org).

7. Darnton's series of review essays and response notes began in the *New York Review of Books,* February 12, 2009, issue.

8. This letter to the court was the initiative of Pamela Samuelson, who— like Darnton—has been a steady critic of the narrow framework in which the settlement is being pursued. See, e.g., Samuelson's "Google Book Search and the Future of Books in Cyberspace": http://74.125.93.132/search?q=cache:hL83 m3sqzdgJ:people.ischool.berkeley.edu/~pam/GBSandBooksInCyberspace.pdf+pa mela+samuelson+google+books&cd=9&hl=en&ct=clnk&gl=us.

9. The settlement was rejected in 2011: see http://en.wikipedia.org/wiki/Google _Book_Search_Settlement_Agreement.

10. I quote from the online Media Commons Press publication of Kathleen Fitzpatrick's *Planned Obsolescence:* http://mediacommons.futureofthebook.org /mcpress/plannedobsolescence/.

11. See the 2006 developerWorks interview with Berners-Lee: http://www.ibm .com/developerworks/podcast/dwi/cm-int082206txt.html.

12. See http://www.rossettiarchive.org. The *Archive* is a complete collection of all Rossetti's textual, pictorial, and design works in all their known material forms and states. There are 845 textual works that exist in some 14,000 distinct documentary states and more than 2,000 pictorial and design works. Each document has an xml transcription as well as a high-resolution image, and with a few exceptions each artistic work is represented by a high-resolution image of both the original work and, in many cases, various later important reproductions of the original. In addition, the *Archive* has some 5,000 files of extensive scholarly commentaries and notes on its materials.

13. SpecLab was the Speculative Computing Laboratory that I founded in 2001 with Johanna Drucker. It was an informal group of students, university staff, and faculty who met regularly to experiment with and explore innovative IT approaches to the interpretation of cultural materials. See Drucker's *SpecLab. Arp* was *The Applied Research in Patacriticism* laboratory I founded with support from the Mellon Foundation in 2002. It was the incubator of NINES and *Juxta* and built the software for *IVANHOE.*

14. *The Valley of the Shadow:* www.valley.lib.virginia.edu.

15. Although the history of social software can be tracked to the earliest days of IT, the period 2002–2004 is widely recognized as especially significant because in 2002 Clay Shirky held his invitation-only "Social Software Summit," and in 2004 Tim O'Reilly convened the first of his annual Web 2.0 conferences.

16. For 18thConnect see: http://www.18thconnect.org/.

17. See: http://www.nines.org/groups/7.

18. Robert Darnton, "The Library: Three Jeremiads," *NYRB* 57, no. 20 (December 23, 2010).


## 8. Philological Investigations I

1. Marjorie Perloff, *The Poetics of Indeterminacy* (Princeton, NJ: Princeton University Press, 1981).

2. Eliza Richards, *Gender and the Poetics of Reception in Poe's Circle* (Cambridge: Cambridge University Press, 2004), 22.

3. Timothy Powell, *Ruthless Democracy: A Multicultural Interpretation of the American Renaissance* (Princeton, NJ: Princeton University Press, 2000), 19. See also F. O. Matthiessen, *American Renaissance: Art and Expression in the Age of Emerson and Whitman* (London: Oxford University Press, 1941) and David S. Reynolds, *Beneath the American Renaissance: The Subversive Imagination in the Age of Emerson and Melville* (New York: Oxford University Press, 1988).

4. Matthiessen, *American Renaissance*. That the problems remain vexed was highlighted recently in the special section of essays devoted to "The State of American Studies" in *New Literary History* 42, no. 3 (Summer 211): 365–418.

5. Scott Peeples, *The Afterlife of Edgar Allan Poe* (Rochester, NY: Camden House, 2004), 159.

6. Richards, *Gender and the Poetics of Reception*, 1.

7. Meredith McGill, *American Literature and the Culture of Reprinting, 1834–1853* (Philadelphia: University of Pennsylvania Press, 2003), 147.

8. The influence of Poe on Baudelaire and Mallarmé is well known. Rossetti discovered Poe in 1847 and immediately began responding to Poe's work with a series of remarkable illustrations (two for "The Raven," one for "Ulalume" and "The Sleepers") and with a number of poems and prose works that show Poe's clear influence. Swinburne regarded Poe as America's most important poet. He contributed to Sara Sigourney Rice's Poe memorial volume and in fact was the person responsible for Mallarmé's contribution, his famous sonnet on Poe's tomb. See *The Rossetti Archive* (http://rossettiarchive.org) and Cecil Y. Lang, ed., *The Swinburne Letters*. 6 vols. (New Haven, CT: Yale University Press, 1960), 3:84–85.

9. Whitman seems to have written a first version of the *Specimen Days* text for *The Critic* (3 June 1882); see Walt Whitman, *Prose Works 1892*, vol. 1: *Specimen Days*, ed. Floyd Stovall (New York: New York University Press, 1963), 230–233.

10. Eric Carlson, *The Recognition of Edgar Allan Poe: Selected Criticism since 1829* (Ann Arbor: University of Michigan Press, 1966), 73–76.

11. Whitman, *Specimen Days*, 156.

12. Ibid., 294.

13. *Democratic Vistas*, first published by Whitman in 1871 (Washington, DC: J. S. Redfield).

14. Ibid., 210–211.

15. Ibid., 231.

16. Quoted in Jean Alexander, *Affidavits of Genius: Edgar Allan Poe and the French Critics, 1847–1924* (Port Washington, NY: Kennikat Press, 1971), 217.

17. Quoted in ibid., 218.

18. Whitman, *Specimen Days*, 158.

19. Important foundations were laid down earlier by Perry Miller (see note 20 below) and Walter Benn Michaels and Donald Pease, eds., *The American Renaissance Reconsidered* (Baltimore, MD: Johns Hopkins University Press, 1985).

20. Perry Miller, *The Raven and the Whale: The War of Words and Wits in the Era of Poe and Melville* (New York: Harcourt Brace, 1956), 4.

21. Matthiessen, *American Renaissance*, xii.

22. Terence Whalen, *Edgar Allan Poe and the Masses: The Political Economy of Literature in Antebellum America* (Princeton, NJ: Princeton University Press, 1999), 38.

23. T.S. Eliot, "From Poe to Valery," in *To Criticize the Critic and Other Writings* (Lincoln: University of Nebraska Press, 1992), 35.

24. Edgar Allan Poe, *Eureka,* ed. Stuart Levine and Susan Levine (Urbana: University of Illinois Press, 2005).

25. James Russell Lowell, *A Fable for Critics* (New York: J.P. Putnam, 1848).

26. Betsy Erkkilä, *Mixed Bloods and Other Crosses: Rethinking American Literature from the Revolution to the Culture Wars* (Philadelphia: University of Pennsylvania Press, 2005), 21, 130.

27. For James and Wilson see Eric Carlson, *Critical Essays on Edgar Allan Poe* (Boston: G.K. Hall, 1987); Laura Riding, *Anarchism Is Not Enough,* ed. Lisa Samuels (Berkeley: University of California Press, 2001), 16; and *Contemporaries and Snobs* (London: Cape, 1928) 201–255.

28. Jonathan Elmer, *Reading at the Social Limit: Affect, Mass Culture, and Edgar Allan Poe* (Stanford, CA: Stanford University Press, 1995), 21.

29. Richards, *Gender and the Poetics of Reception,* 5.

30. McGill, *American Literature and the Culture of Reprinting,* 149.

31. Ibid., 151.

32. Poe, *Eureka,* 21.

33. McGill, *American Literature and the Culture of Reprinting,* 191.

34. Peeples, *The Afterlife of Edgar Allan Poe,* 159.

35. Richards, *Gender and the Poetics of Reception in Poe's Circle,* 1.

36. McGill, *American Literature and the Culture of Reprinting,* 147.

37. Ralph Cohen, "A Note on *New Literary History,*" *New Literary History* 1, no. 1 (1969): 5.

38. Ibid., 6.

39. See http://www.googlizationofeverything.com.

40. Jerome J. McGann, *A Critique of Modern Textual Criticism* (Chicago: University of Chicago Press, 1983) and D. F. McKenzie, *Bibliography and the Sociology of Texts* (London: The British Library, 1986).

41. Richards, *Gender and the Poetics of Reception,* 5.

42. Edgar Allan Poe, *Writings in the* Broadway Journal: *The Text,* ed. Burton R. Pollin, 2 vols. (New York: Gordian Press, 1986). This edition of *The Broadway Journal* is one of the parts of what Pollin projected as the *Collected Writings.* See note 49 below where I take up a commentary on one of the other parts of that project, Pollin's edition of *The Narrative of Arthur Gordon Pym,* in the volume he titled *Imaginary Voyages.*

43. Miller, *The Raven and the Whale.*

44. Poe/Pollin, *Writings in the* Broadway Journal, 1:l–li.

45. McGill, *American Literature and the Culture of Reprinting,* 145.

46. The absence of the text represents Pollin's editorial policy not to print in his edition any Poe texts that are being reprinted from earlier sources. Since the immediate bibliographical context is such a relevant feature of these works, one has to deplore these omissions. Of course the reason for them is plain: Pollin is trying to save paperspace.

47. When these materials were being included *The Broadway Journal* was on the brink of folding. Also, one notes the orthographic difference between "Col-

lier," which is *The Broadway Journal*'s spelling of the name, and "Collyer," the spelling given only a few lines below with the printed text of the letter.

48. The fact that Collyer was a living person who could have exposed the letter as a hoax—if it were a hoax—would be a truly exquisite touch. See Pollin's commentary on the tale and the stir it caused in both England and America.

49. *Pym* is included in Pollin's edition of *The Imaginary Voyages*, ed. Burton R. Pollin (Boston: Twayne Publishers, 1981).

50. Poe was in touch with Harper and Brothers—the eventual publisher of *Pym*—in March 1836 about publishing "A book-length connected narrative" by Poe (Pollin/Ridgely, 31).

51. This is Ridgely's comment in his essay in Pollin's edition of *The Broadway Journal* (30n).

52. J. V. Ridgely and Iola S. Haverstick, "Chartless Voyage: The Many Narratives of Arthur Gordon Pym," *Texas Studies in Language and Literature 6* (Spring 1966): 63–80.

53. McGill, *American Literature and the Culture of Reprinting*, 151.

54. *Eureka*, paragraph 39. See W. C. Harris's discussion of *Eureka* (37–70), and in particular his treatment of the contradictions that are for him the very foundation of "America" (43–61), in *E Pluribus Unum* (Iowa City: University of Iowa Press, 2005).

55. This historical commonplace is splendidly detailed in Daniel Howe's recent and magisterial study of the period, *What Hath God Wrought* (2007).

56. Historians speak of Jackson's "three administrations" because Van Buren so assiduously—often so disastrously—pursued Jacksonian policies.

57. At lines 144–157. The initial exposure of the Poe allusion was made by Joseph M. DeFalco, "Whitman's Changes in 'Out of the Cradle' and Poe's 'Raven,'" *Walt Whitman Review* 16 (1970): 22–27.

58. See http://gibagadinamaagoom.info/cosmology.html.

59. Ibid.

60. See for instance the *Vision of Britain* project (http://www.visionofbritain .org.uk) and the *Shaping the West* project (http:// http://www.stanford.edu /group/spatialhistory/cgi-bin/site/project.php?id=997)—including the interesting discussion of the project "A Data Model for Spatial History: Shaping the West," by Evgenia Schnayder, Killeen Hanson, and Mithu Datta (http://www.stanford .edu/group/spatialhistory/media/images/publication/Railroad_Database_Article .pdf).

## 9. Philological Investigations II

1. Thomas L. Philbrick, "Cooper Country in Fiction": http://external.oneonta .edu/cooper/articles/suny/1978suny-philbrick.html.

2. My vocabulary and analogy are based in the discourse of text markup: see the TEI's online introduction: http://www.tei-c.org/release/doc/tei-p5-doc/en/html /HD.html.

3. The call number of the edition I am studying is PS1414 .A1 1823c. Its boards, while shaken loose, are still present and the original owner has inscribed her name on the half-title (which has bled through to the title page): Arithea D. Parker, March 22, 1823. The two volumes later came into the possession of the literary collector and bibliographer Jacob Chester Chamberlain, who obviously wanted the books because their original boards were still present—an uncommon condition for a work like *The Pioneers*.

4. The standard English treatment of title pages is still Theodore Low De Vinne's *The Practice of Typography: A Treatise on Title-Pages* (New York: The Century Company, 1902). In the context of my discussion here, Part II is the most pertinent section (195–349). But De Vinne is greatly superseded by Arnold Rothe, *Der literarische Titel: Funktionen, Formen, Geschichte* (Frankfurt: Klosterman, 1986). That work then produced the equally important *Il titolo e il testo,* a cura di Michele A. Cortelazzo, premess di Gianfranco Folena. Quaderni del Circolo filologico-linguistico padovano (Padova: Editoriale programma, 1992). For my purposes here, two essays in *Il titolo e il testo* are particularly pertinent: Giovanni Cappello, "Rhetorica del titolo," 11–26, and Arnold Rothe, "Das Titelblatt als System: Interaktion von Wort, Schrift und Bild," 27–56.

5. Work toward a systematic approach to deep interpretive annotation is under development through the "Annotating Literature Project" at the University of Tübingen: see http://www.annotating-literature.org/.

6. For an interesting explication of the general "rhetoric" of title pages see Capello, "Rhetorica del titolo."

7. A proper discussion of the title page's typography would have to begin with (1) an examination of the Charles Wiley title pages in general as well as those for Cooper's novels in particular; (2) an examination of the prevalent American title page designs; and (3) comparisons with different designs from the period as well as designs from earlier periods. I note here, briefly, that Cooper's two earlier novels, *Precaution* (not published by Charles Wiley), and *The Spy* (published by Wiley) both have open-face titles, but the typography is not continued in Wiley's subsequent publications.

8. Jacob Sutherland was a close college friend, sharing similar ideas about America and literature. He also may have been instrumental in firing Cooper's imagination about the landscape that would dominate *The Pioneers:* see Wayne Franklin, *James Fenimore Cooper: The Early Years* (New Haven, CT: Yale University Press, 2007), 214.

9. *The Pioneers,* with Historical Introduction and Explanatory Notes by James Franklin Beard and text established by Lance Schachterle and Kenneth M. Anderson Jr. (Albany, NY: SUNY Press, 1980).

10. For publication details see ibid., and see Franklin, *James Fenimore Cooper,* 355–359.

11. This racism appears as well, differently inflected, in the book's treatment of the two African American characters.

12. *Letters and Journals of James Fenimore Cooper,* ed. James Franklin Beard (Cambridge, MA: Harvard University Press, 1960), IV. 350. And see the discussion of this issue in John P. McWilliams, *Political Justice in a Republic: James Fenimore Cooper's America* (Berkeley: University of California Press, 1972), 2–4.

13. *Notions of the Americans* (Philadelphia: Carey, Lea, & Blanchard, 1835), I. 254. Cooper first published this work in 1828.

14. The character Le Quoi is the chief of the two French references. The other is made briefly, in chapter 13, when Natty Bumppo recollects his service with Sir William Johnson in the French and Indian War—"the morning we beat Dieskau" at the Battle of Lake George (September 1755).

15. For a good discussion of how Cooper presents his native American characters and materials see William A. Starna, "Cooper's Indians: A Critique," in George A. Test, ed., *James Fenimore Cooper: His Country and His Art,* Papers from the 1979 Conference at State University College of New York, Oneonta and Cooperstown: http://external.oneonta.edu/cooper/articles/suny/1979suny-starna.html. Starna's essay makes a critical recovery of the extensive scholarship (to 1979) on this subject in order to clarify the "anthropological accuracy" of Cooper's work.

16. In addition to these geophysical, historical, and ethnographic "sources," Cooper glances obliquely at another source in Dr. Grant's sermon (chapter XI): "The fountain of divine love flows from a source, too pure to admit of pollution in its course." The importance of that divine source for Cooper is very great since a profound belief in the presence of God in both history and nature pervades Cooper's work.

17. In the colonial period this was the site of the important Delaware Indian village of Shamokin, pivotal in the pre-Revolutionary and Revolutionary War years. The British erected Fort Augusta at the strategic site in 1756, and in 1772 the Indians were evicted and sent to the west. See *Bell's History of Northumberland County Pennsylvania,* ed. Herbert C. Bell (Chicago: Brown, Runk and Co., 1891), chapters 2 and 14.

18. See Max M. Mintz. *Seeds of Empire: The American Revolutionary Conquest of the Iroquois* (New York: New York University Press, 1999); Joseph R. Fischer. *A Well-Executed Failure: The Sullivan Campaign against the Iroquois, July–September 1779* (Columbia: University of South Carolina Press, 2007).

19. The most important document is perhaps the 1759 committee report made to George II, *An Enquiry into the Causes of the Alienation of the Delaware and Shawanese Indians from the British Interest* (London: J. Wilkie, 1759); a contemporary-language edition made from the 1867 American edition was produced in 2005 by Donald R. Repsher. See also William W. Campbell. *The Border Warfare of New York During the Revolution; or, The Annals of Tryon County* (New York: Baker and Scribner, 1849); Allan W. Eckert. *The Wilderness War* (New York: Little Brown & Company, 1978); Alan Taylor. *The Divided Ground* (New York: Alfred Knopf, 2006); Jeptha R. Simms. *History of Schoharie County and the Border Wars of New York* (Albany, NY: Munsell and Tanner, 1845).

20. These would include *The Spy, Lionel Lincoln, The Pilot,* the rest of the Leatherstocking series, *The Wept of Wish-ton-Wish, Wyandotté,* and the Effingham novels.

21. See note 12 above and Francis Whiting Halsey, *The Old New York Frontier: Its Wars with Indians and Tories* . . . (New York: Charles Scribner's Sons, 1901), especially sections IV and V. See also Robert M. Calhoon. *The Loyalists in Revolutionary America, 1760–1781* (New York: Harcourt Brace, 1973). Cooper focused attention on the conflict of Loyalist and Insurgent in *The Spy,* but in that book he located the struggle in Westchester instead of Tryon County. The choice made a great difference because the struggle in the Susquehanna frontier region was far more brutal than in the relatively settled and "civilized" region of the Hudson.

22. The third instance, which comes early in chapter 1, calls attention to the ambiguity of the word in *The Pioneers,* referring as it does both to early wilderness trappers and rangers like Natty, and to early settlers like Judge Templeton whose life, like Natty's, spans the periods of early frontier encounter and early settlement (in the case of *The Pioneers,* this period would stretch from approximately the mid-1740s to 1793).

23. See Halsey, *The Old New York Frontier,* section III and in particular page 126. I single out these two men because both figure prominently in the lands in question. Briefly, William Cooper became a vast landholder through some barely legal moves that gained him George Croghan's patents. Members of the Prevost family, who settled Otsego Lake years before William Cooper came, were the first to seek the destruction of Cooper's land holdings in the years after his death in 1809. For a full discussion see Alan Taylor, *William Cooper's Town: Power and Persuasion on the Frontier of the Early American Republic* (New York: Alfred A. Knopf, 1995), chapters 3 and 14.

24. Cooper admired Charles Brockden Brown, as is clear from the gothic character of earlier novels like *The Spy, Lionel Lincoln, The Red Rover,* and *The Bravo.*

25. See for example Franklin, *James Fenimore Cooper,* 460–461.

26. See Barbara Alice Mann, *Forbidden Ground: Racial Politics and Hidden Identity in James Fenimore Cooper's Leather-Stocking Tales* (Toledo: University of Toledo Press, 1997) and her essay "Man with a Cross: Hawkeye was a 'Half-Breed,'" paper originally delivered at the 1998 American Literature Association conference: http://external.oneonta.edu/cooper/articles/ala/1998ala-mann.html.

27. In fact the Iroquois had no right to dispose of the Delaware land, and the Crown claim was based on fifty-year-old treaty documents whose authority was more than dubious. See Bruce E. Johansen, "By Your Observing the Methods Our Wise Forefathers Have Taken. . . .," in Barbara Alice Mann, ed., *Native American Speakers of the Eastern Woodlands: Selected Speeches and Critical Analyses* (New York: Greenwood, 2001), 83–105; William N. Fenton. *The Great Law and the Longhouse: A Political History of the Iroquois Confederacy* (Norman:

University of Oklahoma Press, 1998); and William A. Starna. "The Diplomatic Career of Canasatego," in William A. Pencak and Daniel K. Richter, eds., *Friends and Enemies in Penn's Woods: Indians, Colonists, and the Racial Construction of Pennsylvania* (University Park: Penn State University Press, 2004), 144–163, especially 148. For the treaty of 1742 see Julian P. Boyd, ed., *Indian Treaties Printed by Benjamin Franklin, 1736–1762* (Philadelphia: Historical Society of Pennsylvania, 1938).

28. See Susan Cooper's introduction to *The Deerslayer;* http://external.oneonta .edu/cooper/susan/susan-deerslayer.html.

29. See Francis Paul Purcha, *America Indian Policy in the Formative Years: The Indian Trade and Intercourse Acts 1790–1834* (Cambridge, MA: Harvard University Press, 1962).

30. By the eighteenth century the Delaware had becomes vassals to the Iroquois, and when the British sought to establish their land claims to large areas of Delaware territory, principally in eastern Pennsylvania, the Iroquois (at the Grand Council of 1742) told the Delaware to give way. But the Delaware would not. Cooper used this dispute—which he knew from Heckewelder—to set up the famous antagonism in his Leatherstocking fictions between the Mingwe/Mingoes and the Delaware.

31. See John Heckewelder, *Account of the History, Manners, and Customs of the Indian Nations, Who Once Inhabited Pennsylvania and the Neighboring States* (Philadelphia: Committee of History, Moral Science, and General Literature, 1819), 94.

32. In choosing this meaning Cooper departs from his usual source, Heckewelder, and follows the view of the Quaker jurist Roberts Vaux: see Oscar Jewell Harvey and Ernest Gray Smith, *A History of Wilkes-Barré, Luzerne County, Pensylvania,* 2 vols. (Wilkes-Barre, PA: Oscar J. Harvey, 1909), 1:42.

33. These complex histories are first elaborated in *The Last of the Mohicans* (New York: H. C. Cary and I. Lea, 1826).

34. The Watson Brake and Poverty Point archaeological sites are early and significant (as early as 3500 BCE). See Brian M. Fagin, *Ancient North America: The Archaeology of a Continent,* 4th ed. (New York: Thames & Hudson, 2005); Joe W. Saunders et al., "A Mound Complex in Louisiana at 5400–5000 Years before the Present," *Science* 277, no. 5333 (September 19, 1997): 1796–1799; and on the significance of native American origin myths, Vine Deloria Jr., *Red Earth, White Lies: Native Americans and the Myth of Scientific Fact* (New York: Scribner, 1995).

35. See the journey through the forest to Lake George in *The Deerslayer,* chapters 13–14. Even more pertinent is *Satanstoe,* chapters 21–22, where Cooper stages a contest between forest travel by western compass and by Indian understanding.

36. The essay on the eclipse, written sometime in the 1830s, was discovered among Cooper's papers by his daughter Susan after his death. It was first published in *Putnam's Monthly Magazine* 21 (September 1869): 352–359.

37. This is essentially the perspective of my essay "Fenimore Cooper's Anti-aesthetic and the Representation of Conflicted History," *Modern Language Quarterly* 73, no. 2 (June 2012): 123–156.

38. See Halsey, *The Old New York Frontier,* 359.

39. See Rebecca Hartkopf Schloss, *Sweet Liberty: The Final Days of Slavery in Martinique* (Philadelphia: University of Pennsylvania Press, 2009), especially 93–98.

40. See Taylor, *William Cooper's Town,* 373. The two tales—of William Cooper's shrewd and barely legal speculative gains in the 1786 auction, and the subsequent loss of the Cooper family lands to later speculators—is excellently told in chapters 3 and 14.

41. In later years, as his view of the American republic became more troubled, he denied any personal relation to Templeton and its fictional people.

42. This copy was owned by the distinguished scholar and bibliographer Jacob Chester Chamberlain (d. 1906) and its unusual condition—it is still bound in the original drab boards—reflects his special interests.

## Conclusion

1. Marshall Sahlins, introduction to *Culture in Practice: Selected Essays* (New York: Zone Books, 2000), 27.

2. Sahlins, *Islands of History* (Chicago: University of Chicago Press, 1985).

3. "The Convergence of the Twain," in *The Complete Poetical Works of Thomas Hardy,* ed. Samuel Hynes, 3 vols. (Oxford: Clarendon Press, 1982–1985), 2:12.

4. Hardy, " 'According to the Mighty Working,' " in *The Complete Poetical Works,* 2:336.

5. Sahlins, introduction to *Culture in Practice,* 9–10.

6. Leon Trotsky, *The History of the Russian Revolution,* trans. Max Eastman (Ann Arbor: University of Michigan Press, 1974). Trotsky discusses this foundational axiom of his thought in his first chapter, "Peculiarities of Russia's Development."

7. Translated by M. B. DeBevoise (Cambridge, Mass.: Harvard University Press, 2004).

8. David Harvey, *Paris, Capital of Modernity* (New York: Routledge, 2003).

9. Drucker, *Sweet Dreams: Contemporary Art and Complicity* (Chicago: University of Chicago Press, 2005).

10. *Lord Byron: The Complete Poetical Works,* ed. Jerome McGann, 7 vols. (Oxford: Clarendon Press, 1986), 4:407–408.

11. Herbert Marcuse, *The Aesthetic Dimension: Towards a Critique of Marxist Aesthetics* (Boston: Beacon Press, 1978); Theodor W. Adorno, *Aesthetic Theory,* ed. Gretel Adorno and Rolf Tiedemann (Minneapolis: University of Minnesota Press, 1997).

12. Alexander Gottlieb Baumgarten, *Reflections on Poetry: Alexander Gottlieb Baumgarten's "Meditationes philosophicae de nonnullis ad poema pertinentibus,"* trans. Karl Aschenbrenner and William B. Holther (Berkeley: University of California Press, 1954).

13. Kai Hammermeister, *The German Aesthetic Tradition* (Cambridge: Cambridge University Press, 2002), 4.

14. Marianne Moore, "Critics and Connoisseurs," in *The Complete Poems* (New York: Viking, 1981), 38.

15. "Poetry," in *The Complete Poems,* 267.

# Acknowledgments

My first and longest-standing intellectual debt is to my students, who have always been there for me, in conversations formal as well as informal. I've never been able to think without thinking with them. In the case of this book my debt is deepest to my students at University of Virginia.

No one can properly acknowledge the true scale of the influences on one's ideas and work. But I must recall here some persons who have been special intellectual and personal presences. First and foremost Patricia Spacks and Steve Arata, who patiently endure my requests for enlightenment in our weekly lunches. My life moans round with many other voices, and especially with the voices of Charles Bernstein, Marshall Brown, Virgil Burnett, James Chandler, Adriana Craciun, Johanna Drucker, Nicholas Frankel, Jeffrey Herrick, Cecil Lang, Alan Liu, Michael Suarez, Chip Tucker, and John Unsworth. John Kulka, the distinguished editor at Harvard University Press, has encouraged and supported this project from the first, and I am immensely grateful to him and his associates at the press, Karen Peleaz and Heather Hughes, and my assiduous copyeditor, John Donohue of Westchester Publishing Services. I also want to thank Jama Coartney of the University of Virginia Media Center for her remarkable generosity in helping to prepare the illustrations for print.

Robert Creeley's poem "The Innocence" is here reprinted from *The Collected Poems of Robert Creeley 1945–1975* (copyright © 1962 by Robert Creeley) with the permission of The Permissions Company, Inc., on behalf of the Estate of Robert Creeley.

The book prints revised versions of a number of essays that have been previously published, and I gratefully acknowledge the editors' permissions.

Chapter 1, "Our Textual History," *Times Literary Supplement* no. 5564 (20 November 2009): 13–15.

Chapter 2, "Philology in a New Key," *Critical Inquiry* 39, no. 2 (2013): 327–346.

Chapter 4, "Interpretation," in *Introduction to Scholarship in Modern Languages and Literature,* 3rd ed., ed. David Nicholl (New York: Modern Language Association of America, 2007), 160–170.

Chapter 5, "Marking Texts in Many Dimensions," in *A Companion to Digital Humanities,* ed. Susan Schreibman, Ray Siemens, and John Unsworth (Oxford: Blackwell, 2004), 198–217.

Chapter 6, "Texts in N-Dimensions and Interpretation in a New Key," *Text Technology* (Special Issue devoted to *IVANHOE*) 12, no. 2 (2003): 1–18.

Chapter 8, "Literary History and Editorial Method: Poe and Antebellum America," *New Literary History* 40, no. 4 (Autumn 2009): 825–842.

Conclusion, "Pseudodoxia Academica," *Literary History in the Global Age, New Literary History* 39, no. 3 (Summer 2008): 645–656.

In addition, a version of Chapter 7, "Sustainability: The Elephant in the Room," was published in *Online Humanities Scholarship. The Shape of Things to Come*, ed. Jerome McGann (Houston: Rice University Press, 2010), 1–22. Though still available freely online (http://cnx.org/content/col11199/latest/), the print-on-demand version became inaccessible when Rice University Press went out of business.

# Index